The fourth Ticonderoga (CV-14) was laid down as Hancock on 1 Feb... and Dry Dock Company; renamed Ticonderoga on 1 May 1943; launched or... 1944, Captain Dixie Kiefer in command.

On 31 January 1952, Ticonderoga came out of reserve and went into... September 1954, Ticonderoga was recommissioned at New York, Captain W... her new home port--Norfolk, Virginia. On 2 August 1956, she ente... hurrican bow. Those modifications were completed by early 1957,... California. On 16 September, she stood out of San Francisco Bay an... made four more peacetime deployments to the western Pacific. Earl... Pacific, the carrier cleared Pearl Harbor on 4 May. On 2 August,... (DD-731) reported attacked by by units of the North Vietnamese Navy. ... time to be two unprovoked attacks on American seapower. On 5 Augu... four bases. She returned to the Naval Air Station, North Island, C... and 1966 was her first total combat tour of duty during the America... San Diego to end the deployment.

Following repairs she stood out of San Diego on 9 July to begin... headed south for an overnight stop at Subic Bay in the Philippines... Tonkin. On 28 December, Ticonderoga sailed for her fourth combat d... the coast of Vietnam for five separate periods totalling 120 day... preparations for her fifth consecutive combat deployment to the sou... periods on the line off Vietnam. The aircraft carrier took statio... Ticonderoga arrived in San Diego on 18 September, and Ticonderoga... California coast for the remainder of the year.

During the remainder of her active career, Ticonderoga made... deployments, she operated in the eastern Pacific and participated in... American Samoa during April 1972. The carrier then headed back to Sa...

On 1 September 1973, the aircraft carrier was decommissioned. ... scrap. Ticonderoga received five battle stars during World War II... and 12 battle stars during the Vietnam War.

ary 1943 at Newport News, Virginia; by the Newport News Shipbuilding
7 February 1944; and commissioned at the Norfolk Navy Yard on 8 May

educed commission for the transit from Bremerton to New York.   On 11
liam A. Schoech in command.   In January 1955, the carrier shifted to
d the shipyard to receive an angled flight deck and and enclosed
and, in April, she got underway for her new home port--Alameda,
shaped course for the Far East.   Between 1958 and 1963, Ticonderoga
in 1964, she began preparations for her sixth cruise to the western
ile operating in international waters in the Gulf of Tonkin, Maddox
President Johnson responded with a reprisal to what he felt at the
, Ticonderoga and Constellation (CV-46) launched 60 sorties against
ifornia, on 15 December 1964.   Ticonderoga's winter deployment 1965
involvement in the Vietnam War.   On 13 May, she pulled into port at

normal round of west coast training operations.   5 November when she
the 10th and 11th.   On the 13th, Ticonderoga arrived in the Gulf of
oyment.   Between January and July, Ticonderoga was on the line off
combat duty.   During the first months of 1969, Ticonderoga made
east Asia area, she arrived on the 20th.   Ticonderoga served four
off Vietnam for her last line period of the deployment on 26 June.
s redesignated CVS-14 on the 21st.   The warship operated off the

more deployments to the Far East.   In between these two last
he recovery of the Apollo 16 moon mission capsule and atronauts near
Diego where she arrived on 28 December.
name was struck from the Navy list on 16 November 1973 and sold for
three Navy Unit Commendations, one Meritorious Unit Commendation,

USS TICONDEROGA
CV-CVA-CVS-14

TURNER PUBLISHING COMPANY

TURNER PUBLISHING COMPANY

Copyright © 1996
Turner Publishing Company.
All rights reserved.
Publishing Rights: Turner Publishing
Company

Turner Publishing Company Staff:
Editor: Erik Parrent
Designer: Lora Lauder

Library of Congress
Catalog Card Number 96-061908

ISBN: 978-1-68162-435-8

Additional copies may be purchased directly
from Turner Publishing Company.

This publication was compiled using available
information. The publisher regrets it cannot assume liability for errors or omissions.

*Endsheets: Courtesy of Howard Hoxsie and C. Vern
Higman)*

*Photo this page: Communications Department, To-
kyo Bay, September 1945. (Courtesy of George K.
Ames)*

3

A four-inch shell through right wing and fuselage exploded above plane "Round Trip Ticket" on November 11, 1944. It severed two of the four engine mounts and all cockpit instruments. Higman received shrapnel wounds on his right leg. (Courtesy of C.V. Higman)

TABLE OF CONTENTS

Ticonderoga ships and men have established an impressive naval tradition for nearly two centuries. We have only official records of the *Ticonderoga* men who sailed and fought the earlier ships. In this volume are the vivid memories of those who survive today from World War II to the present.

Love and pride in your ship and fellow shipmates are surely a paramount necessity for a happy and effective crew. Such was the case of carrier *Ticonderoga* during her twenty-nine years of service. From routine operations to deadly combat with her enemies, the men who manned her performed their duties with the highest courage and professionalism.

Herein are some of their stories as best they remember them including that fateful day in January of 1945 when so many gave their lives for their country. Many more, today, still carry the scars and disabling wounds of the attack and the mental horrors will never leave any of those who were aboard at the time.

The Aegis Cruiser *Ticonderoga*, operating with our present day fleet, carries on our tradition in this modern day and has made her powerful presence known to those who would challenge our purposes throughout the world.

We, of the carrier *Ticonderoga*, are sailing with her and her crew in mind and heart as she sallies forth in her quest for peace in a turbulent world.

Charles "Chuck" Large, M 1/c
Plankowner

USS Ticonderoga *(Photography by Bruce Trombecky, courtesy of U.S. Navy Pacific Missile Test Center)*

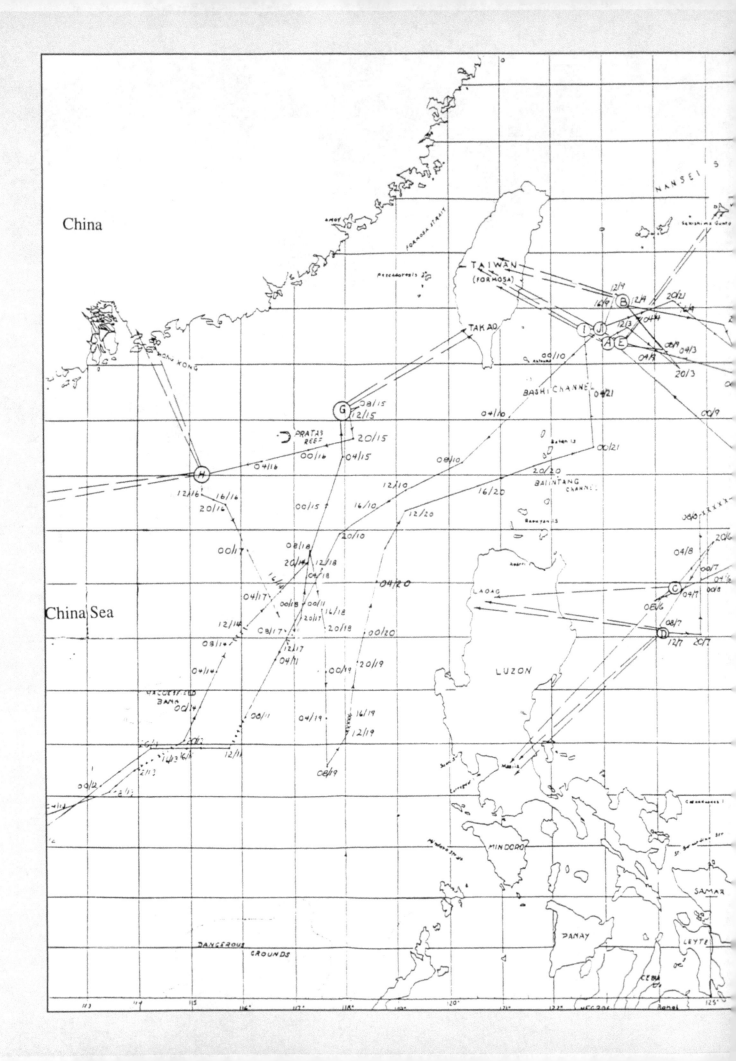

China

China Sea

TAIWAN
(FORMOSA)

LUZON

MINDORO

SAMAR

LEYTE

PANAY

DANGEROUS GROUNDS

Jan. 2 nd Fueled Ship.

A- Jan. 3 rd Launched 3 strikes against airfields in central Formosa.

B- Jan. 4 th Launched 2 strikes against airfields in central Formosa.

Jan. 5 th Fueled Ship.

C- Jan. 6 th Launched 1 strike and 1 VF sweep against Laoag and Clark fields, Luzon, P.I.

D- Jan. 7 th Launched 2 strikes and 4 VF sweeps against Laoag and Clark fields, Luzon, P.I.

Jan. 8 th Fueled Ship.

E- Jan. 9 th Launched 3 strikes and 2 VF sweeps against north central Formosa airfields and Miyako Jira.

Jan. 11 th Fueled Destroyers.

F- Jan. 12 th Launched 3 strikes and 3 VF sweeps against shipping and airfields, Saigon, and Camranh Bay Area, French Indo China.

Jan. 13 th Fueled Destroyers. Fueled Ship. Forced to discontinue fueling operations because of heavy sea.

Jan. 14 th Fueled Ship.

G- Jan. 15 th Launched 2 strikes and 1 VF sweep against shipping and airfields, Takao Area, Formosa.

H- Jan. 16 th Launched 2 strikes and 3 VF sweeps against shipping and airfields, Hainan Island and Hong Kong, China.

Jan. 17 th Fueled Destroyer.

Jan. 19 th Fueled Ship.

I- Jan. 21 st Launched 1 strike and 4 VF sweeps against airfields in central Formosa, and shipping at Toshien.

J- Jan. 21 st TG 38.3 attacked by numerous enemy planes. Five planes shot down by Ticonderoga C.A.P. Three shot down by Ticonderoga. U.S.S. Langley hit by bomb from enemy plane. 1211 Japanese plane crash dived on flight deck of U.S.S. Ticonderoga starting large fires on hangar deck. 1258 second Japanese plane crash dived into island structure of U.S.S. Ticonderoga starting large fire. Ship compelled to retire to Ulithi as result of damage.

HISTORY
OF THE
USS TICONDEROGA

9

USS *Ticonderoga*
The "*Big T*"
Ships That Have Borne The Name

Ticonderoga

A village in Essex County, NY, on La Chute River, 100 miles north of Albany. The name is an Iroquois Indian term which means "between two lakes" and refers to Lake George and Lake Champlain. Here, the French built a fort called Carillon in 1755, but it was captured four years later by British troops under General Amherst. Early in the American Revolution, on May 10, 1775, Ethan Allen and his "Green Mountain Boys" captured the fort from the British. General Sir John Burgoyne recaptured the fort in May 1777, holding it until his surrender at Saratoga, NY on October 17, 1777.

Jet aircraft departing the flight deck of Ticonderoga. *(Courtesy of E.W. Tenpenny)*

I

(Sch: t. 350; l. 120'; a. 8 long 12-pdrs., 4 long 18-pdrs., 3 32-pdr. car.)

The first *Ticonderoga*, a merchant steamer built in 1814 at Vergennes, Vermont, was purchased by the Navy at Lake Champlain and converted to schooner rigging; and relaunched on May 12, 1814.

Ticonderoga rendered gallant service with Captain Thomas Macdonough's squadron during the Battle of Lake Champlain on September 11, 1814. Commanded by Lieutenant Stephen Cassin, *Ticonderoga* compelled sloop HMS *Finch* (formerly USS *Growler*) to surrender after riddling her with shot and forcing her aground. She also assisted in the capture of sloop HMS *Chubb* (formerly USS *Eagle*), and repelled several boarding attempts by British gunboats. Midshipman Hiram Paulding was on board *Ticonderoga* during the battle and used his pistol to discharge a cannon when firing matches proved defective. During the two-and-one-half hour engagement, six members of *Ticonderoga's* crew were killed, and six others were wounded.

After the war, *Ticonderoga* was laid up at Whitehall, New York. A decade later, she was pronounced unworthy of repair and sold at public sale on July 19, 1925.

II

(ScSlp: dp. 2,526; l. 237'0"; b. 38'2"; dr. 17'6"; a. 11 K.; a. 1 150-pdr., 1 50-pdr. D.r., 6'9" D.sb., 2 24-pdr. how., 2 12-pdr. r., 2 heavy 12-pdr.ab.)

The second *Ticonderoga* was laid down by the New York Navy Yard in 1861; launched on October 16, 1862; sponsored by Miss Katherine Heaton Offley; and commissioned at New York on May 12, 1863, Commodore J.L. Lardner in command.

Ticonderoga went south on June 5, 1863, for duty as flagship of the West Indies Squadron and, after stopping at Philadelphia, arrived at Cape Haitien on June 12. She patrolled waters off the Virgin Islands, Barbados, Tobago, Trinidad, and Curacao protecting Union commerce. *Ticonderoga* returned to Philadelphia for repairs in September. She was relieved as flagship of the squadron in October and sent to the Boston Navy Yard.

Operating out of Boston, *Ticonderoga* searched unsuccessfully off Nova Scotia for the captured steamer *Chesapeake* from December 11-16. In June 1864, she hunted Confederate commerce raiders off the New England coast, putting into Portland Harbor, Maine, on June 26. There, *Ticonderoga* received a telegram on July 10 ordering her to track down and destroy the marauding Confederate raider CSS *Florida*. Her search lasted until October and carried *Ticonderoga* as far south as Cape San Roque but was stopped because of mechanical troubles and insufficient fuel. She returned to Philadelphia late in October.

Ticonderoga left Philadelphia bound for Hampton Roads, Virginia, on October 31. She was assigned to the North Atlantic Blockading Squadron on November 4 and deployed off Wilmington, North Carolina. *Ticonderoga* participated in the first, unsuccessful attempt to take Fort Fisher, North Carolina, on December 24 and 25, losing eight men killed and 20 wounded on the first day of the assault when a 100-pounder Parrott rifle exploded. A landing party from *Ticonderoga* assisted in the capture of the fort on January 15, 1865.

Ticonderoga joined the South Atlantic Blockading Squadron on January 19. After a brief tour of duty, she left for Philadelphia in March and was decommissioned there on May 5.

Ticonderoga was recommissioned for service with the European Squadron in 1866. She remained with the Squadron through 1869, visiting ports in the Mediterranean, on the continent, and along the English and African coasts. The vessel was extensively repaired in 1870 and reported for duty with the South Atlantic Squadron at Rio de Janeiro on August 23, 1871. After over two years of service on the coast of South America, she was reassigned to the North Atlantic Squadron in January 1874. The ship was decommissioned at Portsmouth, New Hampshire, on October 24 and remained laid up there until 1877.

Ticonderoga was recommissioned on November 5, 1878 and ordered to embark upon a cruise around the world, Commodore Robert W. Shufeldt commanding. The expedition was of a commercial nature, intended to expand existing trade relations and establish new ones. *Ticonderoga* sailed eastward from Hampton Roads on December 7 and stopped at ports including Madeira, Monrovia, Cape Town, Aden, Bombay, Penang, Singapore, Manila, Hong Kong, Nagasaki, Fusan, Honolulu, and San Francisco. *Ticonderoga* arrived at Mare Island, California, for extensive repairs on November 9, 1880. during the two year mission, she had visited over 40 ports and steamed in excess of 36,000 miles without a mishap.

She left Mare Island in March 1881 and returned to New York on August 23. She was decommissioned there a final time on September 10, 1882 and declared unfit for further service. *Ticonderoga* was sold at Boston on August 5, 1887, to Thomas Butler and Co.

III

(Id. No. 1958; t. 5,130 (gross); l. 401.1'; b. 53.2'; dph. 27.5; dr. 25'6" (mean); s. 11 k.; a. 1 6", 1 3")

Camilla Rickmere (spelled *Kamilla Rickmere* in German), a steamer built in 1914 by *Rickmere Aktien Gasellschaft*, at Bremerhaven, Germany and operated by *Rickmere Raismuhlen Reederei & Schiffbau Aktien Gasellschaft*, was seized by the United States Customs officials in 1917; turned over to the Navy; fitted out as an animal transport; renamed *Ticonderoga*; and commissioned at Boston in the Naval Overseas Transportation Service (NOTS) on January 5, 1918, Lieutenant Commander James J. Madison, USNRF, in command.

Ticonderoga departed Boston on January 16 and reached Newport News, Virginia, three days later. There, she loaded a cargo of automobiles, trucks, animals, and sundry other Army supplies before moving north to New York City to join a convoy which sailed for France on February 20. *Ticonderoga* entered port at Brest on March 7 and began discharging her cargo. She completed unloading operations and departed France on the 23rd to return to the United States. She arrived at New York on April 8 and the following day headed for Norfolk, Virginia, to undergo repairs and take on cargo before returning to New York on the 30th.

On May 3, *Ticonderoga* steamed out of New York Harbor once more, bound for Europe. She reached Brest on May 18 and proceeded southeast along the coast of France to the Gironde estuary where she unloaded her cargo and took on ballast for the return voyage. The transport put to sea on June 10 and entered Hampton Roads 15 days later. *Ticonderoga* took on another Army shipment at Newport News and joined an eastbound convoy at New York on July 12. She delivered her cargo at the Gironde estuary once more, laying over there on July 28 to August 21 before heading home.

Ticonderoga loaded another Army cargo at Norfolk between September 5 and 19. She then steamed to New York where she joined a convoy bound for Europe. On September 22, *Ticonderoga* cleared New York for the last time. During the night of the 29th and 30th, the transport developed engine trouble and dropped be-hind the convoy. At 0520 the following morning, she sighted the German submarine U-152 running on the surface; and she cleared for action. For the next two hours, her gun crews fought the enemy in a losing battle. The U-boat's gunners put her forward gun out of commission after six shots, but the 6-inch gun aft continued the uneven battle. Almost every man on board *Ticonderoga*, including her captain, suffered wounds. Eventually, the submarine's two 5.9-inch guns succeeded in silencing *Ticonderoga's* remaining gun. At 0745, *Ticonderoga* slipped beneath the sea. Of the 237 sailors and soldiers embarked, only 24 survived. Twenty-two of those survivors were in one life boat and were picked up by the British steamer SS *Moorish Prince* four days later. The other two, the executive officer and the first assistant engineer, were taken prisoner on board the U-boat and eventually landed at Kiel, Germany, when U-152 completed her cruise. *Ticonderoga's* name was subsequently struck from the Navy list.

Ticonderoga (CV-19) was renamed *Hancock* (q.v.) on May 1, 1943, when the names of CV-14 and CV-19 were switched.

IV

(CV-14: dp. 27,100; l. 888'; b. 93'0" (wl.); ew. 147'6"; dr. 28'7"; s. 33 k.; cpl. 3,448; a. 12'5", 72 40mm., ac. 80+; cl. *Essex*)

The fourth *Ticonderoga* (CV-14) was laid down as *Hancock* on February 1, 1943 at Newport News, VA, by the Newport News Shipbuilding & Dry Dock Co; renamed *Ticonderoga* on May 1, 1943; launched on February 7, 1944; sponsored by Miss Stephanie Sarah Pell; and commissioned at the Norfolk Navy Yard on May 8, 1944, Captain Dixie Kiefer in command.

Ticonderoga remained at Norfolk for almost two months outfitting and embarking Air Group 80. On June 26, the carrier shaped a course for the British West Indies. She conducted air operations and drills en route and reached Port of

The crash of SB2C #56 - August 30, 1944; Ensign James H. Klein, pilot. (Courtesy of Klein)

Spain, Trinidad, on the 30th. For the next 15 days, *Ticonderoga* trained intensively to weld her air group and crew into an efficient wartime team. She departed the West Indies on July 16 and headed back to Norfolk where she arrived on the 22nd. Eight days later, the carrier headed for Panama. She transited the canal on September 4 and steamed up the coast to San Diego the following day. On the 13th, the carrier moored at San Diego where she loaded provisions, fuel, aviation gas, and an additional 77 planes, as well as the Marine Corps aviation and defense units that went with them. On the 19th, she sailed for Hawaii where she arrived five days later.

Ticonderoga remained at Pearl Harbor for almost a month. She and *Carina* (AK-74) conducted experiments in the underway transfer of aviation bombs from cargo ship to aircraft carrier. Following those tests, she conducted air operations, day and night landing and antiaircraft defense drills, until October 18 when she exited Pearl Harbor and headed for the western Pacific. After a brief stop at Eniwetok, *Ticonderoga* arrived at Ulithi Atoll in the Western Carolines on the 29th. There she embarked Rear Admiral A.W. Radford, Commander, Carrier Division 6, and joined Task Force (TF) 38 as a unit for Rear Admiral Frederick C. Sherman's Task Group (TG) 38.3.

The carrier sortied from Ulithi with TF 38 on November 2. She joined the other carriers as they resumed their extended air cover for the ground forces capturing Leyte. She launched her first air strike on the morning of the 5th. The planes of her air group spent the next two days pummeling enemy shipping near Luzon and air installations on that island. Her planes bombed and strafed the airfields at Zablan, Mandaluyond, and Pasig. They also joined those of other carriers in sending the heavy cruiser *Nachi* to a watery resting place. In addition, *Ticonderoga* pilots claimed six Japanese aircraft shot down and one destroyed on the ground, as well as 23 others damaged.

Around 1600 on the 5th, the enemy retaliated by sending up a flock of planes piloted by members of the suicide corps dubbed kamikaze, or "Divine Wind," in honor of the typhoon that had destroyed a Chinese invasion fleet four centuries previously. Two of the suicide planes succeeded in slipping through the American combat air patrol and antiaircraft fire to crash *Lexington* (CV-16). *Ticonderoga* emerged from that airborne banzai charge unscathed and claimed a tally of two splashes. On November 6, the warship launched two fighter sweeps and two bombing strikes against the Luzon airfields and enemy shipping in the vicinity. Her airmen returned later that day claiming the destruction of 35 Japanese aircraft and attacks on six enemy ships in Manila Bay. After recovering her planes, the carrier retired to the east for a fueling rendezvous.

She refueled and received replacement planes on the 7th and then headed back to continue pounding enemy forces in the Philippines. Early on the morning of November 11, her planes combined with others of TF 38 to attack a Japanese reinforcement convoy, just as it was preparing to enter Ormoc Bay from the Camotes Sea. Together, the planes accounted for all the enemy transports and four of the seven escorting de-

stroyers. On the 12th and 13th, *Ticonderoga* and her sisters launched strikes at Luzon airfields and docks and shipping around Manila. This raid tallied an impressive score: light cruiser *Kiso*, four destroyers, and seven merchant ships. At the conclusion of the raid, TF 38 retired eastward for a refueling breather. *Ticonderoga* and the rest of TG 38.3, however, continued east to Ulithi where they arrived on the 17th to replenish, refuel, and rearm.

On November 22, the aircraft carrier departed Ulithi once more and steamed back toward the Philippines. Three days later, she launched air strikes on central Luzon and adjacent waters. Her pilots finished off the heavy cruiser *Kumano*, damaged in the Battle off Samar. Later, they attacked an enemy convoy about 15 miles southwest of *Kumano's* not-so-safe haven in Dasol Bay. Of this convoy, cruiser *Yasoshima*, a merchant man, and three landing ships went to the bottom. *Ticonderoga's* air group rounded out their day of destruction with an aerial rampage which cost the Japanese 15 planes shot down and 11 destroyed on the ground.

While her air group busily pounded the Japanese, *Ticonderoga's* ship's company also made their presence felt. Just after noon, a torpedo launched by an enemy plane broached in *Langley's* (CVL-27) wake to announce the approach of an air raid. *Ticonderoga's* gunners raced to their battle stations as the raiders made both conventional and suicide attacks on the task group. Her sister ship *Essex* (CV-9) erupted in flames when one of the kamikazes crashed into her. When a second suicide plane tried to finish off the stricken carrier, *Ticonderoga's* gunners joined those firing from other ships in cutting his approach abruptly short. That afternoon, while damage control parties dressed *Essex's* wounds, *Ticonderoga* extended her hospitality to that damaged carrier's homeless airmen as well as to *Intrepid* (CV-11) pilots in similar straits. The following day, TF 38 retired to the east.

TF 38 stood out of Ulithi again on December 11 and headed for the Philippines. *Ticonderoga* arrived at the launch point early in the afternoon of the 13th and sent her planes aloft to blanket Japanese airbases on Luzon while Army planes took care of those in the central Philippines. For three days, *Ticonderoga* airmen and their comrades wreaked havoc with a storm of destruction on enemy airfields. She withdrew on the 16th with the rest of TF 38 in search of a fueling rendezvous. While attempting to find calmer waters in which to refuel, TF 38 steamed directly through a violent, but unheralded, typhoon. Though the storm cost Admiral Halsey's force three destroyers and over 800 lives, *Ticonderoga* and the other carriers managed to ride it out with a minimum of damage. Having survived the tempest's fury, *Ticonderoga* returned to Ulithi on Christmas Eve.

Repairs occasioned by the typhoon kept TF 38 in the anchorage almost until the end of the month. The carriers did not return to sea until December 30, 1944, when they steamed north to Formosa and Luzon in preparation for the landings on the latter island at Lingayen Gulf. Severe weather limited the Formosa strikes on January 3 and 4, 1945, and in all likelihood, obviated the need for them. The warships fueled at

sea on the 5th. Despite rough weather on the 6th, the strikes on Luzon airfields were carried out. That day, *Ticonderoga's* airmen and their colleagues of the other air groups increased their score by another 32 enemy planes. The 7th brought more strikes on Luzon installations. After a fueling rendezvous on the 8th, *Ticonderoga* sped north at night to get into position to blanket Japanese airfields in the Ryukyus during the Lingayen assault the following morning. However, foul weather, the bugaboo of TF 38 during the winter of 1944 and 1945, forced TG 38.3 to abandon the strikes on the Ryukyus airfields and join TG 38.2 in pounding Formosa.

During the night of January 9 and 10, TF 38 steamed boldly through the Luzon Strait and then headed generally southwest, diagonally across the South China Sea. *Ticonderoga* provided combat air patrol coverage on the 11th and helped to bring down four enemy planes which attempted to snoop the formation. Otherwise, the carriers and their consorts proceeded unmolested to a point some 150 to 200 miles off the coast of Indochina. There, on the 12th, they launched their approximately 850 planes and made a series of anti-shipping sweeps during which they sank a whopping 44 ships, totaling over 130,000 tons. After recovering planes in the late afternoon, the carriers moved off to the northeast. Heavy weather hindered fueling operations on the 13th and 14th, and air searches failed to turn up any tempting targets. On the 15th, fighters swept Japanese airfields on the Chinese coast while the flattops headed for a position from which to strike Hong Kong. The following morning, they launched antishipping bombing raids and fighter sweeps of air installations. Weather prevented air operations altogether, and again made fueling difficult. It worsened the next day and stopped replenishment operations all together, so that they were not finally concluded until the 19th. The force then shaped a course generally northward to retransit Luzon Strait via Balintang Channel.

The three task groups of TF 38 completed their transit during the night of January 20 and 21. The next morning, their planes hit airfields on Formosa, in the Pescadores, and at Sakishima Gunto. The good flying weather brought mixed blessings. While it allowed American flight operations to continue through the day, it also brought new gusts of the "Divine Wind." Just after noon, a single-engined Japanese plane scored a hit on *Langley* with a glide-bombing attack. Seconds later, a kamikaze swooped out of the clouds and plunged toward *Ticonderoga*. He crashed through her flight deck abreast of the No. 2 5-inch mount, and his bomb exploded just above her hangar deck. Several planes stowed nearby erupted into flames. Death and destruction abounded, but the ship's company fought valiantly to save the threatened carrier. Captain Kiefer conned his ship smartly. First, he changed course to keep the wind from fanning the blaze. Then, he ordered magazines and other compartments flooded to prevent further explosions and to correct a 10-degree starboard list. Finally, he instructed the damage control party to continue flooding compartments on *Ticonderoga's* port side. That operation induced a 10-degree port list which neatly dumped the fire overboard! Firefighters and plane handlers completed the job by dousing the flames and jettisoning burning aircraft.

Wounded denizens of the deep often attract predators. *Ticonderoga* was no exception. The other kamikazes pounced on her like a school of sharks in a feeding frenzy. Her antiaircraft gunners struck back with desperate, but methodical, ferocity and quickly swatted three of her tormentors into the sea. A fourth plane slipped through her barrage and smashed into the carrier's starboard side near the island. His bomb set more planes on fire, riddled her flight deck, and injured or killed another 100 sailors, including Captain Keifer. Yet, *Ticonderoga's* crew refused to submit. Spared further attacks, they brought her fires completely under control not long after 1400; and *Ticonderoga* retired painfully.

The stricken carrier arrived at Ulithi on January 24 but remained there only long enought to move her wounded to hospital ship *Samaratian* (AH-10), to transfer her air group to *Hancock* (CV-19), and to embark passengers bound for home. *Ticonderoga* cleared the lagoon on January 28 and headed for the United States. The warship stopped briefly at Pearl Harbor en route to the Puget Sound Navy Yard where she arrived on February 15.

Her repairs were completed on April 20, and she cleared Puget Sound the following day for the Alameda Naval Air Station. After embarking passengers and aircraft bound for Hawaii, the carrier headed for Pearl Harbor where she arrived on May 1. The next day, Air Group 87 came on board and, for the next week, trained in preparation for the carrier's return to combat. *Ticonderoga* stood out of Pearl Harbor and shaped a course for the eastern Pacific. En route to Ulithi, she launched her planes for what amounted to training strikes on Japanese held Taroa in the Marshalls. On May 22, the warship arrived in Ulithi and rejoined the Fast Carrier Task Force as an element of Rear Admiral Radford's TG 58.4.

Two days after her arrival, *Ticonderoga* sortied from Ulithi with TF 58 and headed north to spend the last weeks of the war in Japanese home waters. Three days out, Admiral Halsey relieved Admiral Spruance, the 5th Fleet reverted back to 3rd Fleet, and TF 58 became TF 38 again for the duration. On June 2 and 3, *Ticonderoga* fighters struck at airfields on Kyushu in an effort to neutralize the remnants of Japanese air power, particularly the Kamikaze Corps, and to relieve the pressure on American forces at Okinawa. During the following two days, *Ticonderoga* rode out her second typhoon in less than six months and emerged relatively unscathed. She provided combat air patrol cover for the June 6 refueling rendezvous, and four of her fighters intercepted and destroyed three Okinawa bound kamikazes. That evening, she steamed off at high speed with TG 38.4 to conduct a fighter sweep of airfields on southern Kyushu on the 8th. *Ticonderoga's* planes then joined in the aerial bombardment of Minami Daito Shima and Kita Daito Shima before the carrier headed for Leyte where she arrived on the 13th.

During the two week rest and replenishment period she enjoyed at Leyte, *Ticonderoga* changed task organizations from TG 38.4 to Rear Admiral Gerald F. Bogan's TG 38.3. On July 1, she departed Leyte with TF 38 and headed north

to resume raids on Japan. Two days later, a damaged reduction gear forced her into Apra Harbor, Guam, for repairs. She remained there until the 19th when she steamed off to rejoin TF 38 and resume her role in the war against Japan. On the 24th, her planes joined those of other fast carriers in striking ships in the Inland Sea and airfields at Nagoya, Osaka, and Miko. During those raids, TF 38 planes found the sad remnants of the once-mighty Japances Fleet and bagged battleships *Ise, Hyuga,* and *Haruna* as well as an escort carrier, *Kaiyo,* and two heavy cruisers. On July 28, her aircraft directed their efforts toward the Kure Naval Base, where they pounded an aircraft carrier, three cruisers, a destroyer, and a submarine. She shifted her attention to the industrial area of central Honshu on the 30th, then to northern Honshu and Hokkaido on August 9 and 10. The latter attacks thoroughly destroyed the marshalling area for a planned airborne suicide raid on the B-29 bases in the Marianas. On the 13th and 14th, her planes returned to the Tokyo area and helped to subject the Japanese capital to another severe drubbing.

The two atomic bombs dropped on Hiroshima and Nagasaki on the 6th and 9th, respectively, convinced the Japanese of the futility of continued resistance. On the morning of August 15, *Ticonderoga* launched another strike against Tokyo. During or just after that attack, word reached TF 38 to the effect that Japan had capitulated.

The shock of peace, though not so abrupt as that of war almost four years previously, took some getting used to. *Ticonderoga* and her sister ships remained on a full war footing. She continued patrols over Japanese territory and sent reconnaissance flights in search of camps containing Allied prisoners of war so that airdropped supplies could be rushed to them. On September 6, four days after the formal surrender ceremony on board *Missouri* (BB-63), *Ticonderoga* entered Tokyo Bay.

Her arrival at Tokyo ended one phase of her career and began another. She embarked homeward-bound passengers and put to sea again on the 20th. After a stop in Pearl Harbor, the carrier reached Alameda, California, on October 5. She disembarked her passengers and unloaded cargo before heading out on the 9th to pick up another group of veterans. *Ticonderoga* delivered over a thousand soldiers and sailors to Tacoma, Washington, and remained there through the 28th for the Navy Day celebration. On October 29, the carrier departed Tacoma and headed back to Alameda. En route, all of the planes of Air Group 87 were transferred ashore so that the carrier could be altered to accomodate additional passengers in the "Magic Carpet" voyages to follow. Following the completion of those modifications at the Pearl Harbor Naval Shipyard in November, the warship headed for the Philippines and arrived at Samar on November 20. She returned to Alameda on December 6 and debarked almost 4,000 returning servicemen. The carrier made one more "Magic Carpet" run in december 1945 and January 1946 before entereing the Puget Sound Naval Shipyard to prepare for inactivation. Almost a year later, on January 9, 1947, *Ticonderoga* was placed out of commission and berthed with the Bremerton Group of the Pacific Reserve Fleet.

On January 31, 1952, *Ticonderoga* came out of reserve and went into reduced commission for the transit from Bremerton to New York. She departed Puget Sound on February 27 and reached New York on April 1. Three days later, she was decommissioned at the New York Naval Shipyard to begin an extensive conversion. During the ensuing 29 months, the carrier received numerous modificatons: steam catapults to launch jets, a new nylon baricade, a new deck-edge elevator and the latest electronic and fire control equipment necessary for her to become an integral unit of the fleet. On September 11, 1954, *Ticonderoga* was recommissioned at New York, Captain William A. Schoech in command.

In January 1955, the carrier shifted to her new home port, Norfolk, Virginia, where she arrived on the 6th. Over the next month, she conducted carrier qualifications with Air Group 6 in the Virginia Capes operating area. On February 3, she stood out of Hampton Roads for shakedown near Cuba, after which she returned via Norfolk to New York for additional alterations. During the late summer, the warship resumed carrier qualifications in the Virginia capes area. After a visit to Philadelphia early in September, she participated in the sets of three new planes; the A4D-1 *Skyhawk,* the F4D-1 *Skyray,* and the F3H-2N *Demon. Ticonderoga* then returned to normal operations along the east coast until November 4 when she departed Mayport, Florida and headed for Europe. She relieved *Intrepid* at Gibraltar 10 days later and cruised the length of the Mediterranean during the following eight months. On August 2, 1956, *Ticonderoga* returned to Norfolk and entered the shipyard to receive an angled flight deck and an enclosed hurricane bow.

Those modifications were completed by early 1957; and, in April, she got underway for her new home port, Alameda, California. She reached her destination on May 30, underwent repairs, and finished out the summer with operations off the California coast. On September 16, she stood out of San Francisco Bay and shaped a course for the Far East. En route, she stopped at Pearl Harbor before continuing west to Yokosuka, Japan, where she arrived on October 15. For six months, *Ticonderoga* cruised Oriental waters from Japan in the north to the Philippines in the south. Upon arriving at Alameda on April 25, 1958, she completed her first deployment to the western Pacific since recommissioning.

Between 1958 and 1963, *Ticonderoga* made four more peacetime deployments to the western Pacific. During each, she conducted training operatons with other units of the 7th Fleet and made goodwill and liberty port calls throughout the Far East. Early in 1964, she began preparations for her sixth cruise to the western Pacific and, following exercises off the west coast and in the Hawaiian Islands, the carrier cleared Pearl Harbor on May 4 for what began as another peaceful tour of duty in the Far East. The first three months of that deployment brought normal operations, training and port calls. However, on August 2, while operating in international waters in the Gulf of Tonkin, *Maddox* (DD-731) reported being attcked by units of the North Vietnamese navy. Within minutes of her receipt of

Bake shop on the USS Ticonderoga, *West Pacific, 1960. L to R: CS1 McConnel, CS3 Wright, CS3, Balthis, CS3 McGory. (Courtesy of Donald R. McGory)*

the message, *Ticonderoga* dispatched four, rocket-armed F8E, "Crusaders" to the destroyer's assistance. Upon arrival, the "Crusaders" launched Zuni rockets and strafed the North Vietnamese craft with their 20 millimeter cannons. The *Ticonderoga* airmen teamed up with *Maddox* gunners to thwart the North Vietnamese attack, leaving one boat dead in the water and damaging the other two.

Two days later, late in the evening of the 4th, *Ticonderoga* received urgent requests from *Turner Joy* (DD-951), by then on patrol with *Maddox*, for air support in resisting what the destroyer alleged to be another torpedo boat foray. The carrier again launched planes to aid the American surface ships, and *Turner Joy* directed them. The Navy surface and air team believed it had sunk two boats and damaged another pair. President Johnson responded with a reprisal to what he felt at the time to be two unprovoked attacks on American seapower and ordered retaliatory air strikes on selected North Vietnamese motor torpedo boat bases. On August 5, *Ticonderoga* and *Constellation* (CV-46) launched 60 sorties against four bases and their supporting oil storage facilities. Those attacks reportedly resulted in the destruction of 25 PT-type boats, severe damage to the bases, and almost complete razing of the oil storage depot. For her quick reaction and successful combat actions of those three occasions, *Ticonderoga* received the Navy Unit Commendation.

After a return visit to Japan in September, the aircraft carrier resumed normal operations in the South China Sea until winding up the deployment late in the year. She returned to the Naval Air Station, North Island, California on December 15, 1964. Following post-deployment and holiday standdown, *Ticonderoga* moved to the Hunter's Point Naval Shipyard on January 27, 1965, to begin a five month overhaul. She completed repairs in June and spent the summer operating along the coast of California. On September 28, the aircraft carrier put to sea for another deployment to the Orient. She spent some time in the Hawaiian Islands for an operational readiness exercise then continued on to the Far East. She reached "Dixie Station" on November 5 and immediately began combat air operations.

Ticonderoga's winter deployment of 1965 and 1966 was her first total combat tour of duty during American involvement in the Vietnam War. During her six months in the Far East, the carrier spent a total of 115 days in air operations off the coast of Vietnam, dividing her time almost evenly between "Dixie" and "Yankee Stations," the carrier operating areas off South and North Vietnam, respectively. Her air group delivered over 8,000 tons of ordnance in more than 10,000 combat sorties, with a loss of 16 planes, but only 5 pilots. For the most part, her aircraft hit enemy installations in North Vietnam and interdicted supply routes into South Vietnam, including river-borne and coastwise junk and sampan traffic as well as roads, bridges, and trucks on land. Specifically, they claimed the destruction of 35 bridges as well as numerous warehouses, barracks, trucks, boats, and railroad cars and severe damage to a major North Vietnamese thermal power plant located at Uong Bi north of Haiphong. After a stop at Sasebo, Japan, from April 25 to May 3, 1966, the warship put to sea to return to the United States. On May 13, she pulled into port at San Diego to end the deployment.

Following repairs she stood out of San Diego on July 9 to begin a normal round of west coast training operations. Those and similar evolutions continued until October 15, when

Ticonderoga departed San Diego, bound via Hawaii for the western Pacific. The carrier reached Yokosuka, Japan on October 30 and remained there until November 5 when she headed south for an overnight stop at Subic Bay in the Philippines on the 10th and 11th. On the 13th, *Ticonderoga* arrived in the Gulf of Tonkin and began the first of three combat tours druing her 1966-67 deployment. She launched 11,650 combat sorties, all against enemy targets located in North Vietnam. Again, her primary targets were logistics and communications lines and transportation facilities. For their overall efforts in the conduct of day and night strikes on enemy targets, *Ticonderoga* and her air group earned their second Navy Unit Commendation. She completed her final line period on April 27, 1967, and returned to Yokosuka, from which she departed again on May 19 to return to the United States. Ten days later, the carrier entered San Diego and began a month-long, post-deployment standdown. At the beginning of July, the warship shifted to Bremerton, Washington, where she entered the Puget Sound Naval Shipyard for two months of repairs. Upon the completion of yard work, she departed Bremerton on September 6 and steamed south to training operations off the coast of southern California.

On December 28, *Ticonderoga* sailed for her fourth combat deployment to the waters off the Indochinese coast. She made Yokosuka on January 17, 1968, and after two days of upkeep, continued on to the Gulf of Tonkin where she arrived on station on the 26th and began combat operations. Between January and July, *Ticonderoga* was on the line off the coast of Vietnam for five separate periods totaling 120 days of combat duty. During that time, her air wing flew just over 13,000 combat sorties against North Vietnamese and Viet Cong forces, most frequently in the continuing attempts to interdict the enemy lines of supply. In mid-April, following her second line period, she made a port visit to Singapore and then, after upkeep at Subic Bay, returned to duty off Vietnam. On July 9, during her fifth and final line period, Lieutenant Commander J.B. Nichols claimed *Ticonderoga's* first MiG kill. The carrier completed that line period and entered Subic Bay for upkeep on July 25.

On the 27th, she headed north to Yokosuka where she spent a week for upkeep and briefings before heading back to the United States on August 7. *Ticonderoga* reached San Diego on the 17th and disembarked her air group. On the 22nd, she entered the Long Beach Naval Shipyard for post-deployment repairs. She completed those repairs on October 21, conducted sea trials on the 28th and 29th, and began normal operations out of San Diego early in November. For the remainder of the year, she conducted refresher training and carrier qualifications along the coast of Southern California.

During the first month of 1969, *Ticonderoga* made preparations for her fifth consecutive combat deployment to the Southeast Asia area. On February 1, she cleared San Diego and headed west. After a brief stop at Pearl Harbor a week later, she continued her voyage to Yokosuka where she arrived on the 20th. The carrier departed Yokosuka on the 28th for the coast of Vietnam where she arrived on March 4. Over the next four months, *Ticonderoga* served four periods on the line off Vietnam, interdicting communist supply lines and making strikes against their positions.

During her second line period, however, her tour of duty off Vietnam came to an abrupt end on April 16 when she was shifted north to the Sea of Japan. North Korean aircraft had shot down a Navy reconnaissance plane in the area, and *Ticonderoga* was called upon to beef up the forces assigned to the vicinity. However, the crisis abated; and *Ticonderoga* entered Subic Bay on April 27 for upkeep. On May 8, she departed the Philippines to return to "Yankee Station" and resumed interdiction operations. Between her third and fourth line periods, the carrier visited Sasebo and Hong Kong.

The aircraft carrier took station off Vietnam for her last line period of the deployment on June 26 and there followed 37 more days of highly successful air sorties against enemy targets. Following that tour, she joined TF 71 in the Sea of Japan for the remainder of the deployment. *Ticonderoga* concluded the deployment-a highly successful one for she received her third Naval Unit Commendation for her operations during that tour of duty-when she left Subic Bay on September 4.

Ticonderoga arrived in San Diego on September 18. After almost a month of post-deployment standdown, she moved to the Long Beach Naval Shipyard in mid-October to begin conversion to an antisubmarine warfare (ASW) aircraft carrier. Overhaul and conversion work began on October 20, and *Ticonderoga* was redesignated CVS-14 on the 21st. She completed overhaul and conversion on May 28, 1970, and conducted exercises out of Long Beach for most of June. On the 26th, the new ASW support carrier entered her new home port, San Diego. During July and August, she conducted refresher training, refresher air operations, and carrier landing qualifications. The warship operated off the California coast for the remainder of the year and participated in two exercises-HUKASWEX 4-70 late in October and COMPUTEX 23-70 between November 30 and December 3.

During the remainder of her active career, *Ticonderoga* made two more deployments to the Far East. Because of her change in mission, neither tour of duty included combat operations off Vietnam. Both, however, included training exercises in the Sea of Japan with ships of the Japanese Maritime Self Defense Force. The first of these two cruises also brought operations in the Indian Ocean with units of the Thai navy and a transit of Sunda Strait during which a ceremony was held to commemorate the loss of *Houston* (CA-30) and HMAS *Perth* in 1942.

In between these two last deployments, she operated in the eastern Pacific and participated in the recovery of the Apollo 16 moon mission capsule and astronauts near American Samoa during April 1972. The second deployment came in the summer of 1972; and, in addition to the training exercises in the Sea of Japan, *Ticonderoga* also joined ASW training operations in the South China Sea. That fall, she returned to the eastern Pacific and, in November, practiced for the recovery of Apollo 17. The next month, *Ticonderoga* recovered her second set of space voyagers near American Samoa. The car-

rier then headed back to San Diego where she arrived on December 28.

Ticonderoga remained active for nine more months, first operating out of San Diego and then making preparations for inactivation. On September 1, 1973, the aircraft carrier was decommissioned after a board of inspection and survey found her to be unfit for further naval service. Her name was struck from the Navy list on November 16, 1973, and arrangements were begun to sell her for scrap.

Ticonderoga received five battle stars during World War II and three Navy Unit Commendations, one Meritorious Unit Commendation, and 12 Battle Stars during the Vietnam War.

V

(CG-47: dp. 8,910; 1. 563'; b. 55'; dr. 29'; s. 30+k.; a. 1 mis. ln., 2 5", 2 Phalanx, Standard missile, Harpoon, ASROC, 6 15.5" tt; cl. *Ticonderoga*)

Authorized in FY 1978, the fifth *Ticonderoga* (CG-47) was laid down on January 21, 1980, at Pascagoula, Mississippi, by the Ingalls Shipbuilding Division of Litton Industries. Launched on April 25, 1981, she was christened on Armed Forces Day, May 16, 1981, by America's First Lady, Mrs. Nancy Reagan, with Secretary of Defense Casper W. Weinberger as keynote speaker. The nation's first Aegis warship was commissioned at the Ingalls yard on January 22, 1983, Captain Roland G. Guilbault in command. Over fifty (50) members of her predecessor, carrier *Ticonderoga*, attended the ceremony.

CG-47 departed Ingalls a week after commissioning for training and shakedown in the Atlantic and Caribbean. Combat System Ship Qualification Trials and the Follow-on Test and Evaluation of USS *Ticonderoga* were conducted in Roosevelt Roads, Puerto Rico between March 21 and April 22. During this 33 day period, the lead ship of her class proved she was the shield of the fleet. Her final testing, over the summer months, included a four week refresher training exercise, Naval Gun Fire Support certification, Antisubmarine Warfare operations, Final Contract Trials, and Battle Group Operations exercises. *Ticonderoga* was declared "War Ready" in September and sailed in October for her first tour of duty with the Sixth Fleet.

After a stormy crossing of the Atlantic and a short visit to Portsmouth, England, she departed for the Mediterranean area. Shortly after entering the Med, Rear Admiral R.C. Berry, Commander, Cruiser Destroyer Group Eight, assumed the duties of Antiair Warfare Commander, for the battle group that included the carrier *Independence* and the USS *New Jersey*, and made *Ticonderoga* his flagship. On December 13, while deployed off the

coast of Lebanon, USS *Ticonderoga* fired her guns for the first time in anger when, with other United States warships of the Sixth Fleet, she shelled antiaircraft missile and gun emplacements located in the mountains northeast of Beirut. Shelling began immediately after pilots of F-14 Tomcats flying reconnaissance missions reported they were being fired at from the gun emplacements. The Shouf Mountain guns were fired on several times in the days following as *Ticonderoga* maintained her vigil in defense of our forces in the city and overhead. On December 18, CG-47 and DDG-19 (USS *Tattnall*) fired a total of about 60 rounds of 5-inch in about 20 minutes.

Following 47 days of intense operations near Beirut, CG-47 arrived in Haifa for a six day visit to the Holy Land and some R&R. *Ticonderoga* marked her first anniversary by earning eight of the nine operational warfare excellence awards for which all Navy ships compete annually. Ships are judged for excellence in warfare, engineering and seamanship. She received her eight awards in just nine months out of an 18-month competitive cycle. *Ticonderoga* left the Mediterranean on April 10, 1984, to participate in a series of sea tests in the Caribbean on April 19 to April 29. She arrived back in her home port of Norfolk on May 4 after a seven month deployment.

On June 6, Captain Guilbault, on behalf of the crew and officers of *Ticonderoga*, accepted a special team Aegis Excellence Award from RCA Missile and Surface Radar for flawlessly maintaining and operating a new, complex and highly capable system during her Sixth Fleet deployment as part of a multi-carrier battle force.

USS *Ticonderoga* and USS *Yorktown* (second of the Aegis cruisers) underwent individual and joint exercises during joint flight operations off Norfolk in late August. During these exercises, the two cruisers ran 10 miles apart, testing each other's Aegis Combat Systems. CG-47 continued with additional tests of missile firings in the Atlantic during September.

On January 19, 1985, Captain Guilbault, in an impressive Change of Command ceremony, turned over the helm of CG-47 to Captain Raymond M. Walsh to carry on the tradition of *Ticonderogamen* whose motto is First and Formidable and whose trade is Operational Excellence. AND THE NAME LIVES ON.

George A. Garcia (left), AM 1/C, at 1973 decommissioning ceremony in the company of another seaman, Leahy, Radar. (Courtesy of George A. Garcia)

KAMIKAZE ATTACK - USS *TICONDEROGA* CV-14 JANUARY 21, 1945

This was written after a lifelong dream of recording the agonies and glories shared by all who manned the mighty "Big T" one unforgettable day during World War II in the South Pacific. It is dedicated to the USS Ticonderoga, a "Fighting Lady" with one hundred and seventy-five years of Naval tradition, to her officers and crew, past, present and future, and in particular to those brave men who perished in the Japanese Kamikaze attack at noon on January 21, 1945.

-E.B.Sutterley, CPhM, USN

Kamikaze, the "Divine Wind," a treacherous, deadly, unpredictable, merciless attack, the last gasp of a defeated empire.

To read the account of one day of Kamikaze warfare on a US aircraft carrier is to understand both the deadly intent of a defeated yet defiant enemy and the unparalleled courage, resourcefulness, and determination of the men of the United States Navy. The following material is from the records, reports and logs of Commander Tadashi Nakajima of the Imperial Japanese Navy. He was a naval academy graduate, commanded air units on carriers and ashore in China, from 1933 until the outbreak of WW II. He was an air group commander at Bali, Rabaul, New Guinea, the Solomons, Guadalcanal, and Iwo Jima.

He was serving as the flight operations officer for the 201st Air Group in the Philippines when that unit was selected by Admiral Ohnishi for the initiation of suicide tactics as a deliberate weapon of policy. He served as an operations and training officer for suicide units until, in the last few months of the war, he was assigned command of the 723rd Air Group:

A new special attack corps was organized in Formosa. In it were Zeros ("Zekes") and Suisei carrier bombers ("Judy") drawn from the Tainan Air Group. The supply of pilots was limited to the ones who had been evacuated from Tuguegarao and Appari in the Philippines.

The christening ceremonies of this corps took place at Tainan at 1700 on 18 January 1945, and Admiral Ohnishi was personally in attendance. This was the first special attack corps to be formed in Formosa, and it was designated the "Niitaka Unit" after the Formosan mountain of that name.

The decision to launch an attack with the Niitaka Unit was made on 21 January when the First Air Fleet received a report that an enemy task force had been sighted east-southwest of southern Formosa. The unit was divided into three attack sections of the following composition:

No. 1 (from Shinko)
Attackers: 2 Suisei, 2 Zeros
Escort: 2 Zeros

No. 2 (from Taitung)
Attackers: 2 Suisei, 2 Zeros
Escort: 2 Zeros

No. 3 (from Taibu)
Attackers: 2 Suisei
Escort: 2 Zeros

I place special emphasis on two points about the sortie. One was the assembly point after take-off should be to the north of the field, the other that flight to the assembly point should be at minimum altitude. These measures were necessary as precautions against the constant threat of enemy raids. It was essential to get the planes away from the field as quickly as possible, and by flying low they would run the least risk of being observed by the enemy. Every second would count.

Having ordered the planes to be readied, I climbed to the top of a sandbag shelter and looked about in all directions. The weather was beautiful. Scattered white clouds at 1,000 meters covered about 30 percent of the sky. In the direction of Takao all was quiet. There was no enemy plane in sight. I gave the order for take-off.

Within three minutes after the engines were started, the first Suisei was lumbering toward the runway, followed promptly by a second and then a third. My surprise at this performance was accompanied by a sudden thought that the fighters might prove to be a delaying factor, but I was relieved to see them follow immediately.

The first Zero paused for a moment at the south end of the field, gunned its engine, and moved forward, rapidly gathering speed. The rest followed in rapid succession, disappearing to the north in a straight line, flying very low, according to plan. The take-off of the first section was perfect.

The two other sections were ready and standing by. I again scanned the horizon. No enemy planes were in sight, and our search radar still reported no contacts. I ordered both the remaining sections to take off.

When the first of these planes appeared on the runway to take to the air, I was disturbed to find it was the third section and not the second. Its planes got off nicely, however, but I was concerned about that damned second section.

After an interminable delay, during which I expected enemy planes to appear at any second, the planes of the last section rolled over the field toward the runway. My relief in seeing them accelerate and get into the air at last was short lived, for they proceeded to assemble by circling directly over the field. I was just thinking how terribly inferior this second section was, when they capped all earlier errors by flying off to the south.

Then a lookout post reported, "Two Zeros, so and so degree, altitude so and so meters." All that remained was to await reports that had assumed a familiar pattern. This day, unfortunately, the report was not routine.

The second section, delayed in its departure, had met enemy Grummans west of the mountains. Flying low, its planes had been greatly handicapped in the fight that followed, but the escorts had engaged the enemy while the Suisei flew on. As a result of the dogfight the three escorts had lost contact with the Kamikaze planes and could do nothing but return to base. One plane had been so damaged in the fight that it could not land and the pilot had to parachute to safety. The pilots of the escorts were filled with remorse that they had failed to accompany the Suisei to the target area. There was, accordingly, no report on the results achieved by the second section of the Niitaka unit.

Escort planes of the first and third sections returned shortly to base, however, with reports that direct hits had been scored on enemy carriers. One of the targets successfully attacked was identified as the American carrier *Ticonderoga*.

FROM RECORDS OF THE USN:

The *Ticondroga* (CV-14) was damaged this date by suicide planes in position lat. 22*40' N, long. 122*57'E. Also damaged by suicide planes this date were the light carrier *Langley* (CVL-27) at lat. 22*40'N, long. 122*51E, and the destroyer *Maddox* (DD-731) at lat. 23*06'N, long. 122*43' E.

Commissioning of the USS Ticonderoga *CV-14, March 8, 1944. Here are four of the VT-80 pilots. From L to R: Ensigns Higman, Montgomery, Woods, Welch. This photo was taken at Virginia Beach, VA, just before commissioning.*

Body of Hero and Five Others Killed in New York Plane Crash Returned

Memorial services for Commodore Dixie Kiefer and the five other plane crash victims will be conducted at 11:15 a.m. Thursday at Quonset Auditorium. The Commodore's funeral, private, will be at his home on the reservation Thursday afternoon. He will be buried in Arlington National Cemetery, Virginia, Friday at 10:00 a.m.

Plans were being completed today for the funeral of Commodore Dixie Kiefer, wounded hero of Pacific carrier warfare, who was killed Sunday in the crash of a transport in which he was returning from Caldwell, N.J. to Quonset Naval Air Station. He was commanding officer of the air station and commander of naval air bases of the First Naval District.

His body and those of three other officers and two enlisted men were recovered yesterday by 200 men of his former command at Quonset who, with axes and machetes, hacked a way up the steep slope of Mount Beacon, three miles northeast of Beacon, N.Y. to reach the wrecked plane.

Commodore Kiefer, hero of two wars, who survived the carrier *Yorktown* to take command of the *Ticonderoga*, which he later saved after Kamikaze attacks had left it in flames, still carried his wounded arm in a cast when the 160 mile peacetime flight tragically ended his outstanding career.

The plane became lost in fog and was 30 miles off its course when it crashed.

Others killed in the crash, all of whom were stationed at Quonset, were identified last night by the navy as:

LT. COMMANDER IGNATIUS ZIELINSKI, 45, USNR, of Salem, MA assistant medical officer at the Quonset Dispensary and, before entering the service, a medical examiner.

LT. LLOYD P. HEIZEN, 23, USNR senior pilot of the ship, son of Mrs. Alice Rose, 1006 East High Street, Colorado Springs, CO, who frequently flew Commodore Kiefer.

LT. (jg) HANS K. KOHLER, 25, USN co-pilot of the ship, son of Paul Kohler, 28 Division Avenue, Garfield, NJ.

CLARENCE HOOPER, 22, aviation machinist's mate 3c, husband of Doris Marie Hooper, Greensboro, NC.

DAVID O. WOOD, 23, seaman 1c, son of Aime J. Wood, North Franklin, CT.

Kiefer, the famed "Captain Dixie" of the documentary movie, "The Fighting Lady," still wore one arm in a cast from wounds suffered when he was hit 65 times by shrapnel as the carrier *Ticonderoga* was battered by Jap suicide planes off Formosa.

Commodore Kiefer's body and those of the other five crash victims last night were brought back to Quonset Naval Air Station from the scene of the tragedy.

Personnel of the station, who had volunteered for searching parties and for the work of carrying the bodies down the mountainside, accompanied them back to the station.

The commander of air bases of the First Naval District had left Quonset Saturday morning to meet an aviation executive in New York. The aviation executive, an old acquaintance, had met Kiefer earlier last week in New York and had asked him about giving a talk to aircraft workers and had also talked to him about other aviation matters . It was said that after meeting this acquaintance last Saturday, Commodore Kiefer discussed the matters in question and that the two attended the Army-Notre Dame football game Saturday afternoon.

Remaining over Saturday night in New York, the naval hero started for his home base Sunday morning leaving Caldwell, NJ. at 11:23 o'clock in a 2-engined Beechcraft, the type frequently used as transports by navy officers.

Crewmen on the plane radioed Stewart Field at West Point about noon, saying the plane was lost. This radio communication was broken off abruptly, and within minutes, the plane crashed against the mountainside, about 30 miles off the usual air route between Caldwell and Quonset.

A party of 200 officers, sailors and marines set out from Quonset shortly before one yesterday morning with busses, crash trucks and ambulances, loaded with wet weather gear and equipment for rescue work.

Two naval officers in a fast car preceded the party into Beacon, interviewed townspeople and fixed the precise location of the crash.

With daybreak, the 200 volunteers from his command began the arduous task of clearing a way for 2000 yards up the wooded slope to the wreckage. Progress was extremely slow, as the men, with axes or machetes, cleared brush and trees. After two hours work, the party reached the wreckage near the summit of the mountain.

Commodore Kiefer's body was about 25 feet from the fuselage. His gold-braided cap lay near the body, and an enlisted man picked it up and hung it on the broken root of a tree that had been knocked over by the plane. The commodore's wounded arm, still in a cast, was outstretched above his head, and the cast aided in positive identification of the hero's body.

One body, that of a flight captain, was found in the broken fuselage. The body had been slightly burned.

Marines carried Commodore Kiefer's body down the rough slope on a litter. Sorrowing, they recalled that he had reviewed them last Saturday before taking off for New York.

After the commodore's body was removed, bodies of the other five victims were carried down the mountainside in preparation for the sad return to Rhode Island.

News of the commander's death had wrought a marked change in the unofficial life of the station yesterday and today, but necessary duties there were attended quietly by the officers who had been told by Commodore Kiefer, when he first took command, to go out and do their job and "call me if you need me."

Command of the station had been taken over today by the executive officer, Comdr. John T. Workman.

Command of the air bases from Connecticut to Maine was assumed by the chief of staff, Capt. Truman C. Penney.

Numerous calls crowded the station switchboard as friends confirmed news of the tragedy and relayed sympathies to Commodore Kiefer's relatives and associates.

From a hospital at Brunswick, ME, Comdr. Joseph Taylor, navy war hero and commanding officer of the Brunswick air station, telephoned the station to confirm news reports. He was just recovering from a major operation. Kiefer had visited his bedside only last week.

Waves at Quonset today recalled how the commanding officer was "always coming along with flowers from his garden, or a big basket of fruit or some other gift."

Enlisted personnel through the station agreed that because of Commodore Kiefer's activities in their behalf it had become more fun to remain on the station nights for recreation than to go on liberty passes. Station fun under his promotion included clambakes, new boats for sailing, new swim areas, skating parties, sailor-Wave socials, and sunrise steak breakfasts at which the commodore frequently presided. He even procured 150 shotguns so sailors could hunt for game in their free time.

These things were remembered today as officers, enlisted men and Waves quietly prepared to pay their last tribute to their "one wonderful guy."

Recently he underwent another operation for his wounded arm, and he was well on the way to complete recovery.

When he arrived at Quonset last Spring, he said he had one limb that had not been broken and that he was going back into action until it was hit. End of the war disrupted that plan, and Commodore Kiefer then turned his entire energies to Quonset and the air bases command. Much of Quonset's part in postwar naval aviation had already been mapped out by the commodore.

Commodore Kiefer got his title "the indestructible man" from Secretary of the Navy James V. Forrestal when the Navy Secretary gave him the Distinguished Service Medal, one of nine decorations that he earned in battle.

His most famous exploit came aboard the blazing aircraft carrier *Ticonderoga*, which was floundering so badly from kamikaze attacks that a query crackled over the wireless: "Are you going to abandon ship?"

"Hell, no," was Kiefer's classic answer.

For more than 12 hours, Kiefer, then Captain Kiefer and commanding officer of the carrier, remained on deck after the ship suffered almost a mortal blow and he had 65 shrapnel wounds.

Every man at exposed stations on the carrier was either killed or wounded after the kamikaze planes' attack, and Captain Dixie lay on the deck with a 10-inch gash in his arm, a severed artery and his body peppered with bomb fragments. The casualties -337- included 144 dead before the noise of the explosion died away, and the 27,000 ton Essex class carrier, flaming from below the hangar decks, appeared doomed.

Aides were carrying their captain to a safer area below decks, when he asked about the condition of his senior officers and was told they were all casualties. He struggled to his feet and returned to what was left of the bridge.

He ordered the course changed so as to keep the wind from feeding fires that might have reached magazines and fuel stores. After a terrific struggle the crew turned back the fires and within a matter of hours planes were again able to land and take off from the carrier's decks.

Eventually returned to this country for complete hospitalization for his wounds, Commodore Kiefer was assigned to command of the First Naval District air bases with headquarters at Quonset Point. He succeeded Commodore Ben H. Wyatt, USN, on May 3, last.

A midshipman at the United States Military Academy at Annapolis, MD when World War I broke out, he was graduated and was commissioned in 1918. He first served in the anti-submarine patrol and his assignment to the naval aviation section came in 1922.

Holder of nine citations and medals from the navy for distinguished service to his country, he served in the battles of the Coral Sea and Midway and later was assigned as chief of staff at the Naval Air Primary Training Command with headquarters in Kansas City.

It was only five months ago, June 5, that Commodore Kiefer received his latest navy award, the Silver Star, from Rear Admiral Felix X. Gaygax, commandant of the First Naval District.

In addition to the Silver Star, he held the Navy Cross, Distinguished Service Medal, and Purple Heart. He also wore the Victory Medal, Patrol Clasp, the American Defense Service Medal, Fleet Clasp, and the Asiatic-Pacific Areas Campaign Medal.

As a young ensign, Kiefer was first assigned upon graduation from Annapolis, to the cruiser *St. Louis* and later in that same year transferred for assignment to the destroyer force based in Brest, France, for anti-submarine patrol.

He took a post-graduate course in aeronautical engineering at Annapolis beginning in 192? and his varied experiences as a naval aviator included service with observation and scouting squadrons, special studies in engineer officers' duties, assignment to the staff of Admiral Frederick G. Horne as commander aircraft battle force with the USS *Saratoga*.

Later he saw service as an engineer officer aboard the USS *Wright* and for three years was assigned as inspector of naval aircraft at the East Hartford, CT division of the Pratt & Whitney motor company.

He returned to sea as executive officer of the *Wright* and in 1942 was made executive officer aboard the carrier *Yorktown*. During his tour of duty, the *Yorktown* was lost in the Battle of Midway, but not before she had taken part in raids in Salamaua and Lae in the battle of the Coral Sea.

Commodore Kiefer, who was born April 4, 1896, in Blackfoot, IA never married. He lived with his mother Mrs. Christina (Glade) Kiefer, and a sister, Miss Phyllis Kiefer, who came here with him from Kansas City after his assignment as head of the First Naval District air bases. His father, Edward Kiefer, died in 1905.

Two other sisters, Mrs. F.L. Brookhouser of New York City, and Mrs. A.E. Brayson of Salt Lake City, Utah, and a brother, H.G. Kiefer of Los Angeles, Cal. survive.

During his command at Quonset he occupied a dwelling in the officers' colony which he shared with his mother and sister.

THE LETTER LEGACY

The following letters describe the individual actions of the men of the aircraft carrier USS *Ticonderoga* CV-14 on one day of combat in the Pacific during World War II. Even after fifty years, the events of that day remain indelibly etched in the crew's memories and their accounts allow you to share their fears, their deeds, and their courage. It is a permanent remembrance of what they accomplished and, more importantly, a fitting tribute to those who perished on that day.

Richard Alfonso RM2c

I was between watches, reading in my bunk below deck. I heard General Quarters at approximately twelve noon. The Jap planes were coming straight out of the sun at us. I ran up top deck to my General Quarters station in Radio Central in the bridge. I sat at my station with my phones on, typing code, along with George Olsen RM1c, Lt. Gewertz and others.

There was a lot of commotion and gunfire - 5-inch, 40 mm, and 20 mm. When I heard 20 mm going off, I knew they were close. Suddenly we lost all power on our radio sets. I took over with the J.S. phones. I was standing by the table with the "joe pot," which was not turned off. Suddenly we heard a large explosion, which was a bomb going off in the hangar deck. Kamikaze Betty had hit the bridge. It knocked us all down to the deck. I fell forward to the deck and the "joe pot" fell over, spilling hot coffee all over my back. I thought the warm feeling was blood and started calling for a medic. I think the guys laughed about that all the way back to the States.

The J.S. phones were working only one way. We could hear them but they couldn't hear us. The explosion had buckled the door and escape hatch on the deck. We couldn't get out. The heat got so intense from the fire we couldn't walk on the deck; we had to stand on the metal-legged chairs. Fortunately no one was injured in the radio shack. Except my ego!

When the fires were put out on the bridge, they came and forced open the door. We got out and jumped from the bridge to the deck. Because of lack of communications between Radio Central and the outside, they thought we were all dead.

Frank Anci Cox

On the morning of 21 January 1945 I came off 4 AM watch which was the 40 mm mount above the bridge. Sky 1 radar was above us. Went for chow with other members of the watch crew. The one thing that stands out in my mind was Bates from Buffalo telling me how he used to come home under the weather and fall asleep on the couch. His daughter, then very young, would try to wake him up by telling him "I love you Daddy" etc.

As the morning went on with the different work details everything was the normal routine. About 11:00 I met up with Gould and Terril and we ate with the mess cooks - those going on watch. After eating we went up to the hangar deck by the forward starboard crane where we sat and played cards. Before we heard GQ the firing of the guns sounded and we heard a plane. We ran aft to an opening where we saw a Jap plane which had just gone over the ship from port to starboard.

At this point, off we went to our gun stations - mine was the bow, Fifth Division. Had two 40 mm guns on the bow, two off the hangar deck, port side, forward before hangar deck #1. We also had the mount above the bridge. As I ran up the ladder to the forecastle deck and started going to the bow, the first explosion occurred. Everything at that point was vibrating and all you could do was hang on to lines.

Arriving at the gun, everything was ready and when we had to fire we did. To this day I do not know how many had been killed or wounded that were behind me coming up the ladder. As the day went on some of the wounded were brought up to the forecastle deck.

Frank Macey was in our compartment which was on the forecastle deck. As he was coming out of the head during the first explosion something went through the sleeve of his left arm, leaving it detached.

The second plane hit Sky 1 and the 40 mm mount above the bridge and took a great many lives. The Fifth Division lost men there. As for the rest of the day, we stayed at our gun stations until dark. Once GQ ended we all went to see what could be done and view the damage. I remember walking through compartments that were flooded. Sick Bay was overcrowded and the scene was not pleasant.

On the morning of the 22nd everybody had to turn to in more ways than one. The dead, wounded, damages all had to be taken care of. The days that followed were long. I mentioned Bates at the beginning and it is something that will always be with me. As we were walking down the hangar deck I noticed a body lying there with a fuel line across his back. The name on the shirt was Bates.

Lewis Daniel Andrews WT1c

I set the auxiliary watch in #3 fireroom when Dixie took command in May 1944. On January 21, 1945, I had charge of #3 fireroom while we were under attack. My two best buddies, Arthur R. "Doc" Savage WT1c, and Thomas Simpson "T.S." Parker WT2c were with me. "Doc" was checking water for me and "T.S." ran my pumps for me. As a result of pumping so much water to fight the fire, the 3rd deck in our area became flooded and our escape trunk, which terminated on the 3rd deck, became inoperable. As we were unaware of this nobody panicked, but we knew we were in trouble as the demand for steam decreased and the annunciator rang up Stop, and then All Ahead 1/3. We did not get topside until late at night and the rest, of course, is history.

John Armbrust Y2c

I was in the office when GQ sounded, as I had duty at that time. I remember going to my battle station in Main Damage Control. Just seconds out of the office we received the first hit. I stopped for a second and then continued on my way to my battle station.

We were below deck and couldn't see any action but we knew we were in trouble by the reports coming in. If I remember correctly there were seven of us in Damage Control. However, I don't remember the names of these men.

Things happened so fast; some things are very vague. It seems someone said that we were ordered to abandon ship. We were trapped below deck. They said that our destroyers would put the ship on down.

Captain Dixie Kiefer had been injured but was still on the bridge. He said that although he was hit he was still in command of the *Ticonderoga* and that with God's help we would make it.

I remember that I was one scared kid at that time and I'm not sure just what I did when "All Clear" sounded.

James Asadoorian CY

I remember I was just sitting down for lunch at the Chief's Mess and as I reached for some fried chicken, I heard and felt what sounded like a bomb blast. Simultaneously I heard the alarm for General Quarters. That platter of chicken was still there on the table as we abandoned the Chief's Mess and headed for our duty stations.

Since reporting for duty as a nucleus member of the ship's crew in November 1943, I had been assigned to the Executive Officer's office, mainly in charge of personnel records. My GQ station was to assist the XO and to secure and protect the Muster Roll of the ship's crew in a water-tight container. However, just thirty days or so preceeding the Kamikaze attack, I had been assigned to the Chief Engineer's office. This transfer resulted in a change of my GQ station. It was down below in Damage Control Central located in the bowels of the ship and immediately adjacent to the 5-inch gun ammunition storage magazine.

Due to the surprise attack and with no advance warning from the picket line, everyone was scrambling up and down ladders to reach their assigned stations. Water was pouring down from the flight and hangar decks where fires had broken out. The big problem with this was that the water-tight compartments below decks were not yet secured. I finally reached my station, put on my head-set phone and plugged into the direct line to the bridge. Damage reports were coming in faster than we could order the required repair and fire control parties. The first half hour or so was overwhelming but some semblance of normalcy slowly returned with the passing of time. It was then that I realized we were standing in ankle-deep water and the intense humidity was stifling. This was not the way we had drilled and practiced GQ on so many previous occasions. The surprise attack sure threw a wrench into our planning.

Captain Dixie Kiefer, although wounded, was inquiring on my phone as to the degree of list and, "What the Hell are we doing to correct the situation"? His request was relayed to Cdr. Mallory who was responsible for all repairs and fire control. I informed the Captain that sea water was presently being pumped into the empty fuel and oil tanks in order to get the ship back on an even keel.

As time wore on I began to wonder if we would ever be able to get out of this alive. Our situation was very grave due mainly to the fact that the two decks above us were flooded, and we would have drowned like rats if we opened the water-tight door. The Lieutenant who was in charge of the ship's ventilation was studying the blue prints to see if we could escape by squeezing up through the air ducts. This did not

sound like a good idea to me but our options were limited and less than favorable. After what seemed like an eternity, we received word that the fires were under control and the water above us had been pumped out. Believe me, we were all thankful as our prayers had been answered and we were finally able to secure from General Quarters.

My first reaction when I got above decks was to check on my buddy, Chief Boatswain Stanley Scibek who had received shrapnel wounds up on the bridge. I looked for him in the Chief's quarters but that area was now a temporary morgue. After searching through the crew's quarters, I found him lying on a bunk among the wounded who were waiting for medical aid. He was hurt and bleeding but still conscious and I asked if there was anything I could get him. He replied, "I'd sure go for a hot cup of joe." I got it for him and remained with him until they took him into the Sick Bay.

Lawrence Ashman AOM1c

Around noon on January 21, 1945, I was standing forward of the island on the flight deck waiting for the planes to take off. Suddenly the aft 5-inch guns started firing. General Quarters sounded. I looked for the bursts in the sky but couldn't see any. Looking up into the sun and moving to see around the island I was suddenly knocked down by someone who was running like crazy from across the flight deck. At that instant the Kamikaze struck the deck.

I helped man a hose for a while until a Chief came by and told the ordnancemen to get down on the hangar deck aft to unload the planes of bombs and ammo. This we did, throwing everything over the side of the ship. When we were finished I decided to go up on the flight deck and get down on the catwalk on the port side as there was another Kamikaze coming in from the starboard. The catwalks were packed with men and I ended up under a plane with two guys on top of me. That's how many men were up there.

John Austin Cox

On January 21, 1945, I was 19 years of age and only eleven months out of the Sampson, New York Boot Camp. The only experience I had in witnessing disaster and death was an occasional house fire or serious auto accident. It's doubtful that 98% of the young, wet-behind-the-ears crew had witnessed much more than I had, yet my recollection clearly shows that men have a divine sense of direction and courage that is mustered at a time of disaster.

On the day of the attack on the *Ticonderoga*, some things are clearly etched in my mind, others vaguely. I remember having chow with Vinny Maher who was from Worcester, MA and Slim Berzinski from Michigan. Slim had a way of making people laugh. Well, that day he had Vinny and me laughing so hard we were holding our sides. They left to go topside and I remained to finish my lunch. Just as I arose to leave the galley I heard GQ sounded. I dropped my tray and headed off to reach my battle station on the fantail. Ordinarily, I would go up the furthest aft ladder from below decks and make my way along the hangar deck to the fantail. That

day I chose to use the closest ladder as there was a sense of urgency in the GQ sounds. Shortly after reaching the hangar deck just aft of the starboard elevator, there was a tremendous explosion to my rear that sent flying metal and shooting flames from the forward end of the hangar deck. I quickly crouched down and scampered to the fantail to my position on the quad forty millimeters. It was evident to all that the "Ti" had taken a serious hit. Smoke billowed out of the open metal curtains and passed the fantail. As there was no let-up of the smoke for quite some time, it was a strong indication that the fires on the hangar deck and below were far from under control.

Lt. Martin Dibner was the Gunnery Officer of the Day and he calmly informed us of the happenings and kept everyone cool during the fight to save the ship. There was concern by the crew as to why the ship was listing at such a sharp degree. He quickly explained that the voids were being flooded starboard in order to have the fuel fires roll to that side, giving the fire control crew an opportunity to wash the fuel fires over the side. It worked, thank God.

The second Kamikaze that struck the superstructure was out of our sight on the fantail. We were informed by Lt. Dibner of the hit. Even today, knowing all the fire power we had aboard along with the fire power of our accompanying ships, I wonder how in the hell he got through to us. The films of the hit showed tracers disappearing into the fuselage of the plane, but he came right through all that flak.

That evening, after the fires were extinguished, I had watch on the superstructure aft of where the second hit took place. It was a long night. It was then that it all set in as to what had actually happened. In addition, the following morning I was assigned to the burial detail along with Augie Fusco from New Haven, CT, Paul Jaskowski from Brunswick, NJ, George Friedberg from New York City, Willie Williams from Atlanta, GA, Tony Frisenda from Beacon, NY and John Landolina from Windsor, CT, all from the Sixth Division. We grew up fast during those two days.

Jacob F. Auxt AEM1c

I was on the flight deck when the first plane hit and also when the second one hit about one hour later. I remember clearly a piece of metal about the size of a softball rolling down the flight deck after the second one hit the superstructure. A sailor went to pick it up and I told him not to because I knew it was red hot. He didn't listen, grabbed the fragment, and did he ever drop it. After that all I saw was smoke and wounded people.

That night I had the 12 to 4 AM watch on the hangar deck with the dead and the stench of the burned bodies. That smell I will never forget. The day they buried them at sea, every body that went over the side I thought that it could have been me. Then our squadron went to the *Hancock*.

Frank Bach MM2c

My duty at the time was to oversee and maintain the two units of inert gas machines. After every fueling, our inert gas was pumped into gasoline pipe lines to prevent explosions and fire.

At about 1200 hours I was on duty at what was called the gasoline shack, located forward on the hangar deck, port side. A fueling operation had been completed and I was waiting for the chow line to decrease. Our planes were landing. I heard our anti-aircraft guns firing from the starboard side, opposite from me. I then took a quick look out of the open bay door on that side. About the same time, General Quarters sounded. Seeing tracer bullets being fired at us from an oncoming aircraft, I started to run for my General Quarters station which was one of the inert gas machinery rooms about 500 feet back and 4 decks below from my original position. We were under attack. About 475 feet away I heard the first explosion and kept on going toward my station. Upon reaching it, one of my operators informed me that both inert gas units had already pumped their inert gas. All gasoline lines were secure. I was very much relieved to hear that.

We were in contact with our Division Chief by intercom. Hearing that there was fire everywhere on the flight deck, he asked for the two other men with me to report up there to help with the fires. I was to stay because I could control the gas to either station from my position.

I felt a little something on my leg which turned out to be a small amount of blood. I opened a hatch of my station which was very close to, but below Sick Bay. I was going to ask for a band-aid, but seeing shipmates being carried in blankets to the Sick Bay I changed my mind. Either some shrapnel from the blast caught my leg or it happened while running down the hangar deck.

After a very short time, the second blast hit the ship. I felt it down at my station. It was a good thing I had a bucket handy at that time. There was an urgent need to relieve myself. I stayed there for hours. That same day, I had the 2400 to 0400 hour watch on the hangar deck. It was quite weird. Not many bays could be closed. Many bodies were still about, waiting for daylight. The sounds of rusting metal and the odors were quite overwhelming. I was thankful to be a survivor.

O.R. Baird SA(D)3c

My flight quarters and GQ station were up in the island in Air Plot.

I had gone to early chow in order to be ready to launch the afternoon strike and was in the foreward mess hall when they sounded General Quarters.

When I got to the hangar deck, several planes were on fire so I broke out a fire hose with four or five others and went to work. They gave the ship a sharp list to port to run the water and gasoline over the side. It made our job a lot easier.

While this was going on I could see the second plane coming in from starboard. I think the gunners got him, for he started smoking just before he hit. I couldn't see him hit from where I was on the hangar deck. The forward elevator was stopped about eight or ten feet above the hangar deck with a plane burning on it. That was the last one we got out.

After we got the fire out, I went out on the forecastle to try to help with some of the wounded who had been moved out there. I remember one who was badly burned and wanting water. I was afraid to give him too much.

When they started moving the wounded to Sick Bay I went on up to Air Plot and found out about Dixie and Cdr. Burch and Cdr. Miller. I also found out that for a time they thought we might lose her. I hadn't thought about that. I knew we were going to control the fire on the hangar deck and figured they would do the same on the flight deck. Or maybe—I was just too young and dumb to think that they might sink my ship.

Onofrio Biviano MMR3c

On January 21, 1945, I was in the machine shop making a part for a broken machine until General Quarters went off and water started coming in the shop. At that time I left and went topside and started to help fight the fire. In the meantime, we were pushing planes over the side and 500 lb. bombs that were on deck went over the side, too. I tried to help wherever I could. Our clothes were all wet and there was nothing to eat (and I was hungry!). A few days later I helped bury a number of shipmates.

Sal Bonfiglio S1c

I was a Seaman 1c in the Pilots Dept. V-3. I was on board the "Big T" from its commissioning. My job on January 21st was to photograph landings on the flight deck. That day my position was on the port side just past the last barrier. I had gone to early lunch so I could take my position on the flight deck. As I recall, I was standing there when our forty mm from the island started firing and as I looked up I saw a Zero diving toward the island and then veer to his right. I had my K 20 camera and photographed the Zero during his dive. I jumped down to the catwalk and the next thing I heard was another plane hit the deck with both bombs released before impact. I continued through the catwalk under the flight deck to the starboard side and came out on deck close to the 20 mm guns which were firing at another plane that was headed toward the bridge. I can recall 5 inch shells being fired into the water in an effort to knock down the approaching plane, but the plane hit the island. Next I recall going on the deck to help push overboard the planes that were on the aft flight deck. I also recall helping the corpsmen and doctors with the injured shipmates. When darkness came I went down to our Photo Lab and found out we lost two of our photographers. Later on the next day I looked for my buddies. Some I lost, others were safe. I love that ship!

Walter J. Boyling WT3c

I reported aboard the "Big T" in May 1944, in Newport News, VA assigned to the "B" Division - Boiler Room as a Boilermaker/Water Tender 3c. I believe our shakedown cruise was to Scotland Bay, Trinidad, BWI. I initially had the diving gear locker off the hangar deck and made an underwater inspection of the seals on the propeller shafts.

Cdr. Dean, the Damage Control Officer, took over the compartment for storing other gear and I was assigned to boiler room duties from then on. For General Quarters station they assigned me to #3 shaft alley where I was to report to Damage Control any torpedoes entering the hull. (We Were Expendable).

I know one thing - it was about six watertight hatches straight down and they were all dogged down to maintain watertight integrity. I never did know who was in the other three shaft alleys.

When the "Big T" was hit we were in "Condition Yoke," "Condition Zed" being under enemy attack. As such, we would send a section to the mess hall for chow and then return to the boiler room and relieve the other section. As I was climbing the ladder from the mess deck to the hangar deck the Kamikaze crashed through the flight deck and the force of the explosion blew me down the ladder. I broke my collarbone, a memento I have to this day. The next thing was General Quarters sounded and all I could think of was to get to my battle station. I never gave it a thought at the time but have reflected many times since - busting my butt to get to my battle station in the bottom of the #3 shaft alley. Soon thereafter a Jap submarine tried to torpedo us but the Skipper evaded and I understand the USS *Reno*, an anti-aircraft cruiser who was astern of us, took the torpedo. She made it in for repairs. I also vividly recall the USS *Worden* DD349 coming alongside, and when she cast off the typhoon like waves picked her up and slammed her down like a pancake.

Dvon Brogan AM2c

On January 21 I had just come up to the hangar deck from chow. I was standing on the starboard quarter deck watching a small carrier, I believe it was the Langley, operate. I saw a plane dive on it and saw a bomb explode on its flight deck. I took off to the aviation sheet metal shop on the aft port hangar deck - my work place.

I started to put on my battle gear when GQ sounded. Then the first plane hit us. It exploded on the hangar deck. My battle station was a fire hose on the starboard side, mid-deck on the hangar deck. I could not get there because of the fire.

Commander Burch, Exec. officer, came into our shop, grabbed the phone and called Damage Control and ordered several compartments flooded to get a 9 degree port list on the ship so gasoline would run off the hangar deck. He called out the numbers of the compartments to be flooded. I thought then and still think this was an amazing feat. He possibly saved the ship by this action.

I spent the remainder of the day fighting fire and cleaning up the hangar deck.

Harold K. Butcher Lieutenant (j.g.)

I was in Ready Room No. 3, donning my flight gear and getting ready to man a Hellcat for a strike on Formosa. As I recall, it was around 1100 hours. Just as I was heading for the flight deck, I heard what sounded like a 20 mm gun fire three or four rounds and then a loud "Bam" that shook the deck, followed a few seconds later by smoke coming in through the ventilation system. A couple of minutes later the announcement came over the intercom, "Flight Quarter Cancelled." I knew then that we had been Kamikazied, but not much else. I then went out to the catwalk for a "looksee" and was horrified to see several planes on fire.

Then a destroyer came steaming down our port side not more than 100 feet away, going in the opposite direction. Its aft five-inchers were blasting away at a Jap plane, not more than a thousand feet above, that appeared ready to make its attack. I think that they shot it down since no explosion followed, but I didn't stick around to watch and ducked back into the relative safety of the ready room and the company of my fellow pilots—all of us wondering what in hell to do. Being without anything to do while under attack is plain hell!! Then a few minutes later we heard our five-inchers open up, followed shortly by the 40 mms and then we knew that we were again under attack! When the 20 mms got into the attack we knew that the Kamikaze was very close — and sure enough there was a big "BAM" and then silence.

I dashed out to the catwalk to take a look and found a small piece of smoking metal I believed to be from the Jap aircraft right in front of me. Thinking that I might have a souvenir I started to pick it up but quickly thought better of it! Then I noticed a Hellcat right above me on the flight deck was in flames. I was hit in the face with some liquid and immediately thought it was gasoline and I too would go up in flames. I was ready to go over the side if I caught on fire. I ducked back under the edge of the flight deck and then realized that what I thought was gasoline from a ruptured fuel tank was only water from the firefighters' hoses.

That calmed me somewhat, but I was still so shaken up that I was on the verge of panic and raced aft along the catwalk to get away from the flames. On reaching the five-inch gun sponsons, I noticed that the Marines manning the guns were watching me so I forced myself to act natural, and joined a line of men passing foamite cans along to the foamite generators. That gave me something to do and I soon settled down. Then I went up to the flight deck and ambled forward, helping unload bombs and throw them over the side. I helped carry the dead and the wounded and did whatever I could do, just to keep busy.

I particularly remember seeing an enlisted man lying on one of the superstructure decks on the first level above the flight deck. His leg was dangling over the side, held on by just a few sinews but not bleeding much. I pointed him out to a passing corpsman who got together a stretcher party and went up to get him while two of us stayed below to receive the stretcher as it was lowered. The man appeared to be alive, but to this day I have often thought of him and wondered if he survived. If anyone knows, please let me know.

I was on the flight deck for two or three hours after the Kamikaze attacks as the fire ravaged the forward half of the hangar deck, and I didn't want to go below anyway. While on the flight deck I vividly remember watching as our fine Captain, Dixie Kiefer, was carried off the bridge, and the X.O., Cdr. Burch, with many shrapnel wounds, walked down. After some time, I made my way to the after half of the hangar deck which was relatively undamaged and where the walking wounded were being administered to. As soon as we were permitted to go forward, my room mate, Lt.(j.g.) J. Perry Peck and I decided to go to our room. However, it was a mess below the hangar deck with oily water and other debris a foot or more deep in the passageways. The forward half of the hangar deck was littered with bodies and burned aircraft yet some of the aircraft appeared to be intact and only blackened by smoke. But what was really unnerving was the bodies around these aircraft, frozen in death in positions they might have taken caring for the planes. They were blackened by fire and smoke and very dead. It was eerie, to say the least.

We later learned that most of the water below the hangar deck was due to the lack of combing around the hatches leading to the lower levels. This lack of combing allowed gasoline from ruptured aircraft fuel tanks to run down the stairwells, as well as the water being used to fight the fire. One of our ACI officers, Lt. Ford, was trapped in his room and burned to death. Within a matter of days all Essex class carriers were provided with combing about a foot high.

Since all living spaces below and forward of the forward half of the hangar deck were uninhabitable, it was necessary for us to find sleeping space wherever we could. This problem was solved in part by using the spaces belonging to our pilots and air crews that had to land on other carriers since our flight deck was out of commission.

The officers wardroom and galley were both flooded, so we had to go way aft and down three decks below the hangar deck to draw K-Rations for the evening meal and breakfast. It was nightfall before we got the word on the K-ration location, so when I decided to get mine I happened to be alone and this is one time that has stayed sharp in my memory ever since as it was a traumatic experience. I had to walk almost the whole length of the hangar deck to get to the downhatch and the hangar deck was pitch black. After feeling and stumbling about a third of the way, I suddenly was aware that whatever I was stepping on was soft and uneven. You can't imagine my shock and horror at discovering that I was walking upon the bodies of my shipmates, all laid out and covered with blankets for burial the next day. I actually cried out loud to them and to God for their forgiveness. It seemed like an eternity before I was able to extricate myself from the dead, being very careful not to tread on anyone again.

That about sums it up for my day on the 21st of January, 1945—a day that I have lived over many, many times (as I am sure that we all have) as I lay in bed at night and often during the days. As you no doubt recall, Air Group Eighty was transferred to the *Hancock* after we returned to Ulithi. It hurt so awfully much to stand on the deck of the Hancock and watch our beloved *"Big T"* as it disappeared over the horizon on the way back home!! By the way, over the years I lost contact with my old room mate and buddy, J. Perry Peck, who shared most of that fateful day and night with me and was also my roommate on the Hancock.

Clark Carlson RdM2c

I was on duty in CIC. I was usually by the navigation table behind Lt. Commander Ballinger, but there were so many enemy planes in the air I was sitting beside him, directing one group of fighters by radio. Our lookouts that day were Daugherty and McNeely, if I remember their names correctly. Then McNeely said, "One is heading right at me." Machine gun fire was hitting the bulkhead behind us. Ballinger yelled," Cover your heads with your arms." Then there was an explosion when a Kamikaze hit the superstructure and smoke started pouring in, filling CIC and the radar room. We had to get out of there. One of the fellows opened the door and there was smoke and fire so another opened the escape hatch and that was also full of fire. Ballinger yelled," Follow me, I'll get you out of here." He went out the door through the smoke and got out on the starboard side where we went forward on the catwalk around the superstructure. You could look down and see men lying on the flight deck.

Commander Miller came running up saying, " Put me out. I'm on fire." He died instantly. He had taken a breath of fire and burned his lungs.

Emilio J. Casale AOM3c

I remember the Kamikaze attack on January 21, 1945 well. I was in the mess hall and all at once I heard General Quarters, the sound of Battle Stations. This meant that I had to go up to the hangar deck on the port side of the ship. Believe me, this was a task within itself. The ladder was a mess with men going up and others coming down at the same time.

During the mix-up of shipmates and the ordeal of the ladder, someone was hit by a stray bullet and all we could do was pass him down to the deck below to be laid to rest. I finally made my way to the hangar deck and continued on to the starboard side of the ship where I went up another ladder to my destination, my battle station.

While at my battle station I could hear a lot of crying and screaming due to people being shot by the planes coming in and passing over. When I finally got the "All Clear" sound I went up onto the flight deck to help look for any surviving shipmates. Unfortunately, there weren't many and for those who did make it, barely, there wasn't anything hopeful that we could do for them. The dead shipmates were taken down below to be stored until the burial at sea.

Meanwhile, a fellow shipmate, part of the plane handlers, was pushing a plane onto the elevator. The Kamikaze plane was in there, all blown to pieces. As the plane tried to land, it crashed into the elevator and exploded.

In the days following this attack, we had the service for our fellow shipmates. We set up a ramp off the side of the ship, brought the dead bodies up from below, and one at a time we lifted a body up onto the ramp and pushed it over to the sound of Taps, played on a bugle. We all stood at attention as we said our last goodbyes to some of our best buddies. This was definitely the most impressionable time of my life and it will live in my memory forever.

Howard Chamblin Lieutenant (j.g.), Air Department

You ask if I remember the day, the hour, the minute of the Kamikaze attack? There were 3,500 of us with stories about that day. Some off us never lived to tell their tale. Those who did will never forget the grim and sometimes grisly details, and the heroics and gallantry of those who fought to save their shipmates and their ship.

It was right around noontime that I met with Ensign "Shorty" Ewing, one of our photo reconnaissance pilots. We were going over his assignment covering the south tip of Formosa. Just as we stretched out the charts on the wing of an aircraft parked on the hangar deck outside the Photo Lab, the anti-aircraft guns commenced firing. General Quarters had not yet sounded. We immediately decided this was for real, not a drill. "Let's take cover in the Photo Lab," I said.

Within seconds after entering the lab all hell broke loose. I reached for my helmet and first aid kit. The bulkhead where they were hanging imploded, knocking me cold across my desk. I think I was only out for a very short time. There were four of our photographers already in the lab. The explosions continued for some time. The bulkheads around the laboratory began to spew steam and there was the strong odor of exploding ammo and burning human flesh. The sprinkler system started to spray hot water and covered the deck over our shoe soles. By this time we were anxious to get out of the lab, and the only two exits normally available were blocked due to gasoline fires and the explosions of 40 mm shells. We finally partially cracked one door and, at that moment, a young sailor fell through the opening. We had to close this door immediately because of the fires and explosions licking at the entrance. I was the only one in the lab with first aid training so I became this man's doctor. Through a big hole in his back I could

see some inner organs working. His left arm was off at the shoulder, giving the appearance of cooked roast beef. I quickly gave him a shot of morphine since there were no apparent serious head injuries. He came to and recognized me as an officer and said, "Sir, will you please take my girl friend's name and address and notify her that I died loving her." I did my level best to assure him that he was not going to die. In the Photo Lab we did not have the sanitary equipment or materials you would expect in our Sick Bay. I had sulfa powder, adhesive tape used for splicing film and rolls of plain cotton used for cleaning. I poured the sulfa powder in the large hole in his back and all over his shoulder. I stuffed the hole with cotton, taping over it to hold it in place. I used the same procedure on his shoulder, then ran the tape all around his body to provide more stability. By the time we were finished treating this man it was getting too hot to stay in the lab. I ordered the only porthole opened. We were listing about 20 degrees to starboard by this time. By sticking my head out the porthole I saw Lt. Kelly fighting the flight deck fires like a mad man. I finally got his attention and asked him to please tie a line to the deck and get some men to help pull a seriously wounded man up to the flight deck because we were trapped in the Photo Lab. After they got this man safely on the flight deck, he passed the word to me it was too hot for them to stay there any longer. I passed this sad news on to the rest of the men with me in the lab. I said to the men, "I, for one, don't want to be cooked in this hole and conditions are deteriorating rapidly."

I asked PhoM1c Peters, the smallest man in our group, if he felt like he could skinny up that line to the flight deck. He allowed he could, so I said, "Up you go," and we all wished him good luck and up he went and arrived safely. The other three men followed suit and made it safely, leaving Ens. Ewing and myself. So I said, "O.K. Shorty, up you go." "Oh no," he said, "I am much younger than you and I want to make sure you get out safely."

I had to bring my seniority into play for I felt it was my duty to try to see that all hands got out safely. The powerful young officer made it to the flight deck without too many problems. Now it was my turn. You bet I was worried, but out the porthole I went, grabbing the slippery 1" line. Twice I slipped down nearly to the water, hearing the many men already in the drink asking for help. They had been blown over the side when the first Kamikaze exploded on the hangar deck after coming through the flight deck. I finally dug my knees

into the side of the ship and with help from the MAN above, and using my last ounce of strength, I am now able to tell you this factual story. Upon my arrival to the flight deck, the damage from the first Kamikaze was unbelievable. I soon spotted my friend, Lt. John Kelly. He was still fighting the fires and helping people wherever possible and I said, "John, you saved six lives by sending that line down to our open porthole where we were trapped."

He looked up and said, "You'd better duck for here comes another one." I hit the deck facing aft, flat on my stomach, and John fell facing forward with our feet about two feet apart. The anti-aircraft crews were firing at the incoming Kamikaze with all they had. Just before I dropped my head to the deck, I am pretty sure the gunners had him on fire. Then he hit the after part of our island superstructure, wounding or killing most of our senior officers, including 65 shrapnel wounds in our C.O., Capt. Dixie Kiefer, seriously wounding our Exec, Cdr. Bill Burch and our Assistant Air Officer, LCDR "Ace" Barton, and killing our Air Officer, Cdr. Claire Miller, our Gunnery Officer, Cdr. Fuller and Assistant Gunnery Officer, Lt. Bess. Lt. Bess was hit when he was trying to cross the flight deck to reach his General Quarters station. The next senior officer, Cdr. Briner, the Chief Engineering Officer, had to leave his station in the Engine Room and come to the bridge to assume command of the ship. I remained flat on my stomach until the final falling shrapnel pieces dinged off my helmet and the horrible vibrations of the ship from the shock of the blow slackened off. I attempted to get up and survey the damage. The first thing I saw was the worst shock of my life. The bottom part of Lt. Kelly's torso lay with his feet still near mine. The upper part of his body was about 28 to 30 feet up the deck. A large hunk of shrapnel had cut him completely in half. John put up a tremendous fight before he was cut down. In later years while I was on duty at the old Navy Department Bureau of Aeronautics in Washington, DC, I was called to the Pentagon by an Admiral who was reviewing requests received after the war from personnel explaining their actions under fire, wondering if they were eligible for some type of medal. In my opinion, many of these brave people were overlooked. One of the requests under review by the Admiral came from someone who claimed he had saved the lives of six people trapped in the Photo Lab. This was a great shock to me since only Lt. John Kelly and God saved our lives. The Admiral called me later, perhaps after doing further research, and informed me that he was able to have a Navy Cross posthumously issued to Lt. John Kelly, rejecting the previous request.

I lost five of my men during these attacks. As it turned out, one of my top first class Photo Mates, Hughes, was at his station near Cdr. Miller, a terrific location to photograph the second oncoming Kamikaze. I searched for Hughes and finally found his body among some 100 others on the fantail. He still had his beat up camera around his neck. I retrieved the camera, and upon arriving in the Photo Lab to attempt to develop the film, if it was possible, I was forced to tape up many holes to make it light proof. It was necessary to pry the camera open in the darkroom in order to remove the film. I soaked the film in plain fresh water to remove the blood

Naval aircraft poised on the flight deck of the Ticonderoga. *(Courtesy of E.W. Tenpenny)*

and then processed the film with normal chemical procedure. To my surprise the film, even though fogged, showed an identifiable and usable picture of the incoming number two Kamikaze by using image enhancing techniques. Another one of our top notch first class Photo Mates was stationed on the starboard side of the bow of the flight deck. He snapped a 16mm color movie picture of the top of the head of the pilot of the second Kamikaze rolling across the flight deck and being kicked overboard by a sailor. The picture was so clear that the pilot's nationality was identifiable. I want all hands of the "*Big T*" to realize that the ship's photographers aboard contributed some of the most outstanding photographs taken by any crew, showing actions of WW II in which our ship participated. These photographs were forwarded to Washington, DC, where they were used by the Navy Department for historical and publicity purposes, in part to show our civilian population that their tax dollars were well spent. In view of the outstanding work of our Photo gang, especially during my tour of duty as Photo Officer, I wish to take this opportunity to thank all of my Photo Mates, led by Chief Photo Mate Barinoff and my Assistant Photo Officer, CWO Bud Singer, for their unstinting and altruistic performance of duty during some very trying times.

When I finally arrived on the flight deck from my Photo Lab entrapment, only then did I comprehend the massive efforts exhibited by all hands to save our ship. By all hands I mean ALL HANDS, the fire fighters, Damage Control personnel, the entire Medical Department including the dentist, performing all medical procedures from first aid to more detailed acts. I can still see my roommate Father O'Brien, rushing from injured man to injured man, comforting those he could and administering the last rites to so many of our crew. He spotted me trying to give myself first aid to my bleeding knees caused from digging into the side of the ship as I scrabbled my way to the flight deck. He thought I was among the missing. He was to become my lifelong friend.

Later, on the night of the 21st of January, as we sat in the wardroom, we listened to Tokyo Rose saying how sorry she felt for our next of kin since we were unable to meet the challenge of the superior Japanese Air Force. "The *Essex* Class carrier is now at the bottom of the Pacific Ocean," (her words). How she and the entire Japanese nation failed to appreciate the superior fighting spirit of the "*Big T*" and, indeed, of our American fighting men and women!

Robert L. Childers PhM1c

I was in the Sick Bay records office, sitting at my desk typing reports into medical records when "Man Your Battle Stations" sounded and the gong started ringing. I left in a flash for my battle station on the flight deck next to the island just under the two twin five inch guns. I got to the hangar deck and all the guns on the ship were firing. I ran to the rear elevator, which was just behind the ladder leading to the flight deck, when the bomb exploded. I was temporarily stunned by the blast, but quickly collected myself and kept on running for the ladder. I bumped into another sailor running aft. He said,

"Follow me, I know another way to the flight deck." We made it okay but I couldn't get to my first aid bag, life jacket or helmet, as the small deck below the flight deck was filled with smoke.

I found a first aid bag in the balloon room aft of the island and went to work. There was heavy smoke and fire forward on the flight deck where the Jap plane went through. The deck crew was busy working on flames shooting up from the flight deck, when I noticed a sailor lying on the deck near the hole where the plane went through. I got hold of a wire body basket and dragged it out near the fire fighters. Two or three of them helped me get him out of there and over to the balloon room. He was instantly killed and burned beyond belief. He was a steward in the galley below the flight deck. He was blown right out onto the flight deck from the galley.

I was out on the flight deck after covering him up with a piece of canvas. A Chief Petty Officer came running towards me with a gas mask on. He said," Doc, do you think you can follow me up into the island? There are quite a few sailors injured in a couple of offices about halfway up." The passageways were full of smoke and no lights were working. He told me to grab hold of his belt and he would lead me to them. That was the longest climb of my life. I couldn't breathe and my eyes were burning, but we never stopped. There were about twenty men in the two offices, and about ten or twelve were injured - two seriously. The first man was barely alive. He had lost so much blood there was little hope. The second man had his left arm hanging in his flight jacket. It was just hanging by two inches of skin. I removed his arm, bandaged him up and gave him some morphine. I knew he could make it if we could find a way to get him to Sick Bay. He was conscious all the time. The rest of the injuries were not life threatening. The smoke was getting the best of us, so somebody stuck his head out of the porthole and hollered to a couple of guys above us and told them to drop down twenty gas masks on lines and we'd pull them in. They did just that. It helped a little but not much - our lungs were already pretty smoked up. The officer among us hollered to them to drop heavy lines down to the portholes and pull us all up. They got lines down there and pulled us all out and up to the catwalk. I don't know how those four or five guys got the added strength to do that. They did it.

The second Jap plane hit us just forward and above the compartment we were in. We watched through the porthole as he was coming in. We all hit the deck just before he exploded into the superstructure and gun mounts above us. After I got to the catwalk I headed for the bridge. They were calling for a Medic. When I got there, there was a badly wounded sailor right in the gangway. I fixed him up with broom handle splints after stopping his bleeding. We sent him directly to Sick Bay. He needed blood plasma. I then went into Dixie Kiefer's compartment to check up on him. He was doing fine. He asked me a lot of questions about the crew and the ship. I told them they were all doing a great job and the fire was mostly under control. He was pleased but still wouldn't leave the bridge with me to go to Sick Bay. The guys on the bridge dropped me to the flight deck with a line. The island was filled with smoke. I continued forward on the

flight deck to a row of injured sailors laid out in a row. All had received first aid and were doing fine. I headed for Sick Bay to re-supply my first aid kit. When I got to the second deck, I found a compartment full of guys who had not received first aid lying in all of the bunks. I looked them all over - none were serious. I made a list of medical supplies that I needed and sent two of my volunteer helpers to Sick Bay. I had them ask for Chief PhM Sorenson or Sutterley - they would see to it that the order was filled. They came back in a short time and I had all I needed to get the job done. There were about ten guys in there who were not injured and they volunteered to help me. We washed patients and bandaged and treated injuries long into the night. My volunteers stayed right with me through the whole ordeal, and the next day helped me get them all to Sick Bay. Those guys were real heros.

When I arrived at Sick Bay Jan. 22, I changed into clean clothes and shoes and went to the operating room where I assisted PhM1c Robert Tremblay until they were through operating. Tremblay and I laid down on a couple of blankets and went to sleep. When we woke up, the badly injured had already been transferred to a hospital ship. A job well done. Let's go home.

C. Robert Clare AOM1c

I was loading bombs and rockets on the planes to go out on another strike. I told my shipmates in our crew to go to chow, that I would finish loading the rocket heads on the rockets that were not done yet. I had a rocket head on each shoulder when I stepped out on the catwalk.

I heard guns and ammunition going off from the USS *Independence* on our port side. They were shooting at a Jap plane flying directly at us. It flew right over our ship as a decoy. At the same time General Quarters sounded, and everyone was running for their battle stations. I looked up in the sky and I saw a Kamikaze coming at us directly out of the sun with a bomb on the wings and all four guns firing.

I threw the rocket heads I was carrying overboard at the same time the Kamikaze hit us. The plane went through the flight deck and Admirals quarters, where the bomb exploded between the flight deck and hangar deck.

We received orders from the bridge to start pushing the planes that were loaded with bombs overboard in order to keep the fires from getting to them and blowing us up. While we were doing that, another Kamikaze was coming in from the starboard side. We all ran for cover to get out of the line of fire, but before I got under cover I saw our gunners shoot part of the Kamikaze's wing off. The pilot managed to keep flying until it made a direct hit into the bridge.

After the second hit it seemed we were like a duck on a pond floating in the ocean, although we did have a couple destroyers by our side for protection. All we could do after that was fight the fires and help the injured until everything was under control. The next day was the saddest day of my life, for we had to bury 121 men at sea.

Carl Clement ACMM

I know it was my 26th birthday, some of the other details are rather vague by now. I recall that sometime around 1200 I was on my way down to the CPO mess to grab a sandwich before it was time to launch aircraft again. I think they had just launched some fighter planes. The next launch was for TBMs and SB2Cs (a bombing strike on Formosa), and they were spotting planes. I had just stepped through the hatch when there was a loud explosion which shook the entire ship, the ship's guns started firing and I believe GQ sounded also. Everyone in the CPO mess scrambled for their battle stations or whatever.

That was when the first Jap plane (Kamikaze) surprised us and dove through the flight deck forward to the hangar deck, exploding somewhere in between. It set fire to everything forward on the hangar deck.

When I got to the hangar deck I saw that the entire forward part of the ship seemed to be afire and filled with smoke. I went forward with a group of men to attempt to get some of the sprinklers working. We were unsuccessful because we didn't have any tools. Meanwhile, I began finding wounded people whom we helped to go aft and get to the Sick Bay hatch. After that I joined some men who were trying to disarm a TBM which had been sent to the hangar deck with mechanical troubles. The bombs were finally dropped and rolled overboard. I also remember helping disarm a fighter plane which was rolled overboard either then or later on. I know that sometime through the action we rolled quite a few planes overboard because of the fire hazard (loaded with fuel).

While we were trying to control the fires on the hangar deck it seemed as if we were making some headway although fire had spread down to some of the lower decks, washed down by water and gasoline through hatches that weren't closed. It was about this time that the second plane hit the island. Things were getting worse, with many more injured in the island. Everything but the fantail seemed to be on fire. The ship began to take on a heavy list, but still seemed to be under control. Thanks be to the brave men who stayed at their stations to con the ship.

After that it is difficult to say just what we were doing at any one time, between trying to fight fires and carry wounded aft to Sick Bay. That kept us so busy we didn't think of anything else except that we had to keep going to save the ship. This we finally did, although most of us thought we were fighting insurmountable odds. We made it through the night, and the next day we were able to take the wounded off. Most or all of us had friends who we never saw again. The entire ship's crew was deeply sorry to see Dixie Kiefer leave the ship. It was something all would remember. The flag (Admiral Halsey) decided to send us home for repairs too that day, so we left the fleet for Hawaii.

In retrospect, everyone aboard contributed something toward saving the ship. Those who made the supreme sacrifice gave their everything.

There is not much more I can remember now. Every 21st day of January I wonder how we got through it all that day. I guess it was destined that some of us would go on to greater things. What that could be I don't know. May God continue to rest the souls of those that didn't.

Ralph F. Colgain, Jr. FC2c

As a fire controlman just out of Fire Control School, I went aboard the *Ticonderoga* at the Newport News, Va. Shipyard where she was built. I'll never forget how awestricken I was as I looked up from the pier at this enormous ship with the flight deck extending over its curvaceous bow. From that day on I fell in love with her, and as time went on I became more familiar with her and felt more a part of the crew that kept her operating smoothly.

I was given various battle stations, first as a pointer on the forward gun director atop the island. My station on that fateful day of January 21, 1945, was the gun director for the port side Quad mount 40 mm sponson near the bow.

I had just finished noonday chow and retreated to my compartment below for a smoke when the GQ alarm sent me running up the starboard ladders. I got on the ladder that led through the hatch to the hangar deck where my normal path would have been, diagonally across the hangar deck to the forward port Quad mount 40 mm sponson. There were three of us on the ladder, with a bos'n mate ahead of me and a stewards mate ahead of him. The first man at the top of the ladder went through the hatch to his Eternity at the exact moment the Kamikaze exploded through the flight deck on the hangar deck. The bos'n mate and myself were knocked down the ladder by the blast but neither of us were hurt.

Anger steamed within me and the blazing inferno of burning gasoline prevented us from going back up that ladder and out that hatch. We sought an alternate route by retreating to the after part of the ship to get up to the hangar deck. It was obvious we could not make it forward, for the fire was even worse. So we went up to the flight deck where I found one of our fire controlmen who had been coming off his watch station out of the island when the first Kamikaze hit. He was in a complete daze but suffered no physical damage so I led him to the rear of the ship. Just as we arrived there the second Kamikaze hit our forward gun director where he had been on watch before the first one hit and anger once again swelled within my soul for, although we had experienced some bombing attacks before and a near miss by a Kamikaze in a previous encounter, this attack seemed so much more personal and is something I will never forget.

T. Jack Colvin RM3c

It was early chow and then on our way to relieve the radio watch as we had done so many times before. The Chaplain was giving a news broadcast relating the latest threats from "Tokyo Rose." It was rather a light hearted time for us following the successful foray into the South China Sea.

An unexpected explosion brought this temporary euphoria to a sudden end. General Quarters sounded, guns were firing, closed in we did not know what had happened. The voice radio in our place gave information to our sister ships as to our situation. We were still sitting and copying messages.

There was a mixture of fear and excitement as to what was next. The forward 5-inch guns were booming and the quad 40s joined in the cacophony. The concern heightened when the many 20 mms joined in the defense; you knew the enemy was close.

The compartment below the radio shack was an aviation ready room and it was on fire. We had to put our feet on the rungs of the chairs where we sat. One of our officers, a former enlisted man, wondered how these kids 17 or 18 years old would take to this time of combat. Everyone did their job without panic or hysteria. We were quite calm on the surface, but I found the words of the 23rd Psalm, "The Lord is my shepherd," quite comforting.

As the 20 mms chattered the excitement became more intense, and then the loud crash as the second Kamikaze found its mark. We soon realized we were temporarily trapped, with a fire above and below us.

It became apparent the devastation and destruction had created havoc. Lt. Gewertz said all of our radios were out and our only communication with the other ships was a portable radio on the bridge. This was being operated by a radio technician who was not familiar with radio procedure. I volunteered to go up and set up communications with the other ships.

My first sight was a young man standing in a daze, his face looking like it was made of wax that had gotten too close to the fire. It had actually melted and drooped in several places. As I prepared to give him a shot of morphine an officer came up and thankfully administered this merciful procedure.

Being locked in a radio shack during my whole career on ships it was a new experience to see what was happening. I remember as we were burning badly, and it came time for the group to launch planes, the Task Group turned and left us by ourselves. We respected the move because the Third Fleet had a job to do and it did it. Soon as the planes were launched they moved in close to protect us. As they moved in our confidence soared with appreciation and pride.

Dixie Kiefer lay in his bridge cabin in a great deal of pain. We hurt for him, because we knew his pain was that his men and ship had received this terrible blow. Mercifully night came. I recall a bogey was headed for us to attempt a final blow. She made the mistake of flying over some nearby ships and she soon tumbled from the night sky in a ball of flame.

The portable transmitter was taken off my back as action ceased and we were secured for the evening. I remember joining a group of men as we sat on the deck in the Admiral's radio room. We were still numb as the loss of life and damage was reported. There were just soft voices and the consensus of opinion was none of us would ever forget this day. We were right.

Charles E. Conder AOM1c

As I recall, we had two or three GQs during the morning and as noon approached I was pretty well upset. My stomach was in knots. We had fighters out and I was on the flight deck standing between the island and the forward 5-inch gun mount which was where I usually hung out while waiting for the flights to return. It was time

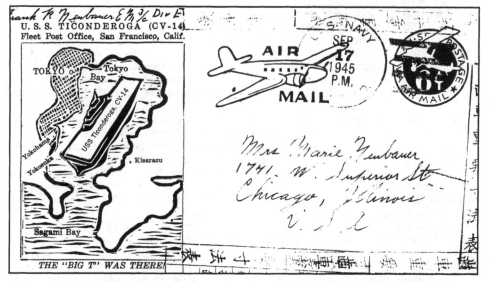

Above and below are examples of V-Mail from the Ticonderoga. *(Courtesy of Frank R. Neubauer)*

Jacob Correll GM3c

I had just finished lunch and was on my way to the hangar deck. General Quarters sounded and I ran up the ladder to the hangar deck to my assigned station. My station was on port side between the hangar deck and the flight deck. When I got there the first plane hit and knocked me off my feet. I'd say that if I had been two minutes later you would not be reading this short story. I checked my station and no one else was there to operate the guns. So I left my station and went to the forward mounts to help. Found the mounts well manned so I passed ammunition from the magazine for them. After that I went along the catwalk of the flight deck on the starboard side to help put the fires out. The second plane must have hit while I was in the magazine. Then we found a shipmate in bad shape. Took him to Sick Bay - bunk and all.

Purl G. Dean Y2c

I boarded the "T" on Christmas Eve, 1944. I was not ships company. I was attached to Commander Carrier Division Six (COMCARDIV SIX) and Admiral Arthur W. Radford was my CO. He wasn't active at that time; another Admiral was running the show. I was, at that time, a Yeoman 2nd Class. As a member of COMCARDIV 6 I had no duties as the "Flag" was not active. My official designation was Intelligence Specialist, but I was rated as Yeoman 2nd Class, pending promotion for a commission.

I had become friendly with a Yeoman 3rd Class and palled around with him some. He was a "talker" in a forward 5-inch gun turret. He told me to come sit with him in the next GQ which I had planned to do.

I was told by the older members of the "Flag" that the 5-inch and 40 mm guns were generally long range weapons, but if I ever heard the 50 cal machine guns start the enemy was right on top of us.

I was always a chow hound and was in the mess when it first opened at about 11:30 A.M. I think we were at GQ then. I can't remember exactly, but it seems to me we had "horse cock" sandwiches.

I got back to the Admiral's quarters and we had started firing the 5-inchers and 40s. I sat down at a desk and started polishing a brass ash tray fashioned from a 40 mm spent shell casing. It was only moments when the 50 cals started firing. Then I really was "concerned" and before I was to the "scared" period — All Hell Broke Loose!

The first Kamikaze had crashed into the forward deck. In seconds smoke had started into the room. My first impression immediately after the blast was warm blood running down my right leg. I started to get up out of my chair to run topside and I collapsed on the floor. More and more smoke was filling the room.

Orville Woodbury, another Yeoman 2nd, picked me up bodily and carried me up one deck and when we got there the ladders were so crowded that he couldn't take me any farther.

There was a small radio room next to the ladder, so he put me in there and laid me on a desk and left. That room filled quickly with ten or fifteen people. The door was dogged.

---

for noon chow and I really didn't feel like eating but my good friend Dick Scholl talked me into going down to the chow hall. I protested that I didn't feel like it but he kept insisting and I finally relented. We had been in the chow line about five minutes when GQ sounded again. We got as far as the ladder on the second deck leading to the hangar deck when "Charlie" came crashing through the flight deck and landed on the hangar deck creating real havoc.

Since we couldn't go up we went back down to the third deck where we were eventually locked in until about three o'clock. I guess in the meantime, after the fires were put out, my division held muster and we were listed as missing. When we finally did get off the third deck and up onto the hangar deck we reported to Chief Hightower and then started to help where we could. In the evening I went to sick bay to see if I could be of any use. As I recall, volunteers were asked for as so many shipmates were badly burned and otherwise hurt. I guess I stayed down until after 10:00 P.M. or so and drew a watch. During the next days, while sailing for home for repairs, I kept busy cleaning and generally keeping our area shipshape. All that happened after that, including a 30 day leave, return to the ship and back to the war zone doesn't need mentioning.

John Connolly EM3c

On that day of Jan. 21st I was in the forward elevator generator room. I had everything operating. As I remember I was alone as the machinist mate never made it down to that station. I felt the ship sort of vibrate and I thought we might have been hit by a torpedo. As I came up out of the forward hatch I encountered a lot of fire on deck; a sad officer I didn't know was trying desparately to get a fire hose but was having difficulty because so much hose was unpacked and was all twisted. A large number of men were lying dead. As I made my way up to the flight deck and proceeded to go aft I noticed men dropping to the deck, and then I realized that the ammunition of the planes on the hangar deck was going off due to fire and it was coming up to the flight deck. As I made my way down to the hangar deck, I met my friend Bob McDowell EM3c. As we were sort of stuck on the hangar deck and could not get to our battle stations, we took up the job of getting the wounded in a safe place. And we did what we had to do at the time. I don't think I will ever forget that day. As President Roosevelt said of the bombing of Pearl Harbor - That day of Jan. 21st was my day of Infamy. But I survived.

Smoke filled the room and soon, against all orders, someone opened the porthole. That helped to some degree but it was obvious that we would all have to get out into the open.

One or two stuck their heads out of the porthole and members of the "Flag" had gone topside and had dropped a line down for us to grab so they could pull us up. The crew inside the compartment immediately said, "Get the injured man out first."

I didn't argue. Some PhM2c gave me a shot of morphine and they helped me up to the porthole. I still had my life preserver around my waist, and as I went out the port the damned life preserver inflated and was inside the ship around my body. I was half in and half out. I could not move until Lt. Rudniki stabbed the inflated life preserver with his shark knife in several places, deflating it. He was later awarded the Bronze Star. Yeoman Woodbury and others who manned the ropes should also have been decorated.

When I was outside the ship they pulled me up and I watched part of the battle from the catwalk.

It was miserably cold. I guess the temperature was in the upper 40s or low 50s. I had only a sweater on over my shirt and dungarees. The ship must have been going about 30 knots, along with a headwind of 10 or 15 miles per hour, so it didn't take long before my teeth were chattering and I was shaking all over, probably from shock as well as cold. We sat there until the battle was over and a corpsman came over with some help and moved me.

I was put alongside many other wounded men and a blanket was put over me. The battle over, members of the "Flag" came over to check on me. They were a great bunch.

Somebody came up with a towel and a basin of water and cleaned me up as best they could. Soon a Chief Pharmacist Mate came by and was checking everyone lying on deck. I supposed a couple of hours passed and some of us on deck were being moved. They put me in the Chief Petty Officers quarters. From time to time a corpsman would come by and check on me. I dropped off to sleep and slept for some time. I guess four or five hours had passed since the attack. A member of the ship's band was sent to stay with me until I was taken to the operating room.

That happened after midnight. When I arrived at the operating room they found out that the fractures were extensive and put a cast on my leg to immobilize it until specialists could reduce the fracture.

I was put in the Officers Mess until I could be transferred to a hospital ship. I was surprised at my "nurses." Commanders and Lieutenant Commanders were bringing ducks (urinals) and bed pans. They were immediately dubbed "bed pan commandos" (not to their faces, of course). They were good and solicitous. Some band members also did wound dressing and more demanding routines.

They transferred me to the Good Samaritan. I left the "T" with nothing but a towel — no clothes or anything. All my gear and possessions were lost. Several days later I was operated on by an orthopedist who set my leg and knee. I owe the use of my left leg to him. After many journeys, hospitals and procedures I was finally home at the Naval Hospital in Jacksonville, Florida. I was given a medical discharge on August 22, 1945.

LARRY DIGAETANO COX

I joined the Navy on November 17, 1943, one day after I turned 17 years old. On May 8, 1944, I was assigned to the USS *Ticonderoga*, 4th Division, 20mm. I was then promoted to coxswain and transferred to the 8th Division (which was lookouts and 20mm) to be in charge of the captain's gig.

On January 21, 1945, I had just finished lunch and went to the starboard side of the hangar deck to check out the captain's gig. I heard 20mm and 40mm firing and immediately ran up the ladder to the flight deck heading toward the bridge to man my 20 mm gun on the starboard side. As I approached the bridge, I saw the Kamikaze plane hit the deck. I proceeded to my gun, manned it, and kept firing at a second plane until it hit the bridge. I was knocked out of my gun but I was not hurt. I looked at my gun barrel and it was warped from firing so many rounds of 20mm. My loader and I changed the barrel and then we stood on our battle station until dark.

C.L. DODSON PFC

On that fatal day I had just gotten back from the mess hall and was on my bench in front of my locker playing Blackjack with one of the guys who also had a locker there. I can't remember who he was, but we had just gotten started when GQ sounded. I put my cards in my locker and headed for the ladder which was only about 10 feet from me but blocked by the lockers. This site was crowded faster than usual for some reason, so I headed another way. My gun turret was on the fantail and I was one deck below the hangar deck.

I was running through the officer's quarters toward the next ladder when all hell broke loose, seemed like right above me at the time, and it was a combination of explosion and lead bouncing off, as if coming from a machine gun. I felt severe vibrations which seemed to make me sway. Then I approached the ladder and saw my Marine friend, can't remember his name now, lying in a puddle of blood around his neck. Someone said a vein had been cut and he bled to death. I paused for a second and continued straight through to the fantail to my 20 mm gun and reported to the Sgt. who had the head-set on.

After this, time became confusing and there was a Japanese plane coming around from the port side. I was on the starboard side, as far as you could get from this gun turret. The plane seemed to be partially out of control, but then seemed to pull back up some as if to regain control. I was the loader and my close buddy, O.C. Harris from S.C., was the gunner. I kept saying, "Get him O.C.! "Get him!" Since we were fully loaded, I got behind him cheering him on, and damned if I don't believe he got him. Although there were a lot of others firing at him, the plane was hit and went down. It was awfully close when it came around from the port side.

The next occurence was another fatal blow. This Jap plane was a good distance away, right in the path of the sun on our starboard side. I think our 5-inch guns were not reaching it at this time and it wasn't diving just yet, but flying from side to side, approximately the width of the sun's rays. Then there seemed to be a pause in firing. Someone said it may be one of our corsairs being flown by the Marines. Then the plane went into a dive toward us at what appeared to be about a 45 degree angle and all hell broke loose again with the firing. How it got through, I'll never know. It just kept coming, diving at an angle that should be hard to penetrate our flak. Our guns on the fantail couldn't fire at it because we would hit our own flight deck. The angle was too strong and we were not set to fire at this direction. Finally, and I use the word because it seemed such a long period from the time we saw it until it hit our superstructure, it hit. From our position it felt like a harsh thud, like sideswiping an iceberg or a small boat being nudged by a whale.

After that we had to stay at our guns on the alert, but the guys on the flight deck, hangar deck and superstructure were still still going through hell with the fire. They moved planes out of the way or overboard etc. and I didn't see all of this because of our location. My buddy O.C. Harris, the gunner on my gun, volunteered to go topside to take the place of one of the Marines that got killed.

We got back into a safety zone until darkness fell and things were under control as much as possible. It was late at night before we got to go back to the sleeping quarters. It was very dark and the feeling reminded me of pictures I've seen of German concentrations camp after they exterminated bodies. I don't recall much conversation that night.

The next day was still a living hell with bodies lined up on the deck, but it was somewhat better than almost bumping into what appeared to be white sheets that covered the bodies in the dark, though my imagination could have taken over after so many years.

CHARLES E. DORE AMM3C

I recall the January 21, 1945, attack as if it was today. I was welding a patch on the right wing of a TBM located back of no. 2 elevator on the hangar deck. I recall mates were lined up for chow when the Kamikaze went through the flight deck and exploded on the hangar deck after no. 1 elevator. We went to help put out the fire and helped with the wounded and the dead. I returned to the aviation metal shop and proceeded with my duties.

Charles S. Downey Lieutenant (j.g.)

On Jan. 21, 1945, I was a LT (j.g.) assigned to VB-80 Flying SB2c Hell Divers. Our squadron had returned from a strike on Formosa that Sunday morning and had been briefed for another strike that afternoon. Our dive bombers had been refueled and ordnance installed and were spotted aft on the *Ticonderoga* flight deck. We were in the Bomber Ready Room, adjacent to the port deck edge elevator, waiting for the signal from the Air Officer to "Man Your Planes." We pilots were ready to go when the close in sound of gunfire - like 20 mm and 40 mm was heard. We were curious and stood up to get our GI Hardhats from the overhead before going out on the catwalk to see what the noise was all about. The very next sound I recall was a very "hurried" GQ signal - like we were late or something - THEN A VERY LOUD EXPLOSION shaking the flight deck.

I wound up on the ready room deck - the lights went out and smoke was pouring in through the air conditioning ducts in the overhead. Minor confusion took place for a few moments until a senior officer, Lt. Wiley Moore, determined that the ship was hit by contacting some squawk box on the bridge. By now we were choking on smoke and our fore and aft passages only led to fire just outside our ready room. It was learned that the only route to safety for us on the gallery deck was to Go AFT! Go AFT! Instructions were given to don gas masks, hold to the pilot in front of you and proceed promptly along the Fore/Aft passage leading to the ship's stern.

While passing through a hatch opening my sheath knife, sewed to my flight suit, tore loose and became separated. I found it the next day and still have it - smells smoky to this day. Finally about 150' from the stern we felt cooler air and began sorting out what happened. I was then among our dive bombers (which was over our battle station) and began helping a "GIANT" ordnance officer lift off 250# bombs from the wing attack points. The other thing I remember was obtaining morphine syrettes from our A/C first aid kits to assist wounded.

The ship was still under attack and I observed an enemy A/C to starboard and above the *Essex*, surrounded by AA fire. He was probably making up his mind on where to hit us then began a shallow glide towards our stbd side. I was in the stbd 20 mm gun tube observing all this when the Marine gunner in charge said, "For Chrissakes Lieutenant get your f_ _ _ _ _ _ head down before it gets hit!" With that I ducked, but peeked up looking forward to observe and feel the impact of the #2 Kamikaze about 400' forward of my location. Later I saw that he hit the forward 5" control unit. Within 30 - 45 minutes the entire fire situation seemed to be under control. The ship had been intentionally listed to port to expedite the flow of uncontrolled gasoline over the side. Lt. Pat Fleming, VF 80 Fighter ACE, was observed waving as he went by us in the water with *Mae West* inflated. LCDR Vorse, CAG 80, thought he would be his own AR Officer. Miller had been fatally wounded on the bridge and the skipper, Dixie, was out of action too. Vorse launched in his F6F Hellcat (there was insufficient wind over the deck, plus the port list) and he promptly slid off the ship and into the water. Uninjured, I saw him climb for the sinking fighter and wave as he/we went by.

Frank Easter EM1c

Our planes were striking the island of Formosa. It was a quiet day with no bogeys showing up. Millham, Marcy and me were taking our after lunch snooze in the After Lighting Shop.

The 5-inch guns were the first to fire, then General Quarters was sounded. We all jumped up - Marcy got my shoes on. I had to call him

back to get them. This probably saved my life as I was headed for the Captain's quarters when the plane hit us right there. After I got my shoes I started forward to my battle station. I was in the passageway under the flight deck after the explosion - black smoke came towards me. I went back and went up on the flight deck to the damage control station.

There was a gaping hole in the flight deck with smoke pouring out. Word came that there were wounded down 2 decks in the CIC Room. Another guy and I grabbed a stretcher and went down there. There were several wounded. We tried to bring one guy out but couldn't keep him on the canvas stretcher.

About that time somebody came in and said the fire had come back and we were trapped. There was a porthole and one guy yelled to a catwalk at flight deck level and they dropped us a line. I got hold of the line and a bow line. I then proceeded to go out through the 2' porthole - life jacket, tool pouch and all. I put my foot in the loop and swung out from the ship. I started climbing until I could almost touch the walk before my arms gave out. I slid back down the line and put my leg through the loop. There I hung while ships all around us were shooting down the Japs. What a Show! The guys on the catwalk dropped down a "bite" of the line and pulled me up to the catwalk. My arms were useless. I couldn't even raise them over my head.

An hour had elapsed and the second plane hit up by the gun director over the bridge. The bomb set planes on fire on the flight deck. It was as close to Hell as I've ever seen. Around 1600 the fires were under control. Went back to the electric shop and made coffee. All the crew straggled back to the shop.

James D. Edwards MM2c

It was January 21, 1945, and I was sitting on the open hatch leading to the next level down. The guns started firing and I went leaping off the hatch to head down below to my General Quarters station, Generator #2 in the main engine room. About that time the explosion came. Immediately, the passage way filled with smoke; the port side had to go against the flow of traffic which was off to starboard. Finally, we reached the engine room.

The engine room was filling up with smoke because the intake fresh air blowers would not shut off. The exhaust fans weren't working either. After a few minutes the fans were put in service. I was standing my watch in a very low position, due to smoke, watching guages. We were trapped below and couldn't get out. There was three feet of water above our heads and communications were out for a while.

I don't remember eating any dinner; supper came later. So much for January 21, 1945.

Dennis W. Farley S1c

I was on watch on #9, 40 mm quad anti-aircraft gun when we were hit by the first Kamikaze. We had no warning of any kind because we had no working radar. It was knocked out by the typhoon in the South China Sea.

We were ready when the next group of Kamikazes attacked and were firing at the plane that hit us in the island superstructure. I was the gunpointer on the gun which was in the after end of the superstructure, just above the two five-inch gun mounts below us. I was the only person wounded in the attack. I was hit in the right shoulder and also in the right leg by the shrapnel

Richard B. Field AOM2c

Shortly after noon on that date, I recall that a General Quarters had sounded but that no enemy planes were observed and the ship was in the process of securing from General Quarters. As an AOM in V-5 division, my battle station was wherever needed on the flight deck. Accordingly, I was standing about thirty feet from the island structure. Nearby, two or three other ordnancemen were standing, one of whom I believe was Johnny Stra, another might have been George Vajda.

Suddenly there was a distant sound of naval anti-aircraft fire. Looking aft I could see in the distance a lone aircraft, presumably Japanese, diving down to the water and then pulling up again. Another look showed me that there was no naval vessel directly in his line of approach. The sound of gunfire came from vessels in the vicinity that had spotted the plane, identified as Japanese, and began firing with guns that were still manned. The thought flashed through my mind that this was a stupid thing to do unless that plane was serving as a decoy for something else. I looked around and didn't see anything until I looked straight up at the sun which was directly overhead. Although the sun was extremely bright, I could see the outline of a plane in a dive heading directly towards our deck. It appeared to me at that time that the impact area would be by the island structure or slightly forward. I immediately pushed the ordnancemen nearby and yelled to them to get aft. I seem to remember Johnny Stra giving me a not so nice look, and saying, "What did you do that for?"

At that point, I lost track of them and rushed aft, getting just behind the after five-inch gun mounts, hitting the deck and hearing and feeling the explosion as that Jap plane Kamikazied between the forward elevator and the island.

Events of the next hour are not clear. I remember many crewmen with fire hoses heading for the impact area which was belching smoke. It appeared that those who were wounded were being adequately cared for, so I looked for something to do to help matters. I soon met other ordnancemen who were approaching the Hellcats, some of which were either burning or very close to planes which were afire. It was immediately obvious that the bombs, which had been installed under the wings, would blow and cause additional damage and casualties if they became hot enough. With other ordnancemen, I helped remove as many bombs as possible, which were then rolled aft on bomb dollies and jettisoned into the ocean.

While we were thus engaged, I directly remember explosions of 50 caliber aircraft machine gun ammunition coming from the wings of planes which were on fire. This did not seem threatening at the time so we ignored this, even when it was as close as four feet away. I recall the ship making some high speed turns during this period and the plane handlers and plane captains (V-1 and V-2) pushing planes overboard from the fire area.

All at once, AA guns began going off on our ship and I heard someone yell, "There's another one coming - starboard side!" I looked and saw this Zero heading for our ship. At this time I was close to where I survived the first Kamikaze hit just aft of the after five inch gun mounts, starboard side. I just had time to hit the deck and realize that this Jap hit forward on the island structure, very close to the bridge.

Again, fires broke out, more high speed turns and the awareness that there were more casualties, but again, it appeared that they were being attended to.

The next thing I remember was a group of ordnancement around Don Noyes (then AOM1c, later Chief) and Don was telling us that there was a fire on the hangar deck and some fighter planes there still had bombs under the wings. He stated he needed some volunteers to go down and remove them. At first, I took the attitude that I wanted no part of that scene, but when I saw several of my friends step forward and when Don looked directly at me, I had to go along. When we went down, I remember thinking it could have been worse.

Things became very blurred after this. The fires were diminishing, the dead and wounded removed and most ordnancemen gathered in their respective armories directly under the flight deck. At this time we were wearing kapok life jackets and battle helmets but I don't remember when I put mine on. Most of us sat on the deck, exhausted, with our backs against the bulkhead. I had quit smoking a month or so earlier, but as we sat there I remember having a lit cigarette in each hand. During this period rumors were coming in quickly but we learned that we had lost our division officer, Kelley, and an ordnance striker, Frazier. We heard that we were high-tailing it eastward towards Pearl Harbor. As darkness began to fall I remember hearing a call for fire fighting parties to report to the flight deck to combat a new outbreak of fires there. A few minutes later we heard that the Japanese were sending out a force of twin engine bombers (Bettys) to finish us off. That immediately caused fear and apprehension on my part, since I did not know that the flight deck fire was quickly extinguished and that, without it, it would be almost impossible to find us during the night. I don't remember anything else that night. We all probably slept in sitting positions in our armory. The next day, we were sailing in an easterly direction, presumably safe from harm. It was then that we toured the damaged areas and the shock really hit us.

Chris Fitzgerald MMR3c

One plane crashed through the forward section of the flight deck. Minutes later the second plane slammed into the ship's superstructure, seriously damaging it with severe loss of personnel.

We were on the chow line below the hangar deck leading to the mess hall for dinner when

SB2C Dive Bombers with Mt. Fuji, Japan, in the background. (Courtesy of Mike Mathias)

the planes attacked. There was a loud explosion and a severe vibration throughout the ship. We didn't realize for the moment what happened. There was no forewarning of an attack until General Quarters sounded about the same time the first plane crashed!

Everyone scrambled to our respective battle stations. My station was at the aft end of the ship in the Refrigerator Equipment Room located on the lowest ship level with the other members of the Refrigeration Group.

We had the auxilliary water and diesel pumps operating to maintain water supply pressure to the fire fighting crews on the hangar deck and elsewhere on the ship.

After prolonged operation of the pumps, especially the diesel pumps which developed a great amount of exhaust here even through the exhaust insulation material, we were developing a serious vacuum situation in the Air Tight Equipment Room because the ventilating system had been put out of commission at the time of the attack on the ship. Consequently, with lack of oxygen in the area (of approximately 25 ft. x 25 ft. x 7 ft. to 8 ft. high) our pumps were becoming seriously affected and we found it very difficult to breathe and very painful to do so.

After reporting the condition a few times to Damage Control we were finally given permission to secure the diesel engines to relieve the situation. We tried unsuccessfully to open the overhead hatch to the Ice-Room Compartment above but in our weakened condition we were unable to push the hatch door up because of the severe vacuum. My shipmate Danny McConnell MMR3c and I found a short section of 4" x 4" lumber and 3 ft. length of pipe which we used to pry the hatch door open and break the vacuum in the equipment room. Immediately the air blasted in from the compartment above like a wind from a Tornado!!

In conclusion, I must say the Good Lord must have been watching over us and providing the means or whatever to help us take the action we did to survive the ordeal.

Eugene R. Forsht Lieutenant, VF-80

I was in the V-3 Division as Aircraft Maintence officer and during flight quarters worked on the flight deck.

On that date, as it approached lunch time, all the fighters were gassed, armed, and respotted for launch. I went down to the ward room for early chow with the flight crews. I had sat down to eat when the first Kamikaze hit. I ran to the flight deck before the hatches were dogged down. There was a hole in the flight deck so no aircraft could be launched. I grabbed a kapok life jacket from the side cleaners locker, and worked with the damage control and fire fighters.

When the second one came in I was next to the superstructure at flight deck control with the group commander "Scoop" Vorse, reporting to him. The only fighters we could launch were on the flight deck. He had on his flight suit, Mae West, and the "lucky green scarf." The next thing (on becoming conscious) I remember was getting up and helping the crews disarm and move the fighter aircraft we could save. I then lost consciousness again. The next thing I remember I was in a wire stretcher and corpsmen were putting a tourniquet on my right arm at the shoulder.

In Sick Bay Dr. Cannon said the only thing that saved me was the kapok life jacket. It was filled with shrapnel. All I had was a shattered right arm.

William R. Frye MM3c

On January 21, 1945, I was on the fantail of the USS *Ticonderoga* talking to Carl S. Gaworecki and other crewmen. It was a beautiful day and at noontime all Hell broke loose! General Quarters sounded and everyone ran. This was the last time I saw Carl.

I ran up a ladder to see what was going on. Halfway up the ladder a Marine pulled me back and went around me. When he was at the top there was an explosion. The Marine fell down the ladder dead. Why did I start up the ladder? I don't know! My GQ station was on the emergency evaporators in the boiler room with Mike Boduch. I arrived in the boiler room but to this day I do not remember how.

I put the evaporators on stand-by and reported to main evaporator room. While waiting for more orders we could hear explosions and things falling down the stack. After the "All Clear" I went topside to look for Carl. I could not find him and no one had seen him. Carl was gone! We had started out our naval service at Sampson, New York and then to school at Wentworth Institute in Boston, Massachusetts. In January 1944 we were assigned to the "Big T." We had asked for submarine duty but were refused.

On the day of the burial at sea I was pulled to help bring the bodies from a compartment below decks to the hangar deck. The smell and feel of them when we loaded them on the stretchers was horrible! I kept looking for Carl but did not find him. Oh God! I looked and looked, but no Carl. When the bodies would slide down the ramp to the sea - all I could think about was, "Is that one him?" Every parade or military function that I attend to this day I think of Carl and I still miss him!

After the attack I was on the flight deck and saw Admiral "Bull" Halsey. I was in a parade in his honor in Philadelphia after the war and was selected to represent the Third Fleet.

Forrest Rex Gambrel AOM2c

On January 21, 1945, as the first Japanese suicide plane crashed through the flight deck and exploded on the hangar deck, I was on the third deck astride a 500 lb. bomb that I'd just fused and banded. It was ready to send up to the flight deck for loading on a plane. The second suicide plane, minutes later, hit the ship's superstructure and almost tipped the "Big T" over! Next thing I knew our compartment was starting to flood. The pumps weren't operating and fire had us trapped inside. Water came waistline high and I thought we were all going to drown. "Submarine Waters" was announced over the PA system. There was a big overstuffed chair floating around and a shipmate jumped into it to avoid leg breaks. This was a bit amusing as I'm sure the water would have prevented that.

Eventually the fire up forward was extinguished. We all scrambled out to the hangar deck. There I saw one brave sailor using some sort of sharp tool to rupture our planes' gas tanks in order for gas to run off the burning ship. My buddy, who had a gas mask but no life jacket, said, "The next bomb that blows I'm going over the side!" I advised him to ride it out. We helped carry wounded and dying sailors to the long Sick Bay line. Over 300 men died that day.

Tokyo Rose announced over the radio that the "Big T" was hit and they'd sink her that night! I was going to my bunk in pitch darkness and stumbled over a dead sailor who'd fallen to the bottom of the ladder on the 3rd deck.

General Quarters was called that night. Being totally exhausted, I never heard the call. Thankfully our night fighters intercepted them before they could attack.

Donald Gatchell Captain, USMC, Gunnery Department

On January 21, 1945, I was in the wardroom eating lunch. When GQ sounded, I headed for the ladder on the starboard side to go to my station which was fire control aft, all 40 and 20 millimeters.

As I started up the ladder I realized that I didn't have my pistol, which was mandatory for GQ. So I turned and headed down the ladder to my room. As I hit the deck below, the first plane and bomb hit forward on the hangar deck. Had I gone up instead of down I probably wouldn't be writing this.

Lights went out, smoke filled the passageway and, due to the fire on the hangar deck I couldn't go up so headed forward and ended up on the bow of the ship. The NCO who was supposed to be in charge of the forward 40 millimeters had not arrived and as I could not get to the hangar or flight deck at that time, I took control of the gun which continued firing at the attacking planes. Finally the NCO showed up and I worked my way up to my station.

The next event that happened was the Kamikaze which hit the forward fire control, the station of the Gunnery Officer, and 5-inch gun just above the pilot house where Captain Kiefer was stationed. The bomb on the plane went through the area and exploded over the flight deck. Those who ran for cover behind the stack were killed, along with the forward fire control personnel. I was spared twice.

It was an event that I will never forget, along with heading back to the States for repairs, running blacked out with escorts for a short time, burials at sea, and letters to the parents of those Marines who lost their lives.

John Giftos HA1c

On the morning of Jan. 21, 1945, it was up as usual for us at the crack of dawn to manage our battle stations. At that time everything seemed pretty much routine. After "All Clear" I went back to Sick Bay from my station which was third deck forward to the officers sleeping area where we had a small operating room set up to be used in case the main O.R. was damaged.

I went about my usual routine of checking any patients we had and then getting them breakfast from the main galley. A few hours seemed to have passed pretty quickly and I was having a cup of coffee with the doctor on duty at that time in the Sick Bay ward. I guess it was pretty close to noon when we heard GQ blaring on the intercom system. The doctor and I said, "Damn, another drill," and started for our battle stations. As we got near the main galley, we started to see smoke and some confusion among the crew that were lining up for chow. It wasn't long before we realized that this was not a drill, but the real thing.

The doctor (Cmdr. Baumgarten) told me he was going back to Sick Bay because he knew he would be needed back there. I continued to head for my station and realized it was getting worse as I could now see flames and dense smoke coming down through the hatches.

As I approached my station I could see that some damage had already occurred in that area.

Just as I was coming to the last hatch I had to secure, an explosion rocked my battle station. I just dropped to the deck and a ball of fire, 100 octane burning gas, passed over my head. I was so lucky not to have been killed right then and there. But if you recall, when you go through a hatch you have to jump over part of the bulkhead sticking up from the deck. The fact that I was lower is what saved me.

After the fire subsided I went into the area and found one officer on the ladder burned to a crisp and, of course, dead.

Then I heard a cry for help coming from one of the quarters and found another officer partially burned, and possibly wounded in some way. About that time one of my stretcher bearers got there. He was part of the band that was assigned to us as helpers.

By now the black, dense smoke was getting so bad that even with our gas masks we were having a hard time breathing and water was coming down through the hatches from the hangar deck. I called damage control and told them of the problem we were having and they gave us permission to secure the area as best we could and to try and get up to the hangar deck. We made our patient as comfortable as we could and started up the ladder.

As we got to the second deck we really couldn't see anything as it was pitch black. We were basically feeling our way along the bulkheads. By now we were also in water that was getting deeper as we went along. At this point breathing was getting very difficult and it seemed our lungs were being seared.

Right about then I was having so much trouble - not being sure where I was and not being able to breathe - my thought was to just lie down. I would drown and all my troubles would be over with. But then I realized if I did that then my patient would also die. With that in mind I seemed to get some extra strength and desire to keep going. Well, it wasn't long before we made it topside and could again breathe easier and tend to our business. I had the bearer get another man and sent them to Sick Bay. I tended to some other men who were very badly wounded. Two of them were dying and all I could do was give them some morphine and have them taken to Sick Bay.

After a while, I too went down to Sick Bay where I helped with whatever I could do. We kept at it for about two to three days without ever getting to our quarters for some much needed sleep. Eventually, things returned to a normal routine.

Wendell H. Gilchrist SK3c

Being in charge of the G-Dunk Stand on the ship meant making ice cream for the crew. Just before noontime I decided to go to the library to see Billy Clifford and have a little friendly talk. Billy was the librarian, also Father O'Brien's assistant. Billy and I were both from Massachusetts and we became pretty friendly.

Just about 12 o'clock GQ went off. I ran for the nearest hatchway, which was very crowded. A lot of shipmates were trying to get up topside. I knew I couldn't make that one so I went forward to the next least crowded one. To this day, I don't know which one it was. I understand most of our shipmates going up that crowded hatch were killed.

My battle station was where the pilots had their quarters. I do not know today one name of my fellow shipmates who were with me in our battle station.

We had the job of carrying our wounded shipmates to Sick Bay. From the time the two Jap planes hit, I was in a state of shock to see our dead shipmates lying on the hangar deck dead. It didn't really hit home until long after.

Louis Giroir ARM2c

Since I was not on board the "Ti" when the Kamikaze attack occurred I was not going to reply, but at the suggestion of my wife I re-considered my decision. So for whatever it is worth, here is an eye-witness report and my thoughts of that eventful day.

I was an aircrewman attached to VT-80 in February, 1944, at Westerly, Rhode Island where the group formed. In June, 1944, the air group reported aboard the "Ti" and was with her through the shakedown, the cut (Panama), Hawaii, and finally, joining the fleet at Ulithi. As you recall, we operated off the Philippine Island for a number of weeks where Air Group 80 took part in a number of aerial combat strikes. On December 4, 1944, the number of dive bombers and torpedo aircraft was reduced to allow for more fighter aircraft on board the *Ticonderoga*. Three pilots and five aircrewmen from VT-80 were transferred to Guam for a new assignment. I was one of the crewmen transferred. Sometime during the early part of January, 1945, my pilot, gunner, and myself reported on board the USS *Langley* (CVL-27) as replacement, so when the event occurred I was on board the *Langley*, which was about three-quarters of a mile off the port bow of the "Ti."

I was down in the galley when I heard a loud bang in the forward end of the ship and then General Quarters sounded. I immediately left the galley, running to the air group ready room. As I came topside, I saw that the "Ti" had been hit by the first Kamikaze and the flight deck was on fire from the bow to the stern. I could see huge columns of flames escaping through openings between the flight deck and the hangar deck. Explosions were seen on both decks, apparently from aircraft gasoline tanks. I saw 5 inch aerial rockets flying into space along with tracer bullets heading toward no apparent target. The ship was an inferno. Through this pandemonium I could see the ship displaying a halo of impenetrable anti-aircraft fire. I believe every gun on board was blasting away at the foe. She was truly a living representation of her heritage. I was amazed to see the ship so full of fight, holding her own against the other two "meatballs" circling her. In addition to protecting herself from other enemy planes in the area, the living hell that was raging inside her had to be reckoned with.

About ten minutes (or so it seems) after I came topside, a second Kamikaze peeled off and headed for his prey. From my vantage point it appeared that the plane struck the flight deck at the bottom of the island. I saw an explosion and a huge fire-ball ascended toward the sky. The Holocaust was made worse - more fire and smoke. During all this time the "Ti" was still fighting an awe-inspiring battle of survival. By now, she was listing and moving slowly. I sensed that if the third pilot completed his attack the "Ti" would be sunk. I watched the "Ti" slowly making her turns. The water sprayed on her decks was unable to extinguish the fire. The toll of the second Kamikaze was devastating. Her listing was so steep that it seemed the ship would roll over. The thunder of her guns had not been diminished as she blasted away at the remaining Kamikaze circling her.

About twenty minutes after the second Kamikaze came crashing down on the flight deck, the third Kamikaze decided to press home his attack. He rolled over and aimed for the *Big T*. I knew this was the end. It seemed that an hour passed from the roll over to the half-way point of his dive when the pilot suddenly aborted his attack and headed away. As soon as he was out of range of the big guns he was shot down by a pair of F6F fighters. The last act of the enemy pilot prevented the sinking of the ship. As you well know, the ship was saved to fight another day.

Jack Goode Y2c

On January 21, 1945, I had finished noon chow and was proceeding toward the ladder leading up to the hangar deck when I heard the 40 mm going off followed by General Quarters. There was a mad rush to get up the ladder and a Marine, James Cardwell, pushed past me and went up the ladder. I was behind him. The Kamikaze hit and tore through the flight deck to the hangar deck. James Cardwell was half through the hatch when he froze and fell backward on top of those behind him. He had been hit in the neck and appeared to die instantly.

After finally getting to my battle station we were dispersed to fight fires on the hangar deck. There were many dead and wounded and smoke and flame everywhere. I vividly recall a crew member of V2 being helped by two others. His right leg was completely blown off and I learned he died a short time later.

I recall the ship listing to port and footing was difficult. We seemed to be getting the fire under control when the second Jap hit the island. CSM Croley and "J" "C" Dillard who were on the signal bridge were killed instantly.

The memory of burial services will always remain with me. Another memory was of the gun control on top of the island structure where several bodies remained until we arrived at Bremerton where a crane removed the charred unit.

William A. Gowder AOM1c

On January 21, 1945, I was a 19 year old sailor working on an F6F on the flight deck of the USS *Ticonderoga*, CV-14. We had just departed from the South China Sea and were going east between Formosa and the Northern Philippines. I was an Aviation Ordnanceman in charge of all the ordnance on six or eight fighters. This included the machine guns, rockets, bombs, and gun cameras. The F6F I was working on was very close to the exact middle of the flight deck. The middle of the island on the carrier was about 2 to 3 planes away on my right. It was around noon. The flight deck was spotted for take-off, planes were loaded for a strike. We were not at General Quarters. The day was quiet and still, the sky clear of clouds with unlimited visibility.

I was checking the electrical circuits before plugging in the six rockets into the F6F. I was standing on the wing stub of the plane, whose wings were folded. I felt a shadow pass over me. I looked up because I knew there were no bridges where we were. I saw nothing but the clear blue sky. Suddenly there was a tremendous explosion approximately 200 feet forward, which was just aft of the #1 elevator. A Kamikaze had gone through our flight deck, exploded with its bomb and bounced off the 3" armor plated hangar deck. Men were blown over the side. We threw kapok life jackets to them which sank because they had been flattened by being used as bedding for many months.

The next hour was chaotic. Fires were throughout the ship. With all the fires we realized we had to deep-six all the bombs, rockets and ammunition on all the planes. Some airplanes were burning and .50 caliber slugs exploded and bounced off our bodies. They were hot but had no force when they were not contained in a gun barrel.

Bomb skids were at a premium, so we carried small bombs and rolled larger ones to the deck edge to be thrown over the side. Don Noyes would cradle his arms under a small wing bomb on the SB2C's. I would trip the bomb rack to release the bomb into his arms. He would then run to the deck edge and heave the bomb over the side. In a matter of minutes all of the wing bombs on the SB2C's were in the Pacific Ocean. The suspension lugs on the 500 and 1000 pound bombs created a very bumpy roll but we knew the bombs were not supposed to go off without a fuse, which we had prudently removed. When we did have a bomb on a skid, sometimes we had to roll it through flaming gasoline which increased the flow of adrenalin substantially!

It was a hectic hour. There was lots of cooperation, which was unusual. Normally, VF men worked on fighters only, VB men on SB2C dive bombers, and VT men on torpedo planes exclusively. Now our main job was to dispose of all the ordnance on all planes. Everyone helped each other in a wonderful display of teamwork! I believe this is what helped prevent other massive explosions.

We were extremely fortunate in gaining control over the fires. Flaming gasoline ran down open hatches on the hangar deck, which is further proof we were not at General Quarters. When we were repaired in Bremerton, Washington, they welded big lips around these hatches to prevent a recurrence of this tragedy.

During this hectic hour I managed to find a Japanese-American dictionary which the Kamikaze pilot was carrying. I intended to keep it as a souvenir. However, we were requested to turn in all of these mementos with the stipulation that they would be returned to the rightful owner. I never saw my memento again. I often wonder who ended up with it. About one hour later we were attacked by another Kamikaze. This one came from the starboard beam. It seemed like every ship in the fleet was trying to shoot him down. We could see pieces of his wing peel off as he was hit by AA fire, but he kept swerving and closing the gap. I had to make a decision. I was on the fantail of the flight deck at the time. A chain going through metal poles kept personnel from falling overboard. I hung on to the chain and the thought went through my head that I would jump if the Kamikaze hit near the fantail. Instead he hit the island structure, but I was one very scared sailor who was afraid he would have to jump into the ocean. I think we had one destroyer for an escort on our way back to Ulithi. Fear settled over the ship, realizing how vulnerable and alone we were. Electrical fires still managed to frighten everyone. The fires continued into the late night. Everytime Gme GQ or Torpedo Attack was played the hair on my body stood up.

Later that afternoon someone, I believe it was a Pharmacist Mate, was making a list of Purple Heart nominees. He asked for my name. I had a wound on top of my head which had saturated my shirt with blood. However, I explained it was not from enemy action but rather a wound received when I hurdled through a relatively high passage way hatch. My head collided with the top of the hatch!

After repairs state-side and a 25 day leave we finished the war at Okinawa. I was much more mature and much more careful - - - but just as scared! Everytime I walked through the passage way where the first Kamikaze went through the Admirals refrigerator I could still smell death, and thought of the loss of life of so many men. I went out of my way not to have to take that passage way whenever possible.

I still carry the card claiming we were in Tokyo Bay for the surrender ceremonies. I also call several shipmates every January 21st.

Charles A. Gray EM2c

The chow line had formed and was backed up onto the hangar deck. I was in the line near the end. GQ sounded and all made tracks for our stations. I made it down one ladder heading for my station, the after diesel generator, some 5 or 6 decks below. When the first Kamikaze hit the superstructure I was on the deck just below the hangar deck. When the second hit, I was at my destination, the after diesel generator. Being so far down I was somewhat insulated from the havoc on the hangar deck. The first hit, however, rattled my teeth.

I spent approximately 4 to 5 hours at my station and then we were allowed to leave our quarters. As we opened each deck hatch to exit, water poured in on us. Upon reaching the hangar deck, WHAT A SIGHT, never to be forgotten. Two days later burial at sea was observed for the dead and missing.

William N. Grijalva S1c

As I recall it was just 12 o'clock, noon. I had been on watch duty and released to go eat lunch. I was on the hangar deck getting ready to go to the galley when the bombs began to go off. I started to run to my battle station. A Kamikaze plane hit our #1 elevator. A second one hit the bridge where Captain Dixie was. When I got to my battle station, one of my buddies was directly

in front of me. A bomb exploded and he was literally bounced to the wall. He hadn't had a chance to get his helmet and life jacket on, but was lucky enough not to be hurt. As I bent to put on my helmet, pieces of shrapnel hit my helmet and made me feel drowsy, but I wasn't hurt seriously either, thank goodness. I did get a piece of shrapnel in my collar bone. One of the boys removed it with a pair of pliers. There was a great deal of blood; it was a real mess.

Our crew leader was right behind me at the time, and he was killed by a piece of shrapnel. A couple of other boys behind him were injured also. One had his stomach torn open. There was nothing that could be done for him and he died. Another, I recall, was wounded on both legs, but survived.

The ship was on fire and floating sideways. Captain Dixie gave orders to abandon, but I guess we wanted to stay with her. None of us obeyed that order. We headed back to Pearl Harbor so we could return the ship to the States for repairs. We weren't travelling very fast, since we were still going sideways.

Frank Guibleo S1c

On the day the suicide plane hit our ship I was at the head of the chow line with the rest of the men from our gun crew. We were to relieve the watch on the gun mount over the bridge. It was a 40mm gun and we were the look-outs.

We had finished our chow and were on our way up to take over our duty. It was at that time that the suicide plane hit the island. The crew tried to get up to the gun to help, but couldn't. We were then told to go help on the 20mm gun at the deck edge.

We were there until we were secured from quarters. When we finally went back to our compartment, the rest of the crew were happy to see us as they thought we had been killed. Thank God for a happy ending. Unfortunately, not everyone was that lucky.

Howard J. Hall MM1c

On the day of the attack I was with my friend Ed Mazur of Pittsburgh, PA. He and I both worked below decks in the machine shop.

We heard over the P.A. system of a TBM bomber returning which had flak damage. We went aft on the hangar deck to see this plane. Then we went forward to the deck edge elevator. While there, Ed asked me to go forward to the weight lifting gym. I had never been there but I declined and said that I was going below to study my 1st class book. Ed went to the gym. Moments later GQ sounded and I flew to the machine shop.

Something told me that this was the real thing so I closed the air intake (my assigned UOB) before being told to do so. The lights went out and smoke filled the shop. We all had to put on our gas masks so we could breathe and water came up on the deck. We all noticed that Ed was not with us.

Later we learned that he had been hit near the forward elevator where a Jap plane blew and a 590 lb. bomb. Ed died that night. God was with me, for if I had gone to the gym I would have been with Ed.

Walter W. Hamilton PhoM1c

It was a twist of fate that I am still here, but I lost my best friend John Hughes PhoM1c. We were both assigned Photo duty on the flight deck and we flipped a coin to see who would go up on the bridge. I won the toss and picked the forward flight deck. The bridge was hit by a Kamikaze plane and we lost a few good men, including John Hughes.

I photographed the explosion when the Jap plane hit the bridge which involved the entire length of the flight deck forward from the bridge. Also, when the second Jap plane went through the forward elevator shaft I tried to get pictures but was pulled back to the catwalk by another man, Kuntzweiler PH, who most likely saved me from getting hit by 50 calibers and explosion.

George L. Hanson S1c

I remember having just sat down to eat our noon meal. It was a good one as it often was when we were in battle zones. We had pie! When the gong and bos'n's pipe sounded I grabbed the pie and ran toward my battle station. I was a Seaman 1c in the F (fire control) Division. My battle station was on the seventh deck, 4 decks below the mess hall, in the Plotting Room which had computers and other controls for tracking and firing the anti-aircraft guns (40 mm and 5-inch-38) remotely from radar and manual input. Almost immediately, the huge explosion from the first suicide plane rocked the ship as we ran to our battle stations. Needless to say, we moved quickly and secured all hatches.

I remember that a few days before, while the ship was in the China Sea, some of us were listening to music and chatter from Tokyo Rose on the PA system in the mess area. As I recall, she cited us by name - *Ticonderoga* - and predicted an unhappy encounter was shortly in store for us. None of us believed her, but she was right!

I remember anxiously waiting to get it straight - what was happening topside!? The Fire Control Plotting Room was next door to CIC and we eventually pooled information. In my mind I seem to recall there being 8-10 people, officers and enlisted men, in the Plotting Room itself. For the most part we were excited, anxious, but calm.

I remember when the second Jap plane hit, about 3 or 4 hours later as I recall, don't know, it hit just below the Mark 37 Director which was manned by our guys, F Division. Communication all but stopped. The ship was listing pretty badly and the general tension and lack of communication caused one guy to panic some. For the most part, we were pretty calm. Our leading officer appointed a volunteer squad under the leadership of a CPO to scout out a possible exit. We were held off, though hoping to get some definitive word on the situation. Finally it came, I believe from CIC, giving us the scope of things. After what seemed like forever, we were able to work our way topside. What a mess we found!

I remember the unbelievable destruction, the burned areas, squashed steel, and the bodies, dead and wounded, and the smells. I looked for my buddy Ted Woods, who was in that Mark 37 Director when the second Jap exploded. He survived and was awarded a medal for heroism in helping others get free from the area. I checked the overloaded Sick Bay looking for another buddy, Jim Dilles. He was OK also, helping out with the wounded.

I remember hearing our charismatic Skipper, Dixie Kiefer, was hit as well as the Exec and the Gunnery Officer. Many friends in the 8th division, lookouts, were casualties. I remember the long, lonely dark night on a new battle station, one of the single mount 5-inch 38s on the port side forward, I believe, wanting a cigarette so bad and being afraid to light up, even under cover! Heard that the Engineering Officer was in command, the senior active officer!

I remember the funeral service, all those men dropped over the side in bags weighted down with a 5-inch 38 projectile, Dixie giving a heart-breaking farewell speech as he was transferred off the ship on a stretcher, and Admiral "Bull" Halsey in his shorts!

Noel Hebard AMM1c

How well I remember that moment. It was about 12:30 and I was working on a tailhook of one of our F6Fs on the hangar deck near the big open bay in the middle of the ship when the first 5-inchers went off and General Quarters sounded. As I was a member of the VF 80 mech crew I had no General Quarters station and sort of kept at my work until I heard the Pom Poms go off. That's when I knew it was close and decided that I better get out of that vulnerable spot and go to a safer area behind the stack at the fuel re-fueling station. As I hurried along I could hear the 508s going off and had just made the turn when the explosion occurred. There was one other crew member behind me and behind him came another crew member with the back of his shirt burned completely off. A little dazed, but not too bad off. That's when I realized why you would be put on report if you were without a shirt or with sleeves rolled up.

There were about six or seven of us in there altogether. We stayed there because there was nowhere to go, debating what to do in regard to the fellow with the burned back. There was no first aid equipment there; fortunately it wasn't life threatening. Being where we were we were unaware of the second plane hit and I can sort of remember looking over the side to see what it would require to take to the water. When the ship lurched to the port side we thought that was it.

We were glad it didn't keel over to the starboard side; everything would have come in on us. Eventually things quieted down and we ventured out to the hangar deck. The destruction was overpowering and one thing I remember was the sprinkler system working all through the wreckage. Our crew chief gathered us together and put us to work helping out as best we could. I remember lifting up some of the men who had lost their lives and being able to recognize them - didn't look hurt at all. Others were just a shell.

Overheard one of the men make the comment, "We'll have to go back to the States to get this fixed up," and he was right. Air Group 80, of which I was a member, had to go over to the Hancock which did not please us very much.

Francis W. Herbert ABM3c

My job was flight deck control. Working with me on the flight deck, on the day we were hit, was Lt. Speidel, Lt. Braine AMM1c, Reno Koznen and S1c James Blair. Our job was to make copies of each plane's location on the flight deck and deliver this information to the proper ready rooms. This also included fighters, bombers, torpedo planes, and their position on the hangar deck. With this information it could be determined how many planes were out on strike and how many had returned.

As each plane left the ship, a forward talker at the catapult would give us the number and type of plane. On the return of the plane, a talker at the landing signal officer station would give us the number and type - letting us know how many returned.

On January 21st we were in the F.D. office at 5:30 a.m. Breakfast was at 4:30 a.m. We started sending strikes off at approximately 8:00 a.m. At about 11:30 a.m. we received information that Bogies had been spotted on the radar screen, i.e., "Here comes Betty with a pickle." Everything was going along okay until after 12 Noon when we heard the firing of all the 40 and 20 mm guns and 5-inch 38s. Our office was at the front of the island, and the guns sounded louder than ever. Lt. Speidel, Lt. Braine and Koznen were out on the flight deck. I was manning the phones, talking to the talkers. All of a sudden the L.S.O. talker said, "There's one coming right on the deck." The next thing I knew there was a huge explosion and the office filled with smoke. I tried to open the door to get out and the door was jammed from the explosion. The Kamikaze had crashed with its bomb right in the front part of the island and had gone down No. 1 elevator.

There was another passageway that led into the plane handlers room, so I found my way in there. Directly opposite the bulkhead was another passageway door and a right turn took me onto the flight deck. I had gone this way a thousand times before, so in the dark it seemed natural.

As I reached the flight deck I couldn't see much because of the smoke. There was a plane on the deck edge elevator and the fire fighters were hosing it down. I went to help them. All of a sudden there were men lying down on the deck and men running for cover of the island. I ran into Repair 8, which was probably 4 ft. wide and 8 ft. long. Men were piled up in there six or seven feet deep. I ended up just about in the middle of the pack.

We could hear the Kamikazes coming in, firing their machine guns. It sounded like a lot of people with hammers hitting the side of the ship. Then there was a huge explosion as one of the planes hit the bridge. The room we were in quickly filled with smoke and we ran out of it. Outside, the ship was listing badly and it looked as though the superstructure was going to fall over. I headed aft, and as I went by the after 5-inch gun I met Nash Haddad. He was all excited. His position was plane handler and his life jacket was in the handler's room. I gave him mine as he was not a very good swimmer. I soon found another jacket that I removed from one of the men who had been hit and no longer needed it . . .

As I went by the after 20 mm a Marine yelled

to me to come and help him. He was in the gun but had nobody to put the 20 mm canisters in. I stayed with him until things cooled down. We then started the terrible job of counting our losses and assessing the damage.

My friend, Jimmy Blair, was lost that day. I guess I was lucky. Many of our shipmates never made it home.

Walter H. Hobby S1c

I don't have much to tell as I had just been released from Sick Bay. I was on light duty recovering from having a 5-inch projectile dropped on my foot. Remember Doc Scherr?

It was Noon; the chow lines were long. I was lying in a bunk, 1st Deck. GQ sounded - I slid out of the bunk to get to Mt 5 upper handling room. Hopping up the ladder to the hangar deck I was pulled back by a Marine who passed me, leaving me falling to the bottom of the ladder. Starting up the ladder again the Marine came tumbling down dead from the explosion on the hangar deck. The hatch was closed. I went back left to the medical hatch which had an escape hatch in it. I climbed the ladder and, sticking my hand through the opening, the hatch came closed, the wheel hit me across the bridge of the nose and to the deck I went. I was out because I didn't know How or What happened.

I got on my feet and went to the torpedo compartment. Comforted by the torpedo men, as I did not know what happened. Smoke was in the air, the battle lanterns were dim and I was scared.

Then there was another explosion. Everyone sat tight. After a while "All Clear" was given. We went topside. It was an awesome sight. The fires were out. Bodies of burned shipmates. Assisted in getting the wounded to Sick Bay. Darkness came and, Oh, the night was long. The smell of burned wood, the creaking of the ship (as it was wounded too). The next day it was sack up our shipmates' bodies and sea burial services. This was a sad day.

Thanks to a great crew and a great captain I'm here today. It wasn't until recently that I learned there were two hours between our hits. Guess I was out for a long while. After we regrouped, I was transferred to the 8th Div. I was on Lookout and 20 mm. Hieter was Cox and we took on new personnel as well as Captain Sinton. But Oh Well, Life went on.

Richard Hodgson SF2c

I was on the mess deck enjoying Sunday dinner, especially since I had gotten a second piece of pie, when GQ sounded. I took off on the run grabbing my second piece of pie, determined not to lose it.

I heard the 40 and 20 mms firing - I knew something was coming in close. I heard Dixie say something like, "Keep calm, don't get excited." Immediately after I heard the explosion and the concussion. I put my pie somewhere and still can't remember what I did with it.

I got to my battle station which was Damage Control Station forward in officer country. There were some minor fires in the officers compartments. We had a R.B.A., but couldn't get the damned thing to function. The smoke was terrible. We were kept busy cooling down the overhead and bulkheads to keep the fire from spreading. It was dark, smoky - we worried about the fire going down to the magazines. After the fires were out we spent the rest of the night pumping water out of the compartments. I had a terrific headache and swore I would never smoke again - that lasted about one day. The next morning we helped to shore the gun director of the island. It was leaning precariously.

A vivid picture is still in my mind of the bodies in bags on the hangar deck waiting for the burial service. I was at the deck edge elevator during the ceremony. Dixie's farewell speech was another thing I'll always remember.

There are so many memories, not all bad. So many names that come to mind - Mr. Bok, Ensign, a great guy and officer. Commander Mallory, Ed Kelly, Tim Harvey, Ted Grindal, Rusty Hegeman, Tont Gierrie, Russ Collins, Andy Hrisko - the three MacDonalds (all killed), Pennell, Petrie.

James Holbrook TM3c

I was stationed at Fairfax Air Base where I met Dixie and asked him to take me when he was assigned to the *Ticonderoga*. After the hit I went up to the hangar deck, as our torpedo shop was right under the hangar deck. The torpedo gang helped with anything we could. Our gang was in the picture with the Captain and Com. Burch just before they left the ship. We also helped with the burial at sea.

George S. Huber SSML3c

I remember when GQ sounded I went to my gunnery station, 20 mm guns, on the starboard side. We were firing, when at "high noon" out of the sun came the Kamikaze. I remember there were 3 pilots, don't know their names, that were hit and were pulled in with us. After the attack there were only 4 men left in our blister. As a result of this attack I lost my hearing and today I have it back with the help of hearing aids.

Gene M. Huckle WT2c

I had just finished chow and had taken my tray back to the scullery when the guns started to fire. I immediately headed for #2 Fireroom as that was where my battle station was.

We were in the Fireroom until close to midnight. It got pretty hot down there. We had to turn our air supply on and off as the smoke would come through the air ducts and get pretty heavy.

We had water in the compartment above us as the hatches didn't get closed immediately. I lost a very good friend on this date, Eugene Herrick. I played football against him and we went through boots together. We were separated when he went to Gunnery School and I went to Water Tender School, then to the Receiving Station in Newport News, going to the ship each day working in the Fireroom.

William K. Hyatt MM1c

A lot of memories. I sure wouldn't want to do it again, but I wouldn't trade the experience either. Sure made a lot of us grow up pretty fast.

I still can't believe that Ski and I could jump

that far but, as it was the only way for us to save ourselves, guess we did what we had to do.

On January 21, 1945, a fellow shipmate and I, Ski Knykowski, were on the superstructure aft of the bridge on the inward side, sunning ourselves, when General Quarters sounded. We both ran down the ladder and across the flight deck to aft of the port side elevator. As we were proceeding down the enclosed ladder to the hangar deck, we were hit with the first Kamikaze plane. The force knocked both of us off our feet. We retreated up the ladder to the lower catwalk where the heat and smoke were bellowing out of the elevator; we seemed to have no place to go. Ski started to cry and I told him we must get out of here. We crawled into a life boat and somehow managed to leap out and pull ourselves up on the upper catwalk, then worked our way aft to the fantail.

It was here we took the second hit. The damage control officer asked us to volunteer to go forward and check for injured, and to secure any water tight doors that were left open. I worked my way forward on the port side as far as I could, then proceeded to the aft engine room, my General Quarters station. There was smoke down there and the ventilators could not pull it out until the ship was turned and the fans and wind helped out. The ship was put at a list so that all the water and gasoline could run off. I cannot imagine a worse hell-hole than the ship was at that time. But the courage of its Captain and Crew was phenomenal, and with everyone working together the fires were put out, our injured were cared for, and the dead were put into body bags in preparation for burial.

After temporary repairs we went to Bremerton, Washington for repairs, which didn't make me unhappy for I had a special someone waiting for me.

Osmond C. Ingram BM2c

I was on the Master at Arms on Jan. 21, 1945. We fed chow early that day. My station was on the hangar deck ladder. The line had gone through and I went down to get some chow. The ship shook and GQ sounded. My station then was on the 2nd deck. I had valves to close and had to close all the hatches. After a period of time I left that space, went across to starboard side to go up to the hangar deck and saw a Marine dead at the bottom of the ladder. It was a bad day but everyone did their job.

Jerome Harry Jadczak EM2c

I was an electrical technician servicing the telephone intercom system aboard the *Ticonderoga*. When the ship suffered the Kamakize attack I was four decks below. I reported for duty and was given the assignment to repair phones which had been disabled on the superstructure (the bridge). I was on my way immediately, taking the most direct route to the place of my assignment. I was about to enter a certain passageway when I had a most unusual experience. I heard a clear, firm voice telling me, "Do not go in there!" I looked around, but there was no one within speaking distance of me so I was inclined to ignore the message. But the same words were repeated a second and third

time. Later I learned that if I had entered that passageway, I would have been swallowed up by flames.

While I was hesitating, an officer appeared and commanded me to lie down on the deck which was covered with three or four inches of water. I remained there until things cooled off. Then I went to an area in the bow of the ship and took the ladder to the officers section where I made the needed repairs on the phone system.

Richard P. Jaycox, Sr. S2c

It was a little past noon on January 21, 1945, and I was located at my gun station, gun No. 4. It was at this time that our ship was hit by a Kamikaze. This Kamikaze hit us just aft of elevator one and abreast of gun mounts No. 2 and 4. At this time, I heard an explosion overhead and shortly thereafter a large portion of the Kamikaze's wing fell and struck gun mount No. 4.

The gun crew present threw the wing portion of the Japanese plane overboard. In doing so, they cleared the gun and we were prepared for any further action.

My first reaction, of course, was surprise. We didn't know what had hit us. It was then that our ship sounded General Quarters and we remained at gun mount No. 4 throughout the remainder of this day and into the next. Within the next few minutes after the first attack, our ship was again hit by a second Kamikaze. This plane struck the island, or the superstructure, of our ship. A large amount of damage was sustained from this attack.

Bryce Johnson AMM3c

We had been at General Quarters all morning because we had two bogies on the radar screen. The aircraft from the morning flight had been recovered, and the Hellcat that I was plane captain on had been respotted on the very aft edge of the flight deck, refueled, and rearmed with the 5 inch rockets and the 150 pound GP bombs. I had secured the aircraft and had permission to go to chow. I had just gone through the chow line and was sitting down when the whole chow hall shook like never before. Scared spitless, I didn't want to be caught below decks. I knew I had to get back topside to my battle station. It seemed like everyone else at noon chow had the same idea. No one was lagging behind. Everyone had some place to go and something to do, and we all started to move at once.

Those of us who needed to be on the flight deck started up the ladders to the hangar deck, but fire was blocking all the accesses to the first and hangar deck. We went down below decks and forward through officer's country to the forecastle and then up to the flight deck. All hell had broken loose. Everything from the forward elevator aft seemed to be on fire. Aircraft had been hit. There was a hole midship twenty to thirty feet in diameter, and there was fire shooting up. The only thing that could have done this was a Kamikaze. We all knew this because the Japanese had made several attempts on other ships in the squadron. This one had gone through the flight deck and the bomb it was carrying exploded in the hangar deck and wiped out our night fighter squadron and the forward elevator. The whole hangar deck was afire.

Although we did know that there were two bogies playing around at high altitude - high enough that the five inchers couldn't reach them (they were high off the starboard side) the situation had started to calm down and we thought we had things under control. However, one of them decided it was his turn. It was an aircraft called Frank. He started his run and nothing seemed to stop him. Forties and twenty millimeter guns didn't phase him. He hit us in the starboard side of the island. I was on the portside catwalk. We all saw him coming and took cover as best we could. You just had to get down out of the way and let the stuff fly.

The officers on the bridge, Captain Kiefer and several others, were wounded at this time. This plane did not do nearly the damage that the first had done. Since he was on the starboard side of the island, he, therefore, wasn't able to do the damage he had hoped for. By this time we had pulled away from the rest of the squadron; left on our own we headed for Guam with two destroyers following us at a distance.

This was the worst part of the whole ordeal. It felt like we were being abandoned. The Japanese might finish us off any time. Would the destroyers be able to help? Would we make it to Guam?

Robert Johnson PhM3c

General Quarters sounded. I headed for my station; third level, starboard side, just forward of the dressing station. At this location we could hear very little but had a sense of activity topside. There were vibrations felt that were uncommon to other General Quarters.

Other than that "uncommon" feeling we experienced, we had a feeling of being insulated to above deck action. We sat around without helmets on and just waited, not knowing what to expect. At the beginning all hatches were closed at condition "Able."

Later the hatches were opened and I took notice of a rescue party heading toward my position from several compartments forward. The rescue party, using life lines, had gone into the smoke filled compartments to bring out the crew that had succumbed to smoke. Norbert Ketza, one of our medical team, was one of the people carried out to my station. We put Norbie on a cot nearby and tried to resuscitate him. We could not get him to come around, so we carried him back to where a doctor could administer adrenaline and whatever care necessary to bring him to consciousness. Norbert Ketza died this day, trying to help others.

I tried helping a man who lost an arm at the shoulder. In some things we feel very inadequate. All we can do is to keep one from bleeding and to make the patient comfortable. I am not sure if this man survived. He had lost a great deal of blood.

After doing all I could at my station I went over to see if I could help out in surgery. Doctor Scherr and "Joe" Tremblay were working as hard and long as they had ever worked in their lives. The next thing I remember is waking up to see the two of them still standing and still at it. God, what dedicated men!!

Richard H. Jones S1c

I was just sitting down for chow when we got hit. Cherry pie was our dessert. I said to my sidekick, "It really is a shame to see that nice pie going to waste." He replied, "Let's hope that's all that goes to waste."

As General Quarters was sounding, I took off for my battle station. It was located on the 7th deck below in a small compartment that held all flooding valves for the forward magazines.

After fighting my way to the forward station, my partner at the station got there at about the same time. I can't place a name with the face. I would say it was a good hour before we got our orders to flood all magazines. That we did. It wasn't long after that we were sent to the hangar deck to help fight fires. Starting up through the compartments to mess hall level we found water above, so we could not get up that way. Returning to our station, we found that the hatch to the heart of the ship was our only way out. We couldn't go down or get through any of the magazines because we had just flooded them. We finally got to the forward officer country passageways and worked our way to the hangar deck. The darkness and smoke was dense and I thought we would never make it to the hangar deck. The ship took the second hit on the bridge when we got to our battle station.

We got to the hangar deck just forward of #1 elevator. Planes were burning all around us. The 20 cal machine gun bullets were exploding in the wings. As we got close to the fire, a Lt. ordered us to get up on the wings of airplanes and yank ammo out. Plane wings were hot, the fire was so bad that we just couldn't continue with our job. We couldn't believe how we were burning, never believing that steel could burn like it did. So many of our shipmates were lying around, stunned and injured, and many dead. We tried going up the forward ladder to below the hangar. Shipmates were dead on this ladder trying to get up to a higher level. This must have happened when we got hit the first time on the hangar deck, when we first took the bomb and then the Jap plane made a climb and came back through the same hole. A lot of the boys were caught by this one.

We were then told to join other crewmen on fire hoses. Things seem to dim at this point. Fire everywhere and the ship listing as if it was kind of weary. It was getting dark and I was just plain tired. We never did get to eat lunch but I did get a piece of cherry pie before I took off for my battle station and ate it on the run.

It seemed the Japanese had us in deep trouble and they tried to finish us off. Our planes could not land because of damage. We found out later they landed on other carriers.

Like I said, things that happened seem to have been dimmed. After a while, don't know what time, we checked into our compartment and heard that our F Division suffered a loss, but we also had a Silver Star given to one of our gunners mates, Sharp. Also, many got wounded in the forward gun control station.

The next day we helped on the bridge, placing people in body bags. I did not care for this job. I picked up a friend, Anderson, from our hometown, Springfield, Mass. I even stopped later at his Mom's home. She would not believe he was gone. He was listed as missing. I found his dog tags. He was 6th Div. or 8th Div. gun mounts on deck side.

William Bennett Jorgensen ARM3c

Dear Mom and Pop,

I'm now listening to the story of the Bunker Hill. And it really makes me wonder. Up until the time of the Franklin, the *"Big T"* was the worst naval tragedy of the war. And we brought our ship back too.

Every carrier that ever got hit has been announced. But who ever heard of the *Ticonderoga*, or Air Group Eighty?

It's not fair. Lots of folks would like to know what happened to their sons. It's not much fun having people tell you they never heard of your ship when you were in the same hell as these "famous" ships. Nor is it fair to our 350-400 dead and missing and 250 wounded. Dixie Kiefer's 65 shrapnel wounds didn't come from a game of cribbage. We didn't stand at attention for three hours while our shipmates were buried to be forgotten.

It's impossible to describe the fury, panic, fear and helplessness while a big, beautiful ship detonates her insides to disintegration. It would also be impossible to describe the awful stench of burned flesh, of the sight of grotesque forms that once were fellows, shipmates you knew. Confidence is suddenly shattered as you see what can happen to a powerful, steel clad man of war. Awe overwhelms the heart as your "home," your haven of security in turbulent, alien waters, suddenly lists to port while smoke billows out and ammunition pops all around like firecrackers on the Fourth of July. The smoke is black, brown, and white, bursting out of the bomb craters or any other vent of escape. Steam is hissing out the stacks and a loss of power is noticeable.

Some men are running around in bewilderment, suffering from shock. Others are jumping over the side. Some are fighting fires or removing gasoline, ammunition or bombs. Human flesh is scattered all over the decks and bulkheads. You can't find anyone you know and you wonder if it is all a bad dream. You wonder why you were spared, or left to suffer a while longer.

Some of the badly burned casualties scream, but most of them just moan or bite their lips. They shiver, even with inches of grease and jelly coating their skinless, black, crisp bodies. Parachutes, blankets, life jackets, mattresses all help to keep them warm. They're taken down to Sick Bay as soon as possible.

Then more specks in the sky appear. Some drop in flames far out, but some get mighty close before we can breathe again.

The next time we're not so lucky. The roar of the five inch batteries snap us out of our daze. Next to the black puffs in the sky is another speck. "Oh please dear Lord. Not again! Please stop him!" That's what you pray to yourself. But soon he's within 40 mm range and their "whoomp, whoomp" is added to the loud bursts of five inch. Still he comes on. Then the 20 mms open up, increasing the crescendo and the deafening roar. Only half the guns are firing because the first plane knocked out the others.

It seems impossible for him to get through that hail of flak but there he is, less than 100 yds. off the stbd. beam. "Where's he going to hit," you wonder. You run, not caring where. Just to do something. Then you see he's heading for the island, so you head aft and port. You try to claw a foxhole in the wooden flight deck, but to no avail. And you can't fit your whole body under the helmet and it seems as though you're all exposed.

You're praying again, only harder. Perspiration beads on your brow and trickles down your entire body. You wonder if this is it, is this where I'm going to get it, here in this vast, empty ocean where no one will ever find me? After all those close calls and sweating out missions I have to get it here where I sought safety and relief. You're scared. More so than before. It's not like the movies at all. There's no glamour, no heroics. We're all scared at the same time. No one stands up and yells, "Come and get us, you Jap rat." We all hope he'll miss. A few lose their heads and jump overboard to be cut up by our screws. But the guns keep firing.

Suddenly there's a loud explosion. The ship shudders, men scream. Shrapnel falls down like rain or big hail stones. The heat of the flash is intense. You look around to see what's happened, glad you're alive but sick at the sight of your buddies, kids mangled or burned or crazed with fear.

The island is riddled full of holes like a sieve. Flames and smoke lap out. Some men crawl out, others worm their way, a few stagger out. The look in their eyes I'll never forget. Most of the men in that island will never see home again, a place where right now you yearn for. If only your mother could wake you from this awful nightmare. Quite a few in that island will never be found.

After the ship has been cleared of those innocent dead and the wounded are cared for, we all fight the fires. Everything by this time is almost red hot. The heat is intense and the smoke brings tears to your eyes. Finally all is under control and now you "sweat" your way back to the anchorage. You're sure that one more sickening sound of General Quarters and that gong will drive you mad.

Then you reach relatively safe waters and you ease up. When the tenseness leaves your body you break out in a cold sweat and shiver. You want to cry, but ycu hold it in until you're in the solitude of your bunk. The coffee they give you doesn't help much and the inches of water in your compartment only serve as a grim reminder of the day.

When the sun rises, it focuses on a battered fighting ship. The burned flesh odor is still strong. Splotches of blood are everywhere, as are fingers, or eyes, or intestines.

After a cleanup comes the morbid task of sea burial. With the mournful wail of Taps, as we stood at attention each body dropped into the ocean, like a rock plunking into water. They slide down a board from under "Old Glory," over 250 once strong. As one of your tears rolls down your cheek you say, "There but for the Grace of God go I."

Then when we get back, no one has ever heard of us due to Navy censorship. Someday the "Big T's" glorious story will be told.

Bremerton Navy Yard, March 1945. Ticonderoga, *undergoing repair, visibile in background. (Courtesy of George K. Ames)*

Joseph Kaskoun AOM3c

We had loaded our planes (F6Fs) with bombs, rockets, and ammo for an afternoon strike and our crew was set to go to lunch. We discovered that one of the aircraft we were responsible for had a defective bomb rack. Since #76 was the one I usually worked on, Billy Gowder (crew chief) asked me to change it and then meet them in the mess hall. The rest of the crew, Dick Fields (Fish), Bob Nowaczyk (Murph), Ed McMullen (Mac), and Bill left me on the flight deck. The plane I was working on was near the starboard side, just aft of the island (about parallel to the after 5-inch gun turret.)

I had just removed the defective rack and was fitting on the new one when I heard an explosion somewhere off the stern and to starboard. I came out from beneath #76, looked in that direction and saw a huge spout of water. Almost immediately the "Forty" mount on the rear of the island opened up, and I looked to see what he was firing at. Because of his quick response, I assume we were probably at "One Easy."

A Japanese plane was racing off to starboard, swerving as he went, and I could see the tracers going just below him. I would guess that he had dropped the bomb that landed just astern. I can remember jumping up and shouting (much as in a game), "Get Im, Get Im."

At about this time I was aware of a shadow behind me, and turning I got a quick glimpse of a plane coming in (I was sure, toward me). I seem to remember that he paralleled the deck for an instant and then rolled over and dived in. He didn't go through very far from where I was and the explosion knocked me down.

Surprisingly, when I got up the first thing I did was to go back to the plane to finish installing the bomb rack. When I saw the plane, I realized it wasn't going anywhere and I ran to the side of the ship to help clear the wing of one of our planes that had fallen on the twenty mm battery on the catwalk, preventing them from firing. Instead, as I looked over the side I could see men jumping into the water from the hangar deck up forward. They were without life jackets and there were a few that obviously could not, or were unable to swim. I started throwing jackets over the side. These were from the twenty mm battery.

When the ship sailed past these men, I went back to the ordnance shack for my helmet but it was completely gone. The Japanese plane had gone through the flight deck in this area. Instead, I met Chief Hightower and he claimed me to join a group he was rounding up and we started to unload the armed planes. Bombs and rockets were just dumped over the side. Bomb racks were triggered and the bombs released onto skids (a drop of three or so feet) and, in many cases, bomb and skid were "Deep Sixed" together. By the time the second plane came in, I was at the port side 5-inch mount and took refuge (hid?) until it hit. I recall seeing a piece of "something" take a long arch to port from the vicinity of the bridge. The rest of the afternoon was spent disarming planes and, for a while, handling a fire hose.

I was sure I had lost my crew because the Jap came through in the vicinity of where the chow line formed on the hangar deck. Fortunately, however, there was no line at that time. Due to loading for the strike we were late and most of the crew had already passed through. Murph and the rest went directly to the mess hall on the third deck.

Need I say how great it was when we all met again the next day?

Robert H. Keenan EM1c

After chow I was relaxing on the fantail of the CV-14 enjoying the sunshine. Off to my left I observed a small carrier I believe to have been the *Monterey* take a bomb hit, then everything broke loose. General Quarters was sounded on our ship, and on my way to my station a young

Marine who was following me below was killed by the force of the explosion on our hangar deck from a bomb hit before we were hit by the Kamikaze that struck our bridge.

William F. Keep TMV3c

I was going up to the hangar deck when the explosion went off. There was a Marine ahead of me. He was hit in the neck with a piece of shrapnel and fell down the up ladder and knocked me to the deck with him on top. He was killed instantly. I went up on the hangar deck and spent the rest of the day doing whatever.

Asa L. Kelly BM2c

On that day were at General Quarters. About noon they passed the word to set condition "One Easy" and that certain gun crews were to go to mess. My mount, #4, was a 5-inch open mount forward on the port side. I was first leader. We were among the first to go.

I was sitting on the ammo locker sharpening my knife. I never went below deck while we were putting up strikes. At this time we had one strike up and another loaded and ready to go.

Suddenly the bugler started to sound G.A. but he never finished. It sounded as if the whole ship was exploding. There was debris flying everywhere. Then came the wall of fire.

Very few of our gun crew made it back to the gun at first as they were forced to run forward on the hangar deck to get to the ladder to reach their gun. The hit was just aft of the forward elevator. Much of the damage was forward on the hangar deck.

Many of the loaded planes on the hangar deck began to burn and explode. The machine gun ammo sounded like bunches of fire crackers going off. Occasionally a rocket would take off through the bow. It's a sound you will not forget. The pointer mechanism on my mount was damaged. Many times I think about this. Being 1st leader I would have been standing in front of the pointer where anything that damaged the pointer would have gone through me.

Those of us who were there unloaded the 40 mm mount next to us; it was burning, fully loaded, with ammo boxes sitting there. We threw it all overboard. We then decided to go forward and help fight the fires. When we got there we found most of the water mains had been ruptured and we were not needed. We then returned to our gun station where we found the Marines getting ready to man our mount. We relieved them and got our mount manned and ready. This was about one hour later when the second Kamikaze hit the island, knocking out everything, including the steering. For a time, before steering could be set up aft, we were traveling without control. I still remember the two destroyers that stayed with us, circling us like Indians around a wagon train, throwing up everything but the kitchen sink to protect us.

One of our fighters flew past us going full speed on the tail of a Japanese plane. Both appeared to be just inches above the water. Next we ran across an airdale who spent a lot of time with us. He had a large hole completely through his thigh. Our corpsman had not appeared. We assumed he had probably gotten it trying to reach us. Anyway, we went into the first aid box and got out sulfa and put it all in the hole. It was not bleeding. Apparently the hot metal had seared the flesh when it went through. We then gave him a shot of morphine, bandaged the wound and carried him to the flight deck where all the wounded and non-essential personnel were being gathered in the event the 1st phase of "Abandon Ship" was sounded. A 1st Class gunner's mate, apparently suffering from shock, came up to me and asked if he was hurt. Without thinking, I said, "Yes, you are burned black." He had probably been burned by the flash, not having his flash gear on. We later heard that both had lived and they had saved the airdale's leg.

We stayed on condition "One Easy" all night, sleeping on whatever we could find. We were all very cold. Sometime during the night the galley made and served some hot soup. It wasn't very much but made us all feel much better knowing we were functioning once more. The officers storage was opened and most of us who had lost our gear were issued blankets. We were leaning over far to the right due to having flooded our ammo magazines. During the night fires flared up twice. We put them out in a hurry, knowing they were looking for us so they could finish us off.

Edward F. Kelly Cox

I received my orders for the *Ticonderoga* in January of 1944, to report to Newport News, Virginia. When I arrived there were no officers there yet. We checked in with a chief who had been recalled when the war started. I'll never forget his greeting: "Our fence is 3 ft. high, we have an open gate every 50 feet. You keep your own liberty card. We'll try to get word to you before we have a morning muster. Let us know if you're leaving the area. Enjoy yourself." My next big surprise was finding out that there were so many of my old shipmates off the USS *Ranger* CV-4. Those first few months were really a ball. The ship yard didn't want us around getting in the workers' way, so we just acted like normal sailors and hung out in a nearby bar. We were having a ball about 10:30 one morning when a 4 striper walked in. He introduced himself as Dixie Kiefer, the Skipper of the *Ticonderoga*, and said that he was staying out near our barracks and anytime we saw his jeep to flag him down and he'd be glad to give us a ride.

I was a 1c shipfitter. Our berthing compartment was A-415 L. Under normal steaming conditions, the main hatch to our compartment was closed and dogged down. Passage in and out of the compartment was through a scuttle. My battle station was in charge of a repair unit. Our area was forward #1 elevator pit, 2nd deck and main deck to the bow.

When GQ sounded on January 21st, I was in our living quarters. Normally, I'd be one of the first through the scuttle, but on this day I had borrowed some Gene Autry records from one of the corpsmen (I think he was a 1c but can't remember his name). I took the record player and records, placed them in the blankets on my bunk and headed out. Whoever was just ahead of me in the scuttle when the first explosion hit, bounced back in my arms but wasn't hurt.

In our part of the ship the biggest problem was fire in the forward elevator pit. We could hear someone calling for help and finally located him standing on the ledge of a rim around the elevator pit with his head close to a natural vent. Two of us were able to go through a door on the 2nd deck and get to him. His clothes were burned off him except around the belt line.

When we were hit we were at GQ but Condition A was not completely set. Some of the hangar deck hatches were still open. We got orders to close the ones in Repair II's area. We had to clear two bodies that had tangled themselves in the hinge area. I recognized one of them as a storekeeper friend who had been on the Ranger with me. The war hit home.

The hangar sprinklers were a godsend. The water from the sprinklers held the flames from the burning airplanes down to where people could get some of the ammo off. But when a list was put on the ship to run the water and gas over the side a lot of it went through those open hangar deck hatches, down to the 2nd and 3rd deck.

Chief Warrant Officer Dearing, a very good friend of mine, told me not to worry too much about the exploding shells on the burning planes, that unless they went through the breech and barrel there would be little velocity. Two or three of us were near the door fighting a fire in the forward elevator pit. I repeated the gunner's story for the boys with me, when a shell that must have met all the qualifications to have power hit the door just over our heads, blew a 4-inch hole in it, knocked it back into the hold open catch and it rattled and shook for 5 minutes.

Cornelius V. Kilbane S2c

I had the 1200 to 1600 watch in the powder/shell compartment #4, 5-inch twin turret on the starboard side of the flight deck. I had early lunch and General Quarters sounded as we were eating. All hands raced for ladders to go to battle stations.

I got as far as living quarters just below the powder/shell compartment. Due to Condition "Z," General Quarters, and fire on the hangar deck, I was able to communicate with the Petty Officer in charge of the powder/shell compartment of #4 turret and was advised to stand by where I was.

While standing by in the quarters, I looked out of an open porthole and saw two planes doing "lazy eights" off the starboard side about midships. All of a sudden, I realized that one of the planes had broken off and before I knew it, I saw the red ball on the side of the plane. It was headed directly for the aft end of the flight deck. The planes in place had been readied for an afternoon strike. As the plane made its approach, it was hit by ship's fire and turned off course. At that moment, I hit the deck and waited for the explosion. As none occurred, I assumed the Kamikaze crashed in the water aft of the fantail. I held position until stand by condition set and reported to my battle station. I continued battle ready until relieved for evening meal.

David C. King AOM2c

Each aviation ordnance dive bomber crew consisted of four men who were responsible for the guns, bombs, ammo and rockets on five aircraft. The planes were all loaded with 500 lb. bombs for a 12:30 strike and I had just finished loading the 20 mm guns with ammunition on the "extra" aircraft. This made me late for noon chow. I stopped in our armory (just beneath the flight deck) to wash my hands when I heard a single 20 mm gun open up, topside. I ran up the ladder at the island, ran out on the flight deck, looked up into the sun and whoosh-boom! The Kamikaze crashed through the deck about thirty feet away. At the same time, a sailor who had seen it coming ran off the flight deck and ran into me. The explosion blew both of us into a safety net and if it weren't for that net we both would have gone over the side.

Climbing back onto the flight deck, an air group officer, Lt. Wehr, grabbed us by the arms and told us, "Go get that man and bring him over here." Then we noticed a sailor lying close to the hole in the deck. About that time the wind shifted and black smoke was pouring out of the hole, covering a large part of the deck. We could not see him or the hole, so we crawled out, located him and dragged him (in pieces) back to the island. The officer, by this time, had gone off somewhere else. We later learned that he was killed by the second Kamikaze.

I can't tell you, in sequence, what happened the rest of the afternoon. I do know that a few of us went from plane to plane stripping the guns of ammunition, pulling the emergency bomb releases and dropping the bombs to the deck. We then rolled them to a deckside chute and dumped them into the sea. Also, I remember being on a firehose with a Marine from a 40 mm mount, pouring water into the hangar deck where several aircraft were burning.

When the second Kamikaze made his run, I was under a 5-inch gun mount watching him come, thinking he would never get through all the anti-aircraft fire. When he hit, high up on the island, the heat was so intense I thought I was on fire. Later I saw a film of that hit and saw the fire roll down past the mount I was under and those flames went down almost to the water line. No wonder I was so hot! A photographer took that film from a forward starboard catwalk.

The rest of the day is hazy now. I do remember Admiral Halsey coming alongside on the *Missouri* looking us over, and the scuttlebutt flying that we only had thirty more minutes to get the fires under control or "get prepared to abandon ship." To this day, I wonder if he really said that. But we did get the fires out shortly after his visit.

Patrick Kitt S2c

After eating I, Ken Bluzard, and Joe Fallacaro, also of the 2nd Div., decided to go below on the starboard side to visit some of our shipmates. After a few minutes of gabbing we heard the sound of 40 mms followed by the sound of 5-inch guns. The ship seemed to shudder. We thought it might be a drill, but seeing the passageways and ladders filled with men running every which way we took off for our stations.

Ken and I made our way across the hangar deck to the forward ladder on the port side leading to the No. 2 & 4, 5-inch gun mounts. I just got to the top of the ladder when a tremendous

explosive sound followed by heat and smoke happened. The #4 mount was out of commission. Smoke was billowing from the flight deck amidship and the forward elevator. We had taken a Kamikaze direct hit. An Ensign made his way to the gun mounts and he and I went to the nearby 40 mm gun mounts and threw hot 40 mm shells overboard. I then entered a smoke filled and burning ammunition compartment to turn on the sprinkler system. Luckily it worked. Joined a bunch of mates handling the water hoses on the flight deck. We scattered when we saw the second Kamikaze closing in on the island structure, which was severely damaged and caused a great loss of life. I found out later Joe Fallacaro was found dead at his station, the forward elevator, and Kenny Bluzard on the ladder to the forward gun mounts. Ken was a few steps slower than I. These actions will never be forgotten.

Otto A. Kjargaard MMR1c

At 1200 hours we were coming out from the South China Sea. The PA system had just piped chow down and added that there were no bogeys on radar. The first Kamikaze hit within seconds, going through the flight deck just aft of the forward elevator, passing through Admiral Radford's quarters and exploding between decks. The planes, fueled and armed, parked, ready to be launched in the forward bay became a flaming inferno.

Immediately, Damage Control put the "*Big T*" into a port list and turned on the overhead sprinklers, causing water and burning fuel to flow to the port side and down an open hatch to compartments below. All hands on duty in the forward bay were killed on the bomb's impact. This was the situation as I came to my battle station, which was on the hangar deck in the island. My compartment was under the flight deck, 15 frames aft of where the plane passed through the flight deck. We were ordered to clear the hangar deck of all planes, ammo, and bombs in the after bays.

One hour later the second plane hit forward of the bridge, hitting Sky One.

Our last task was to go down into compartments below the hangar deck for search and rescue. We brought up many who were trapped in smoke and water. These boys paid a high price on 1-21-1945.

William A. Klein SKV2c

I was in the chow line of the forward mess hall when I heard the 20 mm start shooting. Those of us in line stated the Japs must be close with just the 20s going off and we then started for our General Quarters stations. I started down the ladders to a storeroom on the 4th deck to close a valve, which was my first job. As I started to open the hatch I felt the ship shift and I knew then we were hit. I closed the valve and reported to my battle station, which was the after mess hall repair party. Some of the fellows never did arrive at the station. Most of the party was made up of "R" division, I believe. I cannot recall all of their names.

Soon after arriving, we were told to check the repair party in the forward mess hall as they could not contact them. Some of us put on our

rescue breather masks and went to the forward mess hall. We found the party overcome with smoke and took them back to Sick Bay. I took one more trip back to make sure we did not miss anyone and found one more man. I started back to Sick Bay with him and found it difficult going. Someone came by with a gas mask on. Gas masks do not work well in smoke. He helped me get the man in better position on my back. He went his way and I again started for Sick Bay. To my relief, almost at Sick Bay, three or four men came along and took him from me to continue the trip. I then returned to my station and waited with the rest of our repair party. To this day I often wonder if we made our rescue in time. I sincerely hope so.

Robert C. Knight ACMM

We had been launching strikes all morning. The sky was blue and the ocean calm. We secured from flight operations. It was about noon. As I was the flight deck Chief for VF-80, I was responsible for all fighters on the flight deck. I made sure that all our aircraft were fueled and ready to launch.

I went below to the Chiefs Quarters to eat lunch before flight operations continued. I had just sat down to eat when General Quarters sounded. I had to go up two decks to the hangar deck; our quarters were at the aft end of the ship. Running forward toward the island structure where I usually went up to the flight deck, we were stopped by a red ball of fire in front of us. There was a Marine in front of me and his head just disappeared. I was hit on the right side of my face with several fragments of metal. The wounds were small but I was bleeding quite a bit.

Realizing that I could not go up the island structure ladders I turned aft. On the starboard side aft was a large opening that could be closed by a big metal curtain. At the forward end of this was a solid bulkhead that ran from the hangar deck to the flight deck. I went up that ladder in 3 seconds flat.

Arriving on the flight deck I found everything in one hell of a mess. Fires forward abeam the island. Planes destroyed and burning. We started removing bombs from aircraft and dumped them, as well as damaged aircraft over the side.

All of a sudden the 5-inch AA started firing which didn't bother us too much. Then the 40 mm started. All hell broke loose. Everyone started running. Our storage compartment was at the aft end of the island. I wound up in there with a whole bunch of people. The second Kamikaze hit us above the bridge. We went back to dumping aircraft and fighting fires.

A first aid station was set up just under the flight deck at the bow. I went there to have my face looked at. I was sure lucky; just facial wounds but not deep. They were cleaned and dressed and I returned to the flight deck and back to my plane captains and my aircraft. God, what a day. How we did it, I don't know. Training, I guess. You're under such fear and pressure, how can you cope?

We returned to Ulithi where the Air Group went aboard the USS *Hancock*. I stayed aboard until after the invasion of Iwo Jima, then back to the States.

Joseph K. Knowles Cox

We were bunked in the forward fo'c'sle when General Quarters went off. My station was alone on the fo'c'sle deck twin 40 millimeters.

During the actual battle I could still see the Kamikaze coming right at our position. As God is my Judge, I wouldn't be here if that Jap pilot hadn't chickened out. He was diving straight at us off the port bow; we were firing our 40 mm. At the last minute he dropped one bomb which fell short of the ship and he veered off.

We caught him with his belly up and blew him right out of the sky. I still see that as clear today as if it was yesterday.

Andrew J. Kordziel EM2c

Since it was about noon, I was eating lunch in the mess hall when they sounded the General Quarters alarm. As usual, everyone jumped to their feet and started running to their battle stations. My battle station was to maintain the electrical panel and motors in the Hydraulic Room of the deck edge elevator, just below the hangar deck. Instantly, the first Kamikaze hit the ship and I did not make it to my battle station. I had my battle gear on and remained in the mess hall.

We were then hit by the second Kamikaze and word came to us that help was needed on the hangar deck. I then went to the hangar deck and helped move both the dead and wounded in stretchers to the fantail of the ship. Honest, it was awful and sad to see shipmates burned so bad. I also helped to push a plane over the side. I remember all the bodies placed in canvas bags and set side by side in the fantail of the ship, and the next day or so the burial at sea with the US flag held over the canvas bag as the bodies slid down the slide and into the ocean.

Tony Kowalski RdM2c

On the day we got hit I was in the forward dining hall having lunch. I had been relieved off watch at which there were no Bogies showing on our, or any other ships' radar. We first heard our 5-inch guns firing and then 40 mm all in the same space of time and figured firing practice. But then came 20 mm firing and a loud detonation and General Quarters sounded and we knew we were in trouble. I and other radar personnel knew we had to reach our standby station which was our sleeping compartment. We made our way there just as watertite doors were being closed.

After getting to our compartment, we sat there waiting for further orders as fires were raging above us. I was saying my Rosary as the ship was put alist to drain water off the hangar deck. It was a traumatic situation, not knowing what was going on.

Ships communication was out, ship dead in the water and listing. I thought at 18 I was going down. After about 3 hrs. one of our officers, I think it was Lt. Rossiter, came in to give us some news on what was happening and how we stood.

Later in the P.M. some of the radarmen that were trapped in CIC came into the compartment and told us what happened.

At about 1600 hrs. we were told we had to

make our way to CIC and try to get our gear working; several of us held onto each other and made our way to CIC walking over our dead shipmates on the hangar deck. When we got to CIC nothing was operational and about all we heard was commands issued by Dixie Kiefer and Chief Engineer to get us underway and out of there.

We were assigned a couple of cruisers to accompany us as all of the fleet left us. We finally put out all fires and balanced the ship. Underway at about 12 knots, we headed to Ulithi.

Marvin H. Kurtz RDM2c

Normally my battle station was flag plot as liaison between CIC and the Admiral. However, on that fateful day the Admiral was not aboard. Consequently, my duty was eliminated.

To fill my free time I was "goofing off" in the SC 3 radar shack in the island. The gear was being operated by Ed Mingle and Harold Jenkins. World War II radar was not as efficient as modern gear. No enemy planes were noticed until one was seen by people on deck. Suddenly, the 40 and 20 millimeters chattered wildly and the first Kamikaze struck forward on the flight deck. CIC had a lookout high on the island in "Sky One." "Mac" McNealy, who manned that position, reported to the SC 3 room by sound power phones that a second Kamikaze was headed for him. The 20 millimeters fired rapidly until the plane hit the island. The gunners were engulfed in flaming gasoline and Mac was never seen again. Paint chips from the overhead showered on us, smoke poured from ventilators and a few shrapnel holes appeared in the bulkhead.

Ed and Harold attempted to operate the SC 3 until it became inoperable. We heard much activity outside the hatchway. The three of us donned our life belts but did not inflate them. Much that happened for a while eludes me. We had a compartment one deck below the armored hangar deck. My division had the midnight to 4 AM watch in CIC back up in the island. I recall crawling on hands and knees on a very slippery hangar deck, feeling our way in the darkness, touching debris and some corpses, water dropping from the overhead, a sickening odor - a very eerie sensation.

When we finally located the island hatch and ascended the ladder to CIC we found it to be 95% useless. Broken glass littered the deck and much of the gear was useless.

Robert T. LaBrecque PFC
USMCR

On Jan. 21, 1945, I was in the Marine quarters when General Quarters was sounded. Jim Cardwell and I had attended Mass together that morning; we rushed to our battle stations. As Jim reached the top of the ladder he was hit in the jugular vein and died.

As I ran across the deck I was hit with shrapnel from the second exploding plane. It hit me in my left thigh, above the knee. When I reached my 20 mm gun on the fantail on the port side I strapped myself in and was firing at the attacking planes. My 1st Sgt. noticed a pool of blood around the gun mount and insisted I get out of the mount so that he could see the wound. He

applied sulfa powder and bandages and told me to go to sick bay. I noticed on my way down the many, many people that were much worse off than I was, so I decided not to report to sick bay until later that night. The stench of burnt flesh I will never forget.

All the doctors could do was remove the shrapnel closest to the skin. Most was close to the bone and I was told it would eventually rise to the surface. In 1975 it did, a mass a little larger than a golf ball. It occasionally throbbed in cold weather, but now that I spend my winters in Florida I don't even realize it's there.

You would think it hard to forget a day like that, but I have. This is the best of my recollection. Joe DiSilvestro, a Marine, told me there is a small plaque dedicated to PFC Cardwell in a square in Worcester, Ma, which I hope to find one day.

Edmund J. Laskowski MM2c

I was assigned to the USS *Ticonderoga* at Newport News before she was commisioned on May 8, 1944. My assigned duty was to the Forward Engine Room, M Division, where I was called Ski.

January 21, 1945: after lunch, a friendly mate and I were heading for the flight deck for a breath of fresh air. That was something we did after lunch whenever we were able to do so.

As we ascended the ladder from the lower deck we heard the roar of guns and ammunition. My friend remarked, "They must be having a practice drill." Because the blasting sound was so ear deafening I remarked, "That is not a practice drill. It sounds like real shooting!"

We both turned to go back down the ladder to our quarters and the concussion from the next blast was so strong my friend, who was in back of me, was flipped over my head and landed against the wall. I did not stop to check him as I headed to my quarters and assumed that he continued to his own quarters. Several days later I saw him and he was banged up a bit.

Once I got to my quarters in the forward engine room, I could hear more gunfire. My superior officers were in the quarters and I still remember the look of fear on their faces. I WAS SCARED TOO! Luckily, everyone in my division in the forward engine room made it to their stations safely. When we were all at our stations we had to seal the hatch. Then, when smoke started seeping into the engine room, we had to shut off the blowers as they were drawing smoke from topside.

Actually, all this time I did not know how bad the ship was. The smoke indicated that there must be a fire somewhere. Eventually I was aware that the hatch had to remain closed, as the magazines on the upper deck were flooded to prevent the explosives being set off on the ship. I can vividly remember having the feeling that the ship was listing.

Eventually, orders came to slow down the engines. We learned that there was a fire topside and speed was further fanning the flames above.

I was stationed at my post in the forward engine room, maybe about 18 hours, when we were told that we could open the hatch.

When I exited my quarters, I became aware of what went on and how the ship was hit. When

I came up topside, I saw the body bags of my mates who had perished. I said a silent prayer for them and for their families and thanked the LORD that I had survived this tragedy, as I had a young wife waiting for me at home.

Douglas Latini SM3c

On the day we got hit I was in the laundry room. GQ sounded and I went aft to, I believe, Radio 3 which I was assigned to. Radio 3 was aft on the starboard side. We were a standby in case the island ever went out. When we got hit I was outside of the radio room on the catwalk. I watched as the first plane came along the port side, came up astern and hit the deck forward. A few minutes later I saw a plane dancing in and out of the clouds starboard, way up high. When he started his dive the five-inch went off. That wasn't bad. Then the 40s started which was getting too close.

When the 20 went off I went to the radio room as he was about to hit the island! Radio One was out as the antennas were out. I had to go to the island to get insulators to set up whip antennas so we could send and receive coded messages. When the first plane hit, Radio One was out as was Radio 2, which was forward on the port bow. When the plane hit, it started a fire and bent the ladder going to Radio 2 so the guy didn't get there.

We lost some of our radio crew that got caught on the hangar deck in the fire and explosion.

Ronald F. Law AOM2c

When GQ sounded attack, our TBF Ordnance crew had just completed loading/servicing planes for the next attack scheduled. I was on the flight deck just aft of the island, so I hit the deck and covered my head with my arms when the first Kamikaze was diving in, strafing as he came. His bullets ran a pattern up the deck about a foot away from my shoulder - good miss. I grabbed a fire hose to help extinguish the planes burning on the flight deck until our leaders organized crews to unload and deep-six the bombs. We finished our task on the flight deck and moved to the hangar deck where dive bombers had 1500 lb. A/P's loaded. In unloading these, instead of lifting and lowering as with 200 lb. fighters, a bomb skid was spotted below and the bomb release in the cockpit activated (I didn't see any miss the skid), then with the 35 degree list we headed it to an open curtain and held the skid as the bomb went over. When all planes were unloaded, pushed back to the rear of the decks etc., and the smoke had pretty well cleared, I realized it had been six hours since GQ started and missing lunch (I hadn't eaten since about 3 A:M) and a major headache stopped me cold. After some aspirin and a K ration I settled down for a long night's sleep.

Robert B. Leighton ARM2c

We were in the mess hall when GQ sounded. I made my way back to the flight deck where my GQ station was, just aft of the deck edge elevator, V-1 division arresting gear. We fought fire, mostly burning planes and deck.

When the second plane came in, we jumped into the catwalk just aft of the same deck edge elevator. After this plane hit, we climbed back up on the flight deck and resumed fighting fire and shoved some aircraft over the side.

William S. Leister S1c

On the morning of January 21st, 1945, I had the 8 to 12 watch. At the end of my watch I went to the galley to chow down and then went back to my sleeping quarters, which were directly below the flight deck up forward. We were gathered around shooting the breeze when we suddenly heard a loud explosion. General Quarters sounded and we all took off for our gun mounts.

When I arrived at the flight deck I started running toward my gun mount which was located just above the bridge where the 40 mm guns were mounted. I could see a lot of smoke and flames coming from the forward elevator area. When I finally got to my gun mount I saw a Kamikaze coming in at about 5-inch off the starboard bow. I felt something hit my helmet. I believe it was fire from the Kamikaze. It went through my helmet but lodged in the lining. It was a minor wound compared to what it might have been.

We immediately started returning fire but could not stop him. There was a large explosion as he crashed into us. Although I was unable to see exactly where he hit us, I knew it was near the bridge. As the radar unit crashed down on our gun mount we were surrounded by fire. My friend and fellow shipmate was killed in front of me.

The next thing I remember I was waking up on the bridge below me. I was unable to move, due to a compound fracture of my left leg and burns to my hands and back and a wound to my head.

I stayed there for several hours waiting for help to arrive but knowing there were many others also waiting for help.

When aid finally arrived I was taken below. All beds were full and I was placed on the floor, as were many of the other wounded. My recollections of this time are cloudy but I was there for a couple of days before they were able to get to me and set my leg.

Anthony J. Licci MM3c

On that day I was going to my duty quarters in the aft engine room. As I stepped off the ladder to the main deck of the aft engine room, I heard what sounded like a tremendous sledge hammer hitting the side of the ship. I didn't think it was an explosion because we weren't under attack.

Immediately after that, General Quarters sounded and all hatches were closed and secured. We were down there for what seemed like hours and hours (about 10 of us including a Lt.). Smoke kept coming through the air ducts, but there was enough air in there to get us through it. When we were allowed to go back, we saw the terrible destruction that had occurred.

An interesting note to this story is that previous to the attack I had cut in the chow line so I could eat early and get to my duty quarters on time. I found out that if I had eaten at my regular time I would have been emong the killed or wounded that day.

William H. Long ABM3c

I was a tractor division V1. At that time I was on late chow, just finishing, when things started to happen. I headed for the flight deck to get my battle gear, which was on my tractor. The first plane hit after #1 elevator. I was between the hangar deck and flight deck in the island, going up the stairs. Everything forward was on fire. As I headed toward my tractor to get my gear, the second one came in and hit the island and the 5-inch range finder. Our 40's and 5-inch were shooting at other planes at the time. I remember pulling hoses and getting things back so we could repair the flight deck.

Arnold Lotring F1c

The day of the attack I was in the galley eating with a shipmate. There was a explosion and someone yelled, "We've been hit!"

General Quarters sounded and I ran to my station, a hydraulic valve board. I put on my ear phones and got bits of news about damages and the raging fire on the hangar deck. I heard reports of smoke and fumes being drawn down into the engine spaces. I remember we put a list on the ship to try to run off burning gasoline, etc. from the hangar deck.

Sometime later I was told to secure the board and report to the hangar deck for stretcher duty. This was the first time I saw the magnitude of the damage. By the time I got to the stretchers on the aft end of the hangar deck, as I remember, most of the wounded had first aid. I vaguely remember trying to assist some of the patients who were having trouble breathing, even to the extent of giving some artificial respiration.

A call was made for us to report to the engine spaces, and after going forward and climbing a ladder to look at the bridge I saw what had happened. I returned to the ship engine spaces, got underway, and the realization sunk in that the immediate boiler room group that I worked with had suffered no casualties.

Kenneth E. Loy EM1c

The ship had been on battle alert for quite some time. My battle station was with a damage control party stationed one deck below the hangar deck just aft of the forward personnel hatch on starboard side.

I had been called to replace a lost circuit on the 40 mm gun on the bow, aft of the forecastle one deck above the hangar deck. I had just completed my job when we were first hit. I headed back to my station but couldn't get through the fire and damage on the hangar deck.

Then came the second strike, and a plane came through to hit on the hangar deck. I tried to go back across the deck but was unable to make my way through. I tried several other ways to get to my station and ran into fire. A fuel tank exploded and threw me face first into the bulkhead. I managed to get to Sick Bay where they covered me with vaseline as I was drenched with aviation fuel. A dentist looked at my face, reached in my mouth and lifted out my four front teeth, gave me a gauze pad and said to report when things calmed down.

I stopped at my locker for dry clothes, and as I could not reach my battle station I reported to the electric shop where I was on duty answering trouble calls all night and through the next day.

During the night, on one of the trouble calls when I had reason to cross the hangar deck, I passed rows of bodies laid out on the deck. Until then I hadn't really grasped this result of the hits. What I will always remember was the dim light on the hangar deck and the sight of rows of glowing radium dial wristwatches on the arms of my dead shipmates.

Francis E. Lynch WT3c

On January 21, 1945, I was relieved from the 08:00 - 12:00 watch in No. 1 fireroom and went to my living compartment located portside, off the forward mess hall.

My compartment was #B-320-L just forward of a shower room, and aft of that was a washroom in which, in my birthday suit, I was washing a pair of dungarees, shirt, socks, skivvies and a bath towel, when at approximately 12 noon GQ sounded.

I went forward to my living compartment and put on dungarees, shoes and a shirt when a bomb hit the hanger deck, 2 decks over head. Someone said it was a 5-inch gun firing, but, when we heard what sounded like squirrels on a tin roof, someone else said, "That was no 5" gun."

I ran aft through the two forward mess halls, the electrical shop, the machine shop and the galley into one of the aft mess halls where a trunk was located that led down to my GQ station, the port shaft alley. A fireman from #3 Fireroom, a fireman from the engine room who watched 2 main bearings on the port outer shaft and myself were stationed at this location.

The 2 "B" division people were part of the oil king gang. We monitored 6-10 fuel oil tanks. We opened or closed fuel oil or salt water valves to fill service tanks in the 4 firerooms or took on salt water ballast to trim the ship to keep a level flight deck.

After securing from GQ that night I returned to #1 Fireroom to finish the 20:00 - 24:00 watch.

On returning to my living compartment, I found it had been flooded to the overhead. We all lost our mattresses, most of our clothing and all of our personal gear. All personnel in our fireroom came through the attack o.k. That's what counted.

Daniel M. Madden Lieutenant, Communications Department

I had come off the morning 8-12 watch in the Comm Office and was in my room - I believe it was 204 - in the forward section of the ship on the starboard side of the wardroom deck.

When GQ sounded I rushed into the passageway to head back to the Comm Office, my battle station, on the 02 level of the island. Immense billows of smoke cloaked the forward stairway to the hangar deck, and I made my way to the one at midships.

The hangar deck was a chaotic mix of flames and smoke. The Kamikaze, the first of two, had crashed through the forward end of the flight deck and set ablaze waiting, gassed up planes. The damage control people were already at work.

Gunnery crews were sending streams of firepower into the sky of blue and brightness. The shells were bursting into little puffs, like pieces of clouds that had been somehow detached. From the hangar deck I could see their target - another Kamikaze. It just kept coming. We were the Kamikaze's target. I was in the Comm Office before it smashed into the island.

Commander Burch, the Exec, was at his GQ station aft. Commander Gifford Grange, our Comm Officer, was on the bridge which had taken the second Kamikaze. Joe Morrin, the assistant Comm Officer, had been affected. Communications were shifted to Radio Three in the stern.

Our coding machines were operating on emergency power. Immediate messages on our damage and injuries were relayed visually to nearby ships.

In the hours ahead, the Comm Office encoded and transmitted dispatches to commands within the task force, to ComThirdFlt, to Cincpac in Honolulu and to Cominch in Washington detailing personnel losses and damage. The names of Dixie Kiefer and of Clair Miller, the Air Officer, on the injured list added to the sadness aboard ship.

An incoming message from the task force commander told of our immediate future. The cruiser *Biloxi* was ordered to form a task unit with two destroyers and escort us to Ulithi.

The voyage to Ulithi had aspects of a funeral procession. It was slow. The *Ticonderoga* could not make more than six knots - a terrible comedown for a ship of the fast carrier task force. Lights aboard ship were dimmed, not in a salute to our dead and injured but because main power had been knocked out.

In the evening before going on the mid-watch I sat in Joe Morrin's room in semi-darkness. The sound of GQ blasted through our musings. Our reaction was much slower than usual. In fact GQ was cancelled before we made a move.

There were episodes I shall always remember.

On reaching Ulithi without incident, the *Ticonderoga* sent a warm message of thanks for the safe escort. The response from the task unit commander was short and very sweet; "It has been an honor to escort the finest ship in the fleet."

The saddest moment was the transfer of Dixie Kiefer to a hospital ship. All hands stopped what they were doing and watched in silence. All wished him well.

Crew members had agreed that damage to the ship was more than repair ships at Ulithi could handle. They were right. Our next orders were to proceed to Pearl.

Walter J. Mallett Cox

On January 21, 1945, I remember walking out on the catwalk and thinking that we didn't have to worry about a surprise air attack that day because the weather was so nice we could see a fly in the sky from five miles away. The day seemed particularly nice after two weeks of miserable weather in the South China Sea.

I spent the rest of the morning performing routine duties before heading for early chow. We were scheduled to launch an air strike sometime after noon and I had to be topside when the planes took off.

After chow I was under the flight deck, aft of the superstructure when I heard the sound of gunfire aft of our ship and General Quarters. I immediately came up on the flight deck and saw we had been hit. I guess the old adrenalin started flowing and I was really mad to think they had hit us.

Being assigned to damage control, I went forward to our compartments just below the flight deck to check for damage. Just outside the passageway lay the body of one of my division buddies, Finley, who had been really torn up by shrapnel.

Finley was part American Indian, hailing from Oklahoma, and was married with a beautiful daughter and son. Ironically, he was always worried about making it home and I had assured him as long as he stayed with me he had nothing to worry about.

Upon entering the compartment, I discovered shrapnel holes in the bulkheads adjoining the elevator shaft where a Jap plane had crashed. I got the men to break out the fire hoses and douse the fire below.

I then went back on the flight deck to see what needed to be done there. Someone told me there were pilots trapped in the ready room. To get them out I would have to cut through the wooden flight deck.

During all of this I could see enemy planes. When our 20 millimeter guns started firing I told the men to head for cover, but there wasn't much because of all the smoke and fire.

The next thing I remember, I was lying on the deck alongside a 500 pound bomb. The belly tanks on our planes were aflame after being punctured by shrapnel from the second Jap plane to hit us. I thought I'd better get out of there before the bomb exploded or I burned up.

I finally made it to my feet and headed forward by the deck edge elevator. Suddenly I got so weak I couldn't go any further. I fell down on the flight deck and while lying there I could see a man in the catwalk forward of the deck edge elevator.

I thought he was a fellow in our division (V-1) named McMahon, so I called to him, yelling, "Help me, McMahon." When I got no response, I began feeling sorry for him because I thought he was dead and hanging from the flight deck by his chin. Just then he moved, running forward and away from me. I suppose he went to get help as someone soon came and took me down in the catwalk.

They were fighting fires on the flight deck, and as the ship listed to port the water began to run down in my face. I asked the men to get something to cover my face because I was about to drown without ever being in the ocean. I believe they put a helmet over my face.

I didn't feel any pain at that time but, remembering my first aid, I told them to give me some morphine in case the pain did start. I soon found out that all the morphine topside had been used and the hangar deck fire prevented anymore from coming up from Sick Bay. I don't remember if I ever got any morphine, but I never felt any pain until I was onboard the hospital ship Samaritan.

While waiting to be treated I remember someone saying, "There's Lt. Woods." He was our division officer and apparently had been wounded. My last recollection of that day was someone saying, as they started to treat me, that I had lost so much blood that my veins collapsed. It always seemed odd to me that I was conscious the whole time but later could remember only fragments of what happened.

Later, a dentist at the Naval hospital in Jacksonville told me he was on the *Ticonderoga* and had assisted the doctor who treated me. He also said that they had waited to treat me because they were trying to treat some of the men they thought would live.

I fooled them though. I had to spend 16 months in different hospitals but I was finally discharged in May of 1946.

Owen Markey MM2c

I was coming out of the mess hall when we were attacked by the Kamikaze. There were gigantic holes on the flight deck and men were falling all around me as I tried to get back to my station. Everything was on fire. We tried to put out the fires and get down to the engine room, but the passageways were filled with smoke and fire. All the men were frantic and confused, running back and forth, with men dying all around us. Bodies were lying everywhere. It was a horrifying experience watching friends and crewmates fall beside me.

They finally got the ship stabilized and we headed for Hawaii for repairs. Hawaii couldn't take us, so we had to head for San Diego, California. They couldn't handle us; we were too large and headed for Bremerton, Washington where they took us in. They did their repairs in 30 days and we headed back to sea.

Louis A. Mastellone SK1c

When the first Kamikaze hit the *Ticonderoga* on January 21, 1945, at 12:01 PM, I was on duty in the main general storeroom on the 3rd deck aft of the mess hall. General Quarters sounded and I made my way up along the 2nd deck when a bomb blew up on the hangar deck above me. Due to casualties and a fire in that area, I made my way further forward to another ladder and proceeded up to my battle station which was a quad 40 on the bow of the ship. There we continued to engage other Kamikazes which were attacking us.

Within a short while a second Kamikaze hit the island where Dixie Kiefer and other flag officers and men were wounded.

We were listing to port, and word came that the ship was being flooded on that side to allow burning gasoline to flow off the hangar deck in order to extinguish the fires. All fires were under control without assistance from other ships.

A first aid area was set up on the deck behind our battle station for some of the wounded. When things quieted down, I went back to help comfort some of those men. I spoke with one man who was sitting on deck and leaning against the bulkhead. I asked him how he felt; he said he might be bleeding in his back. I lifted the blanket and saw he had a shrapnel wound in his back. I called for a medic to please help him,

which he did, and he was removed to Sick Bay.

When this initial attack ended, some of our gun crew were relieved to go aft for some food. On our way aft on the hangar deck I witnessed a most unforgettable sight, which to this day remains indelible in my mind. Men were lying all over the hangar deck, burned beyond recognition. We were asked to carry a body on a stretcher to the aft end of the hangar deck where the dead were being assembled. At this point I had no appetite and returned to my battle station, feeling dazed and looking out at the sea, just wondering. The next day the casualty list was issued and I heard names of some very close shipmates who had lost their lives and I said a silent prayer for them.

Robert E. Matisko F1c

I was awakened by the sound of GQ. I put my pants and shoes on as fast as possible and headed for my GQ Station which was #4 fire room. As I ran out of my compartment I heard an explosion. The concussion knocked me down. Others were running and falling down. I looked forward and all I saw was smoke and I heard hollering and screaming. I made it to the starboard side gangway and ran aft to the #4 Fireroom hatch and went to my GQ Station, which was taking care of the burners; however things were pretty hectic down there. Steam lines and water lines were leaking and safety valves were blowing. We all pitched in and did what we had to do to get everything under control.

I don't remember the second hit because we were too busy trying to keep the boiler fire up and on the line. After some time we got everything under control. During this time we had no communication with topside so we really didn't know what was going on. It was some time before we got the news. I don't remember talking to anyone too much because I think we were all preoccupied with our own thoughts. After many hours it looked like we were going to make it.

From then until the next day we were fed information about the damage that was done and learned that we only had one other fireroom operational. The next day when I was relieved, I went above and volunteered to help in any way I could in caring for the wounded and dead and clearing up as much as possible. That's about all I did until we got to Pearl Harbor and then to the States.

We had burial at sea on our way back. As I recall, they were still locating bodies on our way to the States.

Other things that happened during the first day that I remember are; the Chief of the Watch (I can't recall his name) was in full control at all times. He was telling us all which valve to open, which to close, and keeping us all as calm as possible under the circumstances.

I think it must have been on the second hit that I was knocked against the boiler and sustained a pretty bad burn. We found out later one of the sailors on the grades above died during the attack. Apparently he was overcome by the steam.

When I was topside helping out, I was told by a medic to keep giving a sailor water every minute or so - he said he was going to die. I

don't know how long I was doing that. The same medic came back and told me to stop - the sailor was dead.

I also found out that a friend of mine from my hometown was alive. He was on the forty mm aft on the superstructure. He told me they were firing head on at the second plane and could not understand why it did not go down. I was told I was eligible for a Purple Heart but never put in for it. Being alive was worth any medals they could have given me. I bore the marks of the rivets on my back for many years.

Michael Mazzuca S1c

On January 21, 1945, I was in the China Sea on the USS *Ticonderoga*. At five minutes to twelve I was seven floors below deck, putting fuses and detonators in the bombs that were to go up to the flight deck to be loaded on aircraft. I was with 1st class gunners mate "Rollene" and five stewards mates. We were sending the bombs up and they were sending them back down. A 1st class gunner looked up the shaft and said, "There's fire coming down the shaft. I think we've been hit." Five minutes later he said, "We've really been hit." He told me to take the fuse and detonator out of the bomb. Within a half hour the carrier was at a 45 degree angle and we were chest deep in water. We were that way until 1:15 A.M. before they came to check on us. Our whole bodies were wrinkled from being in the water so long. I was very frightened and I still dream about those suicide planes and what they did to us.

Frank M. McAfee Captain, VF-80

On that fateful day I was one of the VF-80 pilots being briefed in the Ready Room for an upcoming mission. Suddenly, a very definite "thump" was heard (and felt) which startled us all. This was followed by smoke coming through the air conditioning vents, which precipitated a mad rush for the exit to the port side catwalk.

The flight deck, aft, was crowded with planes being made ready for launch. Many of us assisted the armament crew in pushing the weapons dollies, loaded with bombs and rockets, overboard. After the bombs were all clear, we disposed of the planes themselves over the fantail. At about this time, we were ordered to disperse to make way for the fire fighters, the true heroes in this tragedy.

At this point, my roommate, Lt. George W. Rauch, and I held a little private "communion service" and decided to repair to the "high side" of the ship's 11 degree list to port. By way of preparation, we entered the aft section of the hangar deck and removed a 2-man life raft and several cans of water from a dive bomber. Our purpose, of course, was to insure our survival and live to fight another day.

We found refuge on a starboard side ladder and waited patiently for the order to "Abandon Ship." Fortunately, the order never came. Thank God for the fire fighters and the emergency repair crews, for without their heroic service we would have buried many more at sea than the 134 lives lost that day.

Roland P. McDermott AFC2c

It was about chow time and we had just finished arming all the planes for the next strike. We were not at General Quarters when I looked up at the sky and saw the Kamikaze bearing down toward our flight deck. I realized what was about to happen, so I jumped down on the catwalk and heard the explosion. We all got together and started to disarm the planes. If the Kamikaze had hit among the planes with their bombs aboard, it would have blown the whole aft end of the ship away.

We continued to disarm the planes manually by having one man catch each 100 lb. bomb as it was released from the shackle and throw it overboard. The larger 250 lb. bombs were caught by two men.

When the planes were disarmed, all we could do was watch as other Kamikazes were attacking. All our guns were firing away at them and the fires were blazing down below on the hangar deck. Unfortunately, all the men on the hangar deck were killed when the Kamikaze hit. It was a time in my life I will never forget.

Donald J. McDonald S1c

I was an original crew member in 1944 on the *Ticonderoga*. I am a plank owner and was transferred off the "*Big T*" just before we went through the Panama Canal. I was reassigned to the *Bon Homme Richard* CV-45. We were in Pearl Harbor in January 1945, when we out to replace the "*Big T*," hit by Kamikazes, "Death Wind" planes.

We were mustered on the flight deck, leaving Pearl Harbor to join the 6th fleet. There were a number of us former crew members of the "*Big T*." We passed the "*Big T*" with our ship's crew at attention in a silence you could cut with a knife. We could see a gaping hole in the starboard side below the flight deck and forward.

We saw the blackened paint and ruined bridge and radar damage. The flight deck had been badly damaged. We wondered how our former shipmates had survived. It gave us an eerie feeling and we wondered if this would be our fate too. It made us want to fulfill our mission and pay back the Japanese 10 times for this. We all closed with a prayer that night for our old friends and our own safety. I, for one, will never forget what I saw. I was eighteen going on nineteen years old then.

Leo McGeehan F1c

We were steaming out of the South China Sea near Formosa and I had just come up from the #4 Firing room because, as you can see, I was a down under "snipe" as we were called (among other names). I was on the 0800 to 1200 watch and decided I wasn't going to get in line for chow. I just went and hit the sack, clothes and all, because I was really tired.

I was just about asleep when I heard our 5-inch guns going off and immediately thought General Quarters was sounded. I jumped from my bunk, headed for the engine room and passed an open hatch just below the hangar deck.

As I passed the hatch, a warm gust of air hit me and knocked me up against the bulkhead

and I just bounced off and kept running to get to my GQ station in the #2 engine room. You see, my job at General Quarters station was to get the long air compressor on the line so that more guns could be firing. When I was tested to see how long I took to do this job, I think I had it on the line in 1 minute and 20 seconds. I was told at the time that was very good. But I think that particular day I broke my record by about 15 seconds.

I got the compressor going and put on my earphones to report I was ready. There was so much activity on those phones, even after everybody had reported in, that they were ready on battle stations. I found out that the concussion I felt as I passed the open hatch on my way to GQ was a Kamikaze hitting the ship. While I was on station I could hear all the shooting going on as each man talked on the phones from top side, and I could feel the big guns, which were our 5-inch, firing from three decks down. Then it wasn't long before another thunderous concussion shook the whole ship and we were hit by another Kamikaze. We took one on the forward deck elevator and another on the smokestack area. What we'll never know is how that smoke watch man ever got down from his perch above the stack when that plane hit, or even before it hit.

After talking to fellows who knew more about the situation, they said he doesn't remember how he got down himself. We were at General Quarters all day and they fed us sandwiches and K-Rations until we set "Condition Able," and then finally secured from General Quarters.

I was below decks on the phones, keeping an eye on the compressor. Most of the news I received was over the phones but I found out about everything when we secured. The ship was on fire but under control. I also understand that in addition to the six planes that our crewmen shot down, we also shoved six of our own badly damaged planes over the side.

When we secured from General Quarters I was looking for a friend of mine from Reading, Pa. His name was Kooistra. I forget at this point what his first name was. Oh yeah, now I remember, it was Peter Joseph Kooistra. He was a big Polak. We called him "Pete" and his GQ station was on the twenty millimeter guns. I looked for him for 3 days and then decided to look on his station after not finding him in that time. When I did find him I got the biggest and saddest shock of my life. He was still at his guns and had been decapitated by enemy fire from the planes that hit us, or near misses, or whatever happened. I don't know and I wasn't able to find out because I learned he wasn't the only one hit up there, but he was the only one I saw there that day.

We limped back to Pearl Harbor and then to the States. I went home for 25 days leave which I sure could use.

John McGonagle MM3c

On January 21, 1945, the day of the attack on the *Ticonderoga*, I was off duty reading a magazine when General Quarters sounded. I went to the engine room to my battle station on the throttle; stayed there until secured by General Quarters, about six hours.

Loading of bombs on the flight deck of the Ticonderoga. *(Courtesy of E.W. Tenpenny)*

Next day I went above to see the damage. My reaction was sadness for those who lost their lives and gratitude that the rest of us were spared.

Hugh T. McKenzie PFC

On 21 January I always toast my shipmates who died that day and my living shipmates who "fought" the ship and saved her that day.

The one thing that always stands out in my mind, (after the first "Zeke" exploded on the hangar deck), just minutes before the second hit, was how lonely we must have looked. Just one burning, smoking carrier and two little "tin cans" on the sea where earlier the whole 3rd fleet had been! How that second "Zeke" got through to hit us I'll never understand! We were firing every gun on the starboard side that was working and he kept on coming right down on the deck, just skimming the waves. You could see our 20 mm tracers going right into the plane, but he flew her right into the fire control turret on top of the bridge and that just about wiped out the command officers left after the first hit.

Heroes? We had a lot of heroes; all who died were heroes and to my way of thinking, the guys in Damage Control were heroes too. It was a long time ago, but that's the way I remember it.

Raymond Means AMM3c

I had just got out of the shower and was in the port catwalk at my flight quarters station waiting for flight quarters to be sounded for the next launch against Formosa. With me was Bernard J. Rousher and Joseph Mayhugh.

We heard planes overhead and looked up to see a dog fight going on. While looking up, the first Kamikaze hit and all three of us received shrapnel. I grabbed the head set and told R.E. Lee to get out of there, we had been hit bad and the cat was out of operation; no need for the engine room to be manned.

I checked Mayhugh and Rousher. Both were

hurt bad and I tried to get them aft to Sick Bay by going down through the fo'c'sle deck and through officers country on the main deck around #1 elevator pit. We could not get onto the hangar deck due to fires.

While passing a scuttle, a sailor came to the top and hung there as we passed. He was burned and bleeding. I could hear shells going off below him. He looked at us and said, "Oh God," and turned loose and fell back down the ladder. I learned later that it was the forward aviation ordnance compartment below him.

The three of us then returned to the fo'c'sle deck and there was a corpsman there taking charge of the wounded and giving morphine and checking everyone. He cut my overalls off and threw them over the side; all my money and pictures, ID, etc. went with them. I would not take the morphine 'cause, even though my left side seemed to be paralyzed, if I was going swimming I wanted to know it and be able to swim.

We lay there on the deck amongst the chains and watched as the second Jap made a run at us from the stbd. side. It seemed like all the stbd. side guns were shooting at him. There had to be a wall of steel out there, but the plane made it through and hit the #1 gun directly in the island.

That's when the bridge caught the shrapnel and Capt. Dixie got hit.

My next memory was being down below in a sleeping compartment around Sick Bay, 2nd bunk from the bottom. The guy below me was lying on his stomach and breathing through holes in his back. You could hear the air bubbling through the blood. Our priest came down and gave him last rites.

On the 22nd they put a bandage on my arm and I was told to get my gear together. I would be leaving the ship at Ulithi as soon as we got there to be transferred to the Hospital Ship *Samaritan.*

Our shower in the sleeping compartment on the 01 level looked like a sieve; the bulkhead was the wall of the #1 elevator pit and a piece of shrapnel the size of a dinner plate had come in one end of the locker and out the other through every peacoat in there.

We got in to Ulithi and I was transferred in a stretcher onto a LST and taken over to the *Samaritan.* I was put in a bunk, then a cart and taken to surgery. As the corpsmen were wheeling me into an operating room, they were wheeling Capt. Dixie out and they were trying to hold him on the cart. He was yelling and screaming and wanted to know why they were only doing nine knots. It seems, I was told later, that he was reliving the sinking of the *Yorktown.* He also had 67 pieces of shrapnel in him that had been removed. I only had 16 pieces and a broken left arm.

Joseph E. Medico S1c

I was working in the forward mess hall on that fateful day. A few of my buddies from the 2nd Division were eating early chow as they had the next watch on the 5 inch single guns aft. One in particular, Art Devine from Lynn, Mass., had gone to boot camp with me and we became good friends.

We were shooting the bull when we heard the forty millimeter guns on the bow firing. At first we thought they were shooting at mines, which happened frequently in that part of the China Sea. Just about the time we heard the bugle blowing General Quarters there was a terrific explosion right above our heads. The last thing I remembered was a black cloud of smoke coming down the double ladder and a great gush of wind. As I was sitting down with my back toward the damage control panel, I was thrown against the panel and was unconscious for a time. I don't know how long. When my sense came back I went to my battle station which was the ships armory, just below in the next compartment by the gedunk stand. I went below and dogged down the hatch.

There were five of us in the ships armory, Gunners Mate 1st class John Harpster, Dan Gallagher, George Popernak, myself and a red headed Gunners Mate named Parker. I remember Dan having to go to the head. It was then we discovered that the mess hall above us was flooded. We didn't know how much water there was over us. We then went to the bomb elevator shaft (hangar deck to the flight deck) that ended in the ships armory. We undogged the hatch but closed it just as fast. Machine gun bullets from the hangar deck were flying around and ricocheting down the shaft. We decided to stay where we were and wait until whatever was going to happen, happened.

It wasn't until after the second plane hit the bridge section that we were able to get out. Once we got out we joined the surviving shipmates in taking care of the wounded and moving the deceased to the fantail.

I served in WW II, Korea and Vietnam but will never forget January 21, 1945. The buckled metal of the hangar deck and bridge, the carrying of the wounded in the stretchers, holding a tarp over them so they couldn't get wet from the sprinklers, the carrying of our departed shipmates who would never joke or laugh with us again. I'll never forget the eyes of one very badly burned shipmate, who I thought was deceased. He opened his eyes as we set him down by the makeshift Sick Bay on the hangar deck. A look I will remember until I join him and our other shipmates in heaven.

Frank Merrill AMM3c

On January 21, 1945, I was an AMM3c plane captain on an F6F fighter flown by Fighting 80 of Air Group 80. I had spotted the plane about even with the forward part of the island for immediate access to the starboard catapult and was lying under the wing when pilot Andy Anderson hurried up to me and said that there were enemy planes in the area and to get the plane on the catapult. He strapped himself in while I got ready to move it up to the catapult.

As I remember, we launched five fighters. It was 11:00 A.M. or shortly thereafter. I walked over to the island and sat down, with my back against it, to wait. Leonard Thorson, another plane captain whose plane had just taken off, came up and said the chow line was going to close and that we should hurry down to the mess hall, which we did via the Captain's ladder.

We then stopped at our quarters where I started to shave before returning to the flight deck and then we were hit by a Kamikaze.

We ran up to the flight deck and shortly thereafter we were hit again, a hit on the island. I watched that plane come in in a shallow power dive from far off starboard. I couldn't believe that he could make it through the wall of tracers. I watched him hit the island.

When I saw the hole in the flight deck made by the first plane, I was glad that Leonard Thorson and I headed for the chow line when we did.

Robert G. Mettauer MM1c

As I remember, I was on duty in the machine shop when General Quarters sounded. I grabbed my gas mask and headed toward repair five forward, my battle station, which was in the forward mess hall. When I reached the mess hall, the two Kamikaze planes had already hit the ship and water from the automatic fire sprinklers was pouring through an open hatch down into our compartment. Accordingly, our first priority was to get the hatch closed to stop the water from entering the ship. When this was accomplished, our compartment was knee high with water. This info was forwarded to battle control who told us to leave and go into a sleeping compartment on the starboard side of the ship. By this time the entire area, all the compartments, were filled with smoke sucked in through the air ducts from outside so we were required to put on our gas masks to avoid passing out from lack of oxygen. Sometime after moving to the sleeping compartment, battle control contacted us and directed us to go into the mess hall aft of repair five forward because they weren't getting any response from the people in that compartment. Things were getting difficult because by now all the lighting in our area of the ship was extinguished and we needed flashlights to get around.

I believe I was one of the first people to enter the quiet mess hall and was astonished to see everyone unconscious and not wearing gas masks. As I entered, there was one sailor sitting at a mess table with a pen-light flashlight lit in his hand. I proceeded to assist in taking one of the unconscious sailors back to Sick Bay. When I returned to the quiet mess hall the sailor with the flashlight was still sitting there. I went to tell him to get out to fresh air only to find that he too was out cold. When I helped carry him back to Sick Bay I heard a voice coming from one of the Sick Bay bunks that I recognized. It was the voice of Ed Mazur crying out for help. Ed worked with me in the machine shop.

In our spare time in the machine shop we built a set of weights for people who wanted to work out. A compartment up forward above the hangar deck and below the flight deck was set aside for those people. That's where Ed Mazur was when General Quarters sounded. Ed made his way to an enclosed ladder at the forward end of the hangar deck, started down when the Kamikaze exploded on the hangar deck. The flames and heat shot up the ladder and burned Ed so badly he did not survive. Ed was listed in our USS *Ticonderoga* war log book as missing in action.

After making the second trip to Sick Bay I went back to the sleeping compartment where I started. From there I went into another companion way with a man named Thompson. It was still completely dark and still filled with smoke. As we made our way, we ran into Chuck Large who was in serious trouble because his gas mask canister had expired and he was gasping for air. Thompson and I grabbed Chuck and led him back to the machine shop. When we arrived there the place was untouched, the lights were on and there was no smoke at all. The people who were stationed there couldn't believe how we looked and what we went through. They couldn't have been more than one hundred and fifty feet from where we were in repair five forward and knew nothing of what we experienced.

From then on things began to get better below decks and we were able to relax and begin to clean up.

Larry Meyer MM2c

I was in A Division. I entered the Navy in March, 1943, and in May I was assigned to the USS Santee, CV-29, doing convoy duty between the States and North Africa. When not employed in that regard we were part of "killer hunter groups" which consisted of one CVE, the Santee, and two or three World War I destroyers. We sank four German submarines for which the entire crew of the USS Santee received a Presidential Unit Citation.

I transferred from the Santee to the Ticonderoga in December 1943. Frank O'Keefe and Frank Bach transferred with me. We were stationed at the Naval Receiving Station at Newport News while the ship was still being built. I was there for Commissioning Day, one of the plank owners.

On January 21, 1945, for some reason or other I was in my bunk so evidently I must have had an earlier watch. A Division, where I slept, was one deck below the hangar deck. When we heard the explosion I jumped out of my bunk and someone in the area said, "They must be firing the five inch guns." I said, "Five inch guns, your ass, we've been hit!" I grabbed all my battle gear and ran to my battle station which was the damage control party in the forward mess hall. When I got there, there were quite a few people there ahead of me. There were several inches of water on the deck and a Chief, I think his name was Taylor, grabbed hold of me and said, "You and Fetters walk to the forward elevator pump room and light off the equipment so the forward elevator can be lowered to the hangar deck." I didn't know at the time but was told later that the fire on the hangar deck had spread to the hangar deck forward elevator pit. I suppose the theory was that if we lowered the elevator down onto the pit it would smother the fire. Anyway, Fetters and myself put on our gas masks and we worked our way forward in the ship, going through officer's country. The smoke was very thick and it was difficult to see. I went through a passageway past probably a dozen or more mess cooks for officer's country, just standing there in their white uniforms - no gas masks or anything, just standing there. I don't know whatever happened to any of them.

Finally we got forward and reached the first hatch which led down to the forward elevator pump room. We opened that hatch, worked our way down, secured it behind us, opened the next one and so on until we got through about four hatches, quite a way down into the ship.

When we got to the pump room there were already two members of A Division manning the equipment there. I can't remember if they had already lowered the elevator or we told them that they wanted it lowered. I guess we were down there two or three days, however long the fires were raging. I know one of us had to go up once in a while and get some K rations. It wasn't bad down there. I guess the only time I really got scared was when they put a list on the ship. I found out later it was to run the burning gasoline over the side, but down there we didn't know whether the ship was going to capsize or not.

Fortunately everything turned out alright for us. None of us were hurt down there but we did lose at least one man from A Division - I think his name was Mazur.

I did have a good friend on the ship, Ollie Breault, a yeoman. He received a Bronze Star for what he did that day on one of the gun mounts. He was on one of the 20 mms. Everybody around him was killed and he took over the gun and kept firing.

Lawrence E. Miles AMM3c

I was a plane captain, AMM3c, V2 Division, assigned to an F6F Hellcat which was fueled and armed on the hangar deck at the time of the attack. Personally, I was with the majority of the division in the mess hall when General Quarters was sounded. I proceeded from the mess hall to the hangar deck and was emerging from the forward hatch of the island exit to the deck as the first plane came through the flight deck and exploded. Due to the fire there were eight to ten men trapped in the island and forced to proceed upward. I was not hit, suffering only slight flash burns; however, the remainder, with the exception of Air Commander Miller, had injuries, some of which were serious and in at least one instance, fatal. Commander Miller and I attended the injured as best we could until Commander Miller exited the compartment in the island to a position on the bridge. Following his exit, the second plane approached from starboard. I watched through the porthole until it crashed just above. As you are probably aware, Commander Miller was killed on the bridge at that time. There were no further injuries to anyone in the compartment where I was trapped and we were subsequently able to reach the flight deck by exiting through the porthole with the aid of lines lowered to our level. Since my discharge I have made several inquiries in Marion, Indiana, which is near my home, as to anyone that had knowledge of Commander Miller's family, without success. Inasmuch as I was one of the last persons to have seen him, I would have liked to express my sympathy to his family. I keep asking and perhaps someday I will locate someone to whom the story of his last minutes can be related.

Norman R. Miner WT1c

When the first plane hit us I was in the chow line, midway down the ladder from the hangar deck. I believe that right after the explosion, General Quarters sounded and I headed for number 1 fireroom. By the time all of us assigned to the fireroom were present, we heard over the phone that it was a Kamikaze. We were working real hard to get the maximum steam out of the boilers because the engine room guys were calling for maximum output. When the second plane hit, the concussion was really felt in the firerooms because of all the open vents we were using to feed the oil burners.

After the second hit, we spent the rest of the day hearing what was going on topside via phone. I never got out of the fireroom until 2100 and went up to the hangar deck to see the damage and the next day I got my first look at the flight deck.

Don Monson Captain

On January 21, 1945, I was on the morning launch. Our mission was to hit Japanese shipping entering Toshien Harbor on the western shore of Formosa. As I recall, we were launched about 0800.

According to my log book, I was flying SB2C Bureau Number 19232. It was a group launch which consisted of fighters, torpedo planes and dive-bombers. We climbed to an altitude of about 15,000 feet as we proceeded towards Formosa. As we cleared the high mountains in the middle of the island, we made a high speed descent into the assigned target area. The antiaircraft was quite heavy and I believe that was the only mission in which I could actually hear the shells exploding close to my airplane as we approached the push-over point. Generally we would see plenty of flak but I had never actually heard it until that day. Our attack on the shipping in Toshien Harbor was highly successful, as evidenced by the many burning ships as we departed the area for our return to the Ticonderoga. I mention this because this entire mission generated a great deal of excitement, but we had survived another mission and we were looking forward to the safety of our floating home. Little did I realize that the real excitement was yet to come.

My logbook shows the duration of that flight as three hours and forty-five minutes, which put me back on deck at 11:45 A.M., just fifteen minutes before the first Kamikaze was to dive through the forward part of the flight deck. As soon as my plane was parked I proceeded to Ready Room Three for the usual post-flight briefing with Lt. Ken Price and the rest of the Air Intelligence Team.

As I arrived in the ready room our Squadron Commander, CDR. E.L. Anderson, was standing up front near the status board briefing the pilots who were about to launch on the next strike. Within minutes of my entering the ready room there was a loud explosion which shook the ship from bow to stern. This was followed immediately by the sound of the ship's anti-aircraft batteries opening up. Since this first attack came in undetected, I'm quite sure the ship was not at General Quarters, thus the ventilating system to the ready room was still operating. Within a few seconds the room was completely filled with dense black smoke. CDR. Anderson borrowed Wiley Moore's flashlight, then told everyone to stand fast while he went to check on what was happening. Within a minute or two after he left, the heat and smoke became unbearable. I decided it was time for me to do some exploring on my own.

I groped my way to the back of the room and went out the door leading to the enclosed passageway leading fore and aft along the port side. Since the ready rooms were situated on the gallery deck, that put us below the flight deck and above the hangar deck. At the time I had no way of knowing that the main fires were on the hangar deck, so I proceeded forward along the passage way until the heat drove me back into the ready room.

Upon re-entering, I realized that the room was still as crowded as before judging from the noise level and general commotion that prevailed. I then decided that this was still not the place to be, so I set out to try the port side passageway again, with firm determination that this time I would NOT turn around again, no matter what I encountered. But in spite of these good intentions, I was once again forced back when I realized that the bulkheads, which I had been sliding my hands along, were sizzling hot and my hands were being burned. So it was back into the mclee of the ready room.

I worked my way up to the front, climbing over upturned chairs, until I was up near the status board. For some reason, the smoke had cleared just enough so I could make out the form of Wiley Moore. Apparently he had decided it was time to forget CDR. Anderson's instructions to stand fast. He said he was going to try going out the front (midships) door into the central fore and aft passageway and try to find a way out by going towards the stern. This sounded like a real good idea to me because I knew the other route was out of the question.

Wiley started out the door and I followed with a firm grip on his belt. Someone else was holding onto my belt and I can only assume that many others followed in similar fashion. We snaked our way along the passageway and soon the smoke began to clear away. In another few moments we saw daylight and we made our way out onto the catwalk, and from there up onto the flight deck.

We were met on the flight deck by our Air Group Flight Surgeon, Doc Cannon. He noticed that I had received some burns on my face and hands so he started to administer some burn ointment, although I didn't feel I needed it. I guess he just felt that he should be doing something, but the real casualties up to that time were down on the hangar deck where the fires were still burning and there was no possibility of getting down there.

As in any situation such as this, there was a great deal of confusion. The ship's skipper, CAPT. Dixie Kiefer, had ordered a port list to permit the burning gasoling on the hangar deck to wash over the side, but this contributed to the uncomfortable feeling that the ship might be going down. Frequent calls, "Man Overboard" were heard, and several swimmers were spotted in the ship's wake.

The AA batteries opened up again as another pair of Kamikazes were attacking from the port side. This time the batteries were ready and these sundowners were blown out of the sky in short order. This was followed by resounding cheers, louder than ever heard at even the greatest of sporting events. I crossed the flight deck and joined up with several other bomber pilots who had gathered just aft of the island structure. It

was there that I noticed CDR. Anderson being administered to on a Stokes stretcher. He appeared to be in very bad shape. Someone, I don't know who, found him unconscious in one of the passageways and had carried him out onto the flight deck.

Shortly after I got settled in with some of my squadron mates aft of the island, another Kamikaze came in low over the water on the starboard side. I could see the AA shells going through the wings and cockpit but it kept coming, striking the island right at the level of the bridge. About that time, we were sure we would soon be hearing the bugle call "The Bear Went Over The Mountain" which is the call to abandon ship. But the *Ticonderoga* was not ready to die.

Unbeknown to LTJG Bob Mullaney, and I believe LT Forbes Perkins, many of us who had escaped from the ready room were holed up aft of the island. Bob was sure we were still trapped, so they had rounded up some help and were trying to cut a hole in the flight deck immediately over the ready room. They were valiantly engaged in these efforts when the second Kamikaze crashed into the island. Bob and Forbes were badly wounded; fortunately, both recovered.

From that point, things began to improve. The fires were brought under control, the rest of the task force took up positions around *Ticonderoga* to protect us as we headed for the haven of Ulithi Atoll.

All in all, it was an experience I can't forget, even the parts I would like to—for instance, the most poignant memory is of a scene I'm not sure I can adequately describe, but I'll try. Some brief time after the fires were out and we were steaming east, I went down to the hangar deck to view all the damage. It was awesome, but as I walked through the aft hangar bay I came to an area where dozens and dozens of charred bodies were laid out. All the bodies had been tagged for identification. One in particular caught my eye. This one young hero lay on his back with one arm reaching skyward. Attached to his outstretched hand was his tag. My immediate thought at that moment was, "That is his ticket to heaven."

Richard T. Morgan PFC

Three of us were sitting on the deck reading one of those off color stories the yeoman used to run off on the mimeograph machine. PFc Cardwell asked, "Have you guys had chow yet?" "Yeah, we jumped the line that comes down from the hangar deck," said Bob Labreque. "The M.A. always yells at those damn Marines jumping the line but he never catches us," said Red Morgan. Cardwell took off and we never saw him alive again. I understand he got to the hangar deck at the moment of the 1st explosion. Labreque was a little luckier. Since his battle station was on the fantail he had a long run aft. He was strapped into the 20 mm when they noticed him bleeding so he was sent to Sick Bay. He tells me he still feels pain from the shrapnel they were able to remove. He was wearing the Purple Heart proudly when a pretty girl in San Francisco noticed. We joked, "Show her your wound Bob." Since he was wounded in the hip he blushed. Crimson.

Many times I thought how lucky I was the

only one of the three not scratched. The Good Lord must have been watching over me. I escaped from a couple of bad auto wrecks the same way.

I got halfway up the stairwell when something like a huge sledge hammer hit. When the second one came in I hit the deck. It wasn't long before our 20 mm gun mount was burned out by the fire. Another PFc from Connecticut was sitting with me under the wings of a plane when the third one came in. That was the most frightening moment of my life. The guns on the starboard side knocked him out of the air.

A little later Sgt. Vaughn ordered me into a burning plane to release the bomb and gas tank so they could throw them overboard. All the time the crazy sergeant was hosing me down with cold water. When we got back to the gun mount I was jumping around shivering. The Lieutenant looked at me and said, "Are you cold, Morgan?" "Yes, Sir," I answered. I figured he'd send me below for coffee. "Well, grab a broom and sweep the deck. That'll warm you up." He laughed and the whole gun deck laughed with him.

George P. Mumper SC3c

I boarded the *Ticonderoga* CV-14 in August 1944 directly from Boot Camp (Camp Perry, Virginia). I was told I was the youngest sailor on board.

On January 21, 1945, I was assigned to S-1 Division as a ship's cook. We worked on 24 hour tours, changing at noon. My battle station was the 5 inch gun if we were off duty and the magazine when on duty. The attack came a few minutes after noon. As I was running up the ladder to my station, a friend, William (Bill) McCravy, was trying to come down to go to the magazine. He yelled for me to go to his station and he would go to mine. As I turned around and was running to go to the magazine, the first Kamikaze hit. I found out later my friend Bill was killed instantly. I spent the next 6 hours in the magazine. Another good friend, Barney Morgan, was also killed that day. He was on smoke watch at the very top of the smoke stack. His duty was to tell the engine room what kind of smoke we were making - white in daylight and black at night. We found his body by following the telephone wire he was still wearing.

Robert O. Nauman RDM1c

The Radar gang had just come up from the chow hall to our V-4 compartment, just forward of the quarter deck, when a terrific explosion rocked the ship. I ran out forward to the hangar deck to see a huge fire. I ran back to my sack for my life and flash gear but found it was gone. I went aft from the compartment and was enlisted by a Chief to help push armed torpedo planes (TBM's) back away from the fire - tough work for a young, but out of shape, Radarman. All of a sudden the fire sprinkler sustem came on and with a natural response to get out of the "rain" I crawled under the wing of a TBM to stay dry and rest a minute. After a minute or two, I bent my head down and looked into the bomb/torpedo bay, only to see it filled with 500 pound bombs. With all the TBM's pushed aft, a group of us worked our way aft and down below, ending up in the torpedo room.

At approximately 1400, we felt another shudder. Shortly before 1600, we went back on watch in C.I.C. only to find the radar and radio equipment knocked out by the second Kamikaze that struck the forward 5-inch gun control turret. I spent the 4-8 watch in C.I.C. talking and listening.

Frank R. Neubauer EM3c

The best I can remember, I was assigned as the electrician mate on one of our two 36" searchlights. During GQ that's where I would go. On the day we were hit, it was my turn to go below and get some chow. I remember that we had chicken and I was sitting by the ladder. The next thing I remember is that someone at the top of the ladder shouted, "WE HAVE BEEN HIT!" Then a shipmate came falling down the ladder. I was scared and made my way up to the flight deck, only to see my battle station was where we were hit. Then someone said, "Help me dump the ammo from the planes before they catch fire." We pushed planes over the side. That is the best I can remember.

Edgar L. Newlin AMM3c

As I remember, it was a nice calm day, which influenced a later decision.

I was a plane captain. For anyone that doesn't know what that is, I took care of an airplane, a fighter to be exact. I was supposed to keep it fueled, tied down, cleaned etc. We were supposed to stay with the plane anytime we were at flight quarters if it wasn't tied down.

At this time we were at flight quarters, but for some reason the launch had been delayed so my plane was just sitting there. I would have been the third plane launched, one on each catapult, and then mine.

It was past noon and we hadn't had chow when another plane captain came along and talked me into going. Remember, we were not supposed to leave our plane in that condition, but we did and it probably saved my life. We had just reached the mess hall when the fantail 40s started firing, maybe three or four rounds. Then they started General Quarters, maybe two or three boings, when a suicide plane hit and blew up on the hangar deck. It sounded like a bucket with rocks in it; more of a rattle than an explosion.

I dropped my tray and started back up to the flight deck, but by then smoke was everywhere and some of the hatches had been closed so I had an awful time getting back to my battle station, which was my plane, and when I got there it was gone! That was where the Jap had hit. He must have aimed for my plane; it went through the flight deck and blew up on the hangar deck. That was what I heard when I was in the mess hall.

I didn't have a battle station so I just wandered around kind of in a daze. I had no idea what to do. I tried to help others, but I seemed to be in the road.

I don't know how much later it was, it seemed like hours but was probably not over thirty minutes, when I found myself standing on the flight deck, forward of the five-inch guns, watching a second Jap plane heading straight for the island. I just stood there watching because I was sure he would go down. I could see the tracer shells going through the plane and the pilot.

It soon became clear that he was going to hit us. About then I realized where I was standing. I looked around; all I could do was jump down to the catwalk and head for the port side under the flight deck. When I was about half way across I heard the plane hit the island.

From then on I remember only flashes of what happened. I remember wandering around, trying to find where I was needed but I don't recall doing anything specific.

I still smell the smell and feel the hopeless feeling of not being able to do anything for my friends. I don't remember many names - Selbe walking around holding a big wad of cotton on what was left of his arm, blown off just above his elbow. He died about 2:00 the next morning - shock they said. There was a little boy named Menard, blown in half. He always wore his dog tags on his belt loop, so we could identify him from that. I don't think he was much over fifteen at the time.

I remember they used our compartment as part of Sick Bay that night so we slept wherever we could. The next day the hospital ship took the wounded and we had burials at sea all afternoon.

I have never had any doubt that I was saved by divine intervention. If I had been where I was supposed to be I would surely have been killed. If we had started two minutes later we would have been caught on the hangar deck where all the casualties of the first plane were. If we had gone sooner we might have been back to my plane and I would have been killed then.

To this day I do not know who talked me into leaving my plane. I can't even see his face - it seems he was a little heavy but that is all I remember about him. If anyone recognizes himself, please let me know. I would like to thank you.

Glenn Noffsinger RDM2c

There are two memories that will remain with me forever. One, after the two planes hit us, a medic asked me to stay with a wounded sailor until he expired. The sailor begged me to keep him alive so he could go back home to his wife and children. As I held his body together he passed away with his family on his mind until the end. To this day I do not know his name or remember his rank. His last words to me were, "Don't let me die."

The second memory was being selected at random to serve on the Burial Preparation Detail. We took the remains after preparation to the fantail for burial at sea the next day. With the greatest of devotion and with Honors the remains were slipped into the sea to rest there forever.

Those families left back home may still be wondering what happened. Believe me, I know. They can now rest in peace as can those sailors who gave their lives in serving their country. Those sailors will be etched in the memory of those of us who came back forever.

We had the greatest skipper the Navy ever had, Dixie Kiefer. When we went to sea he said he would do his best to bring us back and he did his very best to do just that.

J B Nowell AMMH2c

I joined the Navy at age 17 years and 3 months on April 2, 1943. After graduation from Naval Air Technical Training Center and Catapult School I was assigned to the Ticonderoga, then being built at Newport News. I went on the shakedown cruise aboard the USS Franklin as part of the training, and by the time we got back the Ticonderoga was ready. We were a very proud bunch of sailors to be the first crew on the "Mighty Ticon."

Our planes had been involved in numerous strikes against bases and airstrips around the South China Sea coast in preparation for the liberation of the Phillipine Islands. When this mission was complete we had to come back out the same way we went in and evidently the Japs knew it because they had really fortified the Formosa Peninsula. After fighting our way back into the Pacific, the Fleet Admirals Halsey and Nimitz decided that Formosa needed to be neutralized so we turned around and headed right back. This proved to be a rough day for the Ticonderoga but a devestating day for the Japs. They sent everything they had at us and they had brainwashed their pilots to dive their planes into our aircraft carriers. Believe me, that was obviously their goal.

Our planes must have knocked out most of the bases and airstrips because our planes that made it through the strike were back on the ship and we were moving along peacefully about ready for lunch when GQ sounded. Our ships guns started firing on our starboard side (decoys). Because of these decoys flying just out of range on the starboard side, we were a little late in noticing the Kamikaze plane coming in low on the port side. It was right on us before the gun turrets could get turned around and aimed. I believe some of the 20 mm and maybe some of the 40 mm got in a few shots. The Jap pilot dived his plane into the forward part of the flight deck behind the forward elevator. It penetrated the flight deck and set fire to the planes on the hangar deck that were loaded with ammo and waiting to be sent up to the flight deck. The forward elevator had just started up with a load of fighter planes and the explosion stopped it about three to four feet up from the deck.

This was just high enough that the explosion blew several of the plane handling crewmen under the elevator and into the elevator well. The floor of the elevator well just happened to be the roof of the starboard catapult machinery room, which was my GQ station. I believe all of that plane handling crew was killed.

I was crew chief in the starboard catapult room. We had been launching planes as fast as they could get them hooked up to our catapult but as soon as we were hit, our catapult room immediately filled with smoke. Our catapult officer, Lt. John W. Padgett, ordered us to get out and come top side. My telephone man, Tommy Kirkman and I were the only two in the machinery room, which was three decks below the hangar deck. When we emerged to the forward part of the hangar deck, all the planes were

Red Steward and John Williams in #2 elevator pump room, January 6, 1963. (Courtesy of John Williams)

on fire and fifty caliber shells were going off like the fourth of July. Dead and wounded men with their clothes and hair all burned off were lying all around. The planes had been filled with gasoline and were fully charged with 50 caliber ammo.

Fire fighters were trying to fight the fires, so I did what I could to help the wounded.

I was on the fo'c'sle deck when the ship's guns began firing again toward a Jap plane on the starboard side. I looked up and the plane was very low over the water headed straight toward us with shells bursting all around it. I could see the tracer bullets streaming from both wings coming right at us. Every cubby hole that I tried to duck into for protection was full of people. I finally ducked down behind a large roll of cable on the deck and figured this was it. It looked like he was headed straight for me. The big explosion came and debris started falling all around me. I couldn't believe I was still around without a scratch. The Kamikaze had made a direct hit on the forward five-inch gun director turret. The entire crew inside the turret was killed.

The director turret is located pretty high up on the ship's island and after the Kamikaze explosion it had been shifted off its base and looked as if it would teeter over and fall down to the flight deck. The ship's welders were called out to weld braces on it to secure it.

I immediately joined in trying to help the wounded, all of whom were severely burned. We broke the emergency station medical boxes and gave morphine to those in excruciating pain. We had to move several dead bodies out through the hatches. If you've ever been down wind carrying a badly burned body, you know how hard it is to breathe.

Things finally calmed down after dark. Of course we were blacked out. We couldn't have any lights on that could be detected by the Japs. An announcement was made over the P.A. system that C-Rations would be served in the mess hall. I had missed lunch and my 19 year and 21 day old stomach was growling pretty bad. I was exhausted, but hungry. It was a long way to the mess hall and I almost turned back when I tripped over a few dead bodies while crossing the hangar deck.

My normal sleeping compartment was forward above the fo'c'sle deck. When I finally went up to go to bed, my bunk had been ripped in two by shrapnel. I didn't have a problem finding an empty bunk. Final count was 79 dead and 116 missing and never accounted for.

There was one good part to the story; we were able to get back to Puget Sound, Washington under our own power. We all got port and starboard leave while our ship was being repaired and re-outfitted. We had several new revisions on our guns and ship prior to rejoining our fleet.

Don Noyes ACOM

On the day of the attack my crew and I were elated, celebrating our good fortune in the China Sea, and were in the mess hall on the third deck when the first Kamikaze struck. One bomb went off on the flight deck, the second on the hangar deck, and the last on the second deck, which was right over our heads. As we jumped over tables to get out of there, I looked up and saw the steel floor of the second deck hanging over the tables. I imagine another 1/4" and the last bomb would have exploded in the mess hall killing many more, including myself. I swore to myself that if I got out of this I would live the rest of my life as if every day were a Saturday and every Saturday were New Year's Eve and I have kept that promise.

After fighting my way to the hangar deck hatch (I've always had a fear of getting caught below decks) I got to the top of the ladder to find the Marine on watch there cut in two by the bomb that had gone off on the hangar deck. Hurrying to my battle station on the flight deck, I found my division officer, Lt. Kelly, cut in two coming through the island hatch to the flight deck. Fires had broken out everywhere and our job was to keep our own bombs from exploding which, thank God, we did. We had our 35 F6F fighters fully loaded with ammo and a 500 lb. bomb on each. If one bomb had gone off they all would have gone - along with you and I. I looked around for some supervision. All I saw was Chief Ordnanceman Hightower. We knew we had to get the bombs defused and over the side. There was no time to get the bomb cradle from the armory to let them down to the flight deck, so we had some of our crew members go from amid ships aft, taking the fuses out of the bombs while others climbed into the cockpit of each plane and dropped the bombs on the deck. We all prayed that they would not go off. Without the fuses there was not much chance.

Chief Hightower and I, together, rolled at least 20 of the 500 lb. bombs to the edge of the flight deck which was easy as, by then, we were listing to port. We lifted them high enough to throw them over the catwalk. I was 6' and 185 pounds. But Hightower was only 5'4" and 150 pounds. His was superhuman strength under those conditions. The rest of the crew took care of the rest of the bombs.

Eventually we lost all 35 of our fighters on the flight deck. Those that did not burn we pushed over the side. The TBF's and SB2C's were all on the hangar deck loaded with torpedos and 2000 lb. bombs so there were only three fighters left on the extreme aft of the flight deck on the starboard side.

My good friend, and member of my crew, John Henry Ford AOM1c and I were on our way aft to disarm those last 3 F6F's when we saw the second Kamikaze headed toward the *"Big T."* We crouched under the remaining planes waiting to see where he was going to hit. We agreed that if it looked like he was going to hit aft, where we were, we would jump 90 feet into the ocean. We also agreed to keep each other afloat in case either became unconscious. At the last second I saw the plane was going to hit the island and turned around to see Ford going over the side. I reached out and grabbed his belt from behind and pulled him back on the flight deck. His remark was that he was leaving this son-of-a-bitch and swimming home.

We slept in the armory that night after getting the fires out. The scuttlebutt was that they were sending night fighters out to finish us off. I don't know if that was true or not but we got away to fight another day.

Rev. Msgr. Cornelius O'Brien
Lieutenant, Chaplain

As to my memory of the ship being hit, I recall that I was on my way back to my own room. I was coming up from the library and I had just gotten through the Marine quarters when the first Kamikaze hit the ship. The men were already going up the ladder from that deck to the hangar deck when the crash came. The fellows were knocked down the ladder to the hangar deck and the first casualty I came across I will never forget. It was a young Marine, who only a week before had told me of his strong wish to own a jeep at the end of the war and wondering how much it was going to cost. I hope he's driving that jeep in Heaven now.

It took some time to get to our battle stations because things were kind of clogged up. I remember getting to my battle station which was on the after end of the island and just getting inside when the second Kamikaze hit the ship and caused considerable damage.

From then on I was busy doing what I could to help out and I haven't any definite recollection of just what I did except I took care of everybody that I could and I answered any requests from men who took me to one part of the ship or another where there were men in trouble. I don't like to recall some of the incidents and others I have put out of my memory, but I will say that I consider myself very fortunate to have been with such a great group of men who reacted to this horrible emergency and carried out their obligations as men, and I might say as heroes, in the way in which they did everything which was necessary to bring the ship back in.

I can't say much more except that I hope you are well and that you keep well. I hope that God will bless you and take care of you in all your efforts.

Louis W. Oppici ARM2c

We had returned from a strike on Toshien Harbor and were in the ready room when a tremendous explosion occurred just outside the inner door. Someone opened the door and smoke and flames engulfed the room. All hands evacuated by the outer hatch which leads to a catwalk and a ladder to the flight deck.

There was a huge hole amidship and smoke and flames were spewing out of it. People were running everywhere and someone said, "Let's man the guns in the planes," and I jumped into the rear seat of one of the dive bombers on deck and broke out the guns. When I did, it was apparent that we could not fire effectively because the planes were stacked together and the wings were folded up. I got out and went to help the ordnancemen who were unloading the bombs from the planes so as to prevent any explosions if there were any other hits on deck. From somewhere, maybe the intercom from the bridge, came an order to push the planes over the side, which we did.

Another Japanese plane was sighted coming in on the starboard side and, although you could see our anti-aircraft shells hitting the plane, it just kept coming and as he got close he fired his machine guns and I dove to the deck next to the tire of one of the remaining planes on deck. The Kamikaze plane hit the bridge area of the ship. One of the aircrewmen said that the 20 mm guns on the starboard side aft were unmanned and we should go down and man them, which we did.

I remember "Abandon Ship" signal being given, whether it was over the intercom or by word of mouth, but almost instantly a belay order was given.

At one point, I remember the ship pitching on its side and flaming gasoline pouring out of the hangar deck. I was told later that Dixie ordered that maneuver and if he hadn't, we probably would have sunk.

Irving L. Patterson Ensign

On January 21, 1945, I had just landed back on board the *Ticonderoga* from a bombing mission over Formosa. I was sitting in Ready Room #1 and had just lit up a pipe. I sat in the aisle seat instead of my usual seat next to the aft bulkhead, 5 rows back from the front of the ready room. Suddenly the first Kamikaze plane went through the flight deck across the passage from Ready Room 1. I became Airbourne when the bombs went off and came down in a jumbled mess of seats and debris. If I had been in my regular seat I would have been killed. Huge pieces of shrapnel went through the seat and through the flight deck bulkhead. I remember the Skipper yelled, "Stay put, I'll find a way out and come back and get you." He didn't come back and smoke filled the ready room. The only thing we could see was the red light on the squawk box. We called operations via the box and were told to go amidship and aft to get out. I was so glad to see daylight and smell fresh air.

We went to the port catwalk, then to the flight deck where we saw our Skipper, E.L. Anderson, on a stretcher. He was burned and yelling, "Throw me overboard."

The second Kamikaze started to dive on the ship and Lt. Blatchford and I headed aft to the chain guard rail. We talked about jumping off the carrier but decided against it. The Kamikaze pilot took aim on the island as his target instead of the parked planes on the flight deck.

Blatchford and I watched the Jap hit the island. I guess we threw our arms over our heads as we had no other way to protect ourselves.

A lot of officers and men spent the night on the fantail. V-B 80 pilots and crew transferred to the USS *Hancock* and finished out the tour.

Rex K. Pearson Lieutenant, VB 80

The Japanese Kamikaze attack on the USS *Ticonderoga* on January 21, 1945, effectively ended my career as a pilot with the US Navy. The memory of that day and events immediately following come and go. Some things I think I remember are hazy at best; other memories are as plain as if the event was recent. This is what I remember of that day.

According to my flight log, my gunner, Bob Bennett, and I had returned with the VB 80 squadron from an air raid over Formosa. We had finished de-briefing when the first Kamikaze hit the deck. For some reason, I do not remember why, I had already left the ready room and was in my room when it hit. I opened the door, but the smoke was heavy and bulkheads were hot. It seemed safest go get out some other way, so I chose the porthole.

Being rather small at this point was an advantage, although I had to remove my helmet and leave it behind. I got out halfway, yelled for a rope and climbed to the deck hand-over-hand. Once there, I went to a gun emplacement, thinking I could help as there were other Jap planes coming in for the kill. Then the second one struck about 50 feet from where I was standing. The gunners did a great job, their shots were accurate, bits and pieces of the plane were flying everywhere. The pilot was undoubtedly dead by then, but the plane stayed in the dive. Seconds before he hit, I grabbed a swabbie bucket, put it over my head and crouched as low to the deck as I could.

From here is where the picture gets hazy. I got up, started moving, blood pouring, smoke and fire everywhere, men shouting. I saw Lt. Everett Wehr and he called to me, "Rex, I'm dying, I'm dying." He had been hit mid-section, his body almost cut in half. I put my arm around his shoulders and patted him. It was all I could do.

Somehow, I got to the flight deck. My roommate, Lt. George Walsh, apparently stayed with me and told me later they poured plasma into me, in and out of consciousness. Lt. Paul Dull later held me in the shower to help me clean up and wrote to my wife to explain, as best he could, what had happened.

I cannot remember how long it was before I went with the other wounded aboard a hospital ship, nor what happened subsequently. I do know that Lt. Forbes Perkins helped me out by persuading the doctors to send me, along with him to the hospital in San Diego where we stayed several weeks before going home on medical leave. Perkins had to talk for me, the head wound apparently knocked out my speech, and I had some difficulty with locomotion as I had lost all feeling in my left side.

Olin J. Perkins, Sr. AMM2c

We were in the Aircrew Ready Room between the flight deck and the hangar deck. Af-

ter the ship got hit we were unable to leave the Ready Room from the inside hatch because of the fire on the hangar deck. We were told to go out the outside hatch and to go aft. The smoke was very thick and we needed our gas masks but there weren't enough to go around because a lot of them had been lost overboard. So, if you didn't have one you had to use your handkerchief over your nose and mouth. The smoke was so thick you couldn't see, but about the time you thought you couldn't make it, we had followed one another aft. I was thinking about jumping in the waves, but about that time I got to some clear air and was able to make it to the flight deck. After getting there the second plane was coming in. We got under the planes on the flight deck aft which would have been a disaster if he hit aft as the planes were loaded with fuel and bombs, but he hit forward.

After the war was over, I found out I had a friend on the USS *Bronson* and they were picking up our crew who had jumped overboard.

Walter Pielocik AMM2c

As a plane captain on the SB2Cs I spent a lot of time on the flight deck. On this particular day my plane was in the air when the first Kamikaze hit us.

I had just finished early chow and was headed back to the flight deck planning to exit onto the flight deck on the starboard side out of the hatch in the center of the island.

I was just pushing the hatch open in front of me when the first one hit us. Thank God the hatch opened out instead of in since the blast pushed the hatch closed and protected me. I don't know how long I was there until a few others came up the ladder and we exited onto the flight deck. I tried helping the fire fighting crew for a while; sometime during this I noticed I had only one shoe on. I don't know how I lost the other one.

When they spotted the second Kamikaze I jumped down into the catwalk on the port side of the ship and went as far forward as possible. I ended up in a small compartment just under the flight deck. I don't remember who got there first, but it ended up with 6 or 7 of us, including 2 officers - I'm not sure how long we stayed there until we finally were able to leave after the second Kamikaze hit us. To this day I don't remember who any of this group were.

When we did get back on the flight deck it was a mess, with fire fighting crews working to put out the fires and the medical personnel tending to the wounded.

Kenneth H. Platt AOM2c

I was in the act of loading rockets to the wing of an F6F when I noticed, from the corner of my eye, a very low flying aircraft off our port beam. It made a sharp ascent and dove over the stern, down the flight deck, just over my head. I was located about midship, aft of the island.

Fear gripped me! I looked forward to the sound of the impact explosion. What I remember during the next thirty minutes (?) is unclear, except to say that I have a hazy memory of going aft, then working to save planes . . . others . . . ship.

I had the hangar deck watch that night, 2400 hrs., after the day's activity. The horrible stench of fire and bodies is something that haunts me to this day.

Felix P. Radleigh AMM2c

It was about noon. Many of the crew were having chow or were in the chow line. I was forward of the deck edge elevator on the flight deck when suddenly the Marine 20 mm battery aft opened fire on an incoming "Bogie." Almost at the same time there was the sound of General Quarters. Then came the roar of a suicide plane passing along side of me and it crashed forward on the flight deck. The area was ablaze. Men were shouting orders; others were calling for corpsmen or for help. Men were dying; others were dead. The Kamikaze passed so closely to me that the impact of it hitting and exploding knocked me to the deck. I was fortunate that I was not hit by the plane. However, I did get a few wounds to my arms and face, but nothing serious. I proceeded to get a hose hooked up to the foam hopper which kept backing up and was ineffective. I called a seaman, and we both sat on the hopper lid. Out combined weight finally got the foam going.

Shortly after 1300, another suicide plane came on the starboard side parallel to the water. The plane was afire from being hit by our gunners, but it kept coming with its guns blazing. It crashed into the superstructure killing the Gunnery Commander and the Air Commander as well as many others in the area. Several were wounded, and among them was Capt. Dixie Kiefer. Parts of the airplane and its fuel poured on top of us on the flight deck. Then came the explosion.

I was in a squatting position, manning a fire hose which was punctured by shrapnel. Water from the punctured hose poured over me which kept me from getting seriously burned or worse. Others were not so lucky. A shipmate pulled me from the fire, and to him I owe my life. He laid me among the dead and wounded until I received medical attention from a corpsman. Approximately six to seven inches of my shin were blown off, my collar bone was broken and a few of my ribs were damaged or broken. My body was riddled with shrapnel around my face, arms and groin area.

The long road to recovery began aboard the *Ticonderoga* where physicians performed initial surgery on me. When the carrier arrived at Ulithi Atoll, I was transferred to the hospital ship USS *Samaritan* and had additional surgery. Then, the other wounded and I were flown by a Navy hospital plane to Los Negroes in the Admiralty Islands. An Army hospital plane took us to Guadalcanal where I received more surgery. It was there, at Guadalcanal, that I was awarded the Purple Heart by Gen. Lemmuel Shepherd, USMC.

The hospital ship USS *Tryon* brought us back to the States via San Francisco. The dock was lined with ambulances as far as the eye could see. When an elderly woman laid a flower on my chest and said, "Welcome home, Son," I was overwhelmed by emotion and a flood of tears. After countless operations and years of hospitalization, I am still being treated as a result of

that 21st day of January, 1945. And, like many of my shipmates, I still carry metal particles in my body that were "Made in Japan."

Every January 21st at noon, Shipmate Richard Johnson and I meet for lunch. Richard, a Silver Star recipient, was also severly wounded on the USS *Ticonderoga*. We call this annual meeting "Glad to be Alive Day" to thank the Lord for sparing us. Because we were both so near death, each day that we live we call "Bonus Days."

Reames W. Rainey MM3c

On Jan. 21, 1945, I was sitting with Carl Gaworecki MM3c on my bunk at about 12:45 hrs. My bunk was on the port quarter, one deck below the hangar deck and just a few feet from the last hatch going down from the hangar deck. Gaworecki and I heard the 20 mm guns firing and ran up to the hangar deck to see what was happening. We could not see the incoming plane. In a few seconds General Quarters sounded. Gaworecki went forward on the hangar deck and would have had time to be near the deck edge elevator when the first plane struck. I believe Gaworecki's General Quarters station was at the fire pumps, forward, on the starboard side and below the hangar deck. The obvious route would be the one he took. The last time I saw him he was running forward on the hangar deck. I turned around and went down the hatch we had just come up, forward on that deck to the hatch midship on the port side, and down to #3 Fire Room. I never saw Gaworecki again.

Vernon F. Rampa CMM

As close as I can recall, I was having a cup of coffee in Chiefs Quarters when I felt our beautiful lady shudder like a dog shaking water off its back. I believe we were on condition "Baker"; of course we went into General Quarters immediately. I ran from Chiefs Quarters to my GQ station which was Repair 5, the machine shop, 3rd deck amidships.

Lt. Zafran was the officer in charge and I was the phone man. The crew of Repair 5 came in one by one until we were manned except for Ed Mazur who, I found out later, was killed on his way.

We closed all water tight doors and I waited for instructions. I got orders to close some valves and open others which I relayed to the crew. Then I felt the shake again as the second one hit the bridge. All of a sudden I felt the ship list to port. I was sure we were sinking - then water, oil and gasoline started to fill our compartment. I found out later a hatch was sprung on the hangar deck and couldn't be closed. We put on our gas masks as the fumes from the gasoline got to us. The water and oil made the deck quite slippery so we all stayed put - closing some valves, opening others.

I got a call from Sick Bay asking if there was some way we could cut the rings off the officers and men who had their hands burned. The rings were cutting off their circulation. The men came to the machine shop where, with the help of Bob Mettauer, I took a hand grinder with thin wheels. Bob had long nose pliers and some rags soaked in water to keep the heat from the grinding away

from the finger. After grinding both sides of the ring, Bob broke the rest of it until we got it off. I can't remember how many men we did this for. Finally we got orders to secure.

Gregg Ransburg Lieutenant, Air Department

I was a Lieutenant, the fighter director officer in Div V4, CIC (Combat Information Center, often known as "Christ I'm Confused").

My duty for the 1200 watch was to have charge of the strike against Formosa. At lunch in the ward room I happened to sit next to George Taylor, one of our officers of the deck. He was 23 years old, about twelve years my junior. He asked me if I thought his time in the Navy would hurt his chances in the business world. I answered that I was leaving to relieve the watch since I was in charge of the strike. He said he also had the watch but was going to eat his pie. We usually relieved the watch fifteen minutes ahead of time, but because of being in charge of the strike I wanted to be there fifteen minutes earlier to be sure I had everything under control.

Shortly after I arrived in CIC the first Kamikaze bomb exploded on the flight deck where our planes were all armed and loaded for the forthcoming strike. Broken fuel lines and fire created havoc and the Captain ordered a nine degree list to port to dump flaming gasoline over the side. The island seemed to act as a chimney, which meant there was much smoke in our compartment - then I think within fifty minutes the second Kamikaze hit the island in the starboard side. Our lights went out, we lost communication, full of smoke, and our Div. Commander Carl J. Ballinger said to pass the gear and go over the side thinking the ship was sinking. By the way, leaving 15 min. early to relieve the watch saved my life. George Taylor and the others leaving the ward room at the normal time on the ladder to the hangar deck were all blown over the side My roommate was at the bottom of the ladder and survived (Donald C. Howarth V-2). Talk about fate.

Our CIC compartment was so crowded, with about 35 men, that we could not easily wear our helmets and battle dress, which also somewhat hampered our activities. There were two hatches, one forward and one aft. I opened the forward one to see nothing but flames and I said, "Can't we get out the other way?", to which he replied, "Come on, God Dammit - I'll get you out of here," reached and grabbed a cable over his radar unit, vaulting to the deck, and opened the after hatch which opened on to the signal bridge. It was usually kept locked to keep people from interfering with a status board as I remember. How it happened to open I don't know.

Carl went to port, I to starboard. When I looked down from the weather deck about 85' above water, I took off my helmet and tied a line to a stanchion intending to go down via line as far as possible before dropping into the water. I had never gone off a ten foot diving board. Then I looked ahead and saw only a little patch of fire but a lot of ship, so I decided to stay on board. I ran to the flag bridge and started giving instructions to any one left in CIC. My boss, Carl Ballinger, returned to CIC to see if anyone had been unable to get out and it was a very brave act. Soon after there were calls for help on the bridge, so I climbed to the bridge to find Capt. Dixie Kiefer on the deck and the place in a shambles as far as personnel was concerned. I had gotten well acquainted with the Capt. for I had been assigned to the bridge for a period of time as his Radar Interpretation Officer. He had always called me Ranse and said, "Ranse you are a good kid. I'm glad you weren't with me."

The Air Officer, Commander Miller, was dead on the deck. The Exec, Commander Burch, was wounded and the relatively new Navigation Officer had taken command of the ship.

We lowered Commander Miller over the side to the deck below after lifting Capt. Kiefer onto a mattress. He was bleeding profusely and complained of his arm, which turned out to be filled with shrapnel.

The Nav Officer turned to a Lt. nearby and asked him to climb up the island to put a fire out in a forty millimeter mount. Not being able to tell one plane from another, I asked him to watch for Jap planes and I would put the fire out. I worked on it with a hose passed up to me.

Then time seemed to go fast and I found my roommate who was o.k. I caught the mid watch in CIC, prior to which I was sitting with others in the radio shack when a supply officer came by asking if anyone was hungry. I followed him to the crews mess and a big kettle of vegetable soup, another with water and plenty of crackers. I think it was the best meal I ever had. I was introduced to the same officer, Ev Miller, by a mutual friend in Detroit twenty-five years later and he told me I'd gained so much weight he didn't recognize me.

Before we lowered Commander Miller to the deck below, my boss Carl Ballinger (both Annapolis) cut off his ring finger to send his ring to his wife.

Carl G. Ritter EM2c

I was sitting on the fantail writing a letter to my fiance, Irene. Air Group 80 was returning from a strike. I can very vividly remember thinking it was probably not the smartest position to be in. If a plane being waved in was damaged it might crash short of the flight deck onto the fantail. I dismissed the thought quickly since the forty mms were manned and we were in this together.

At that instant the forty mms opened up and General Quarters sounded. My battle station was three decks below the starboard hatch by the forward elevator on the hangar deck, a long distance away from Combat Information Center. My first impulse was to run down the hangar deck to that hatch when my training command kicked in and said, get to the battle station by the quickest, safest route. I was better than halfway to the down hatches to CIC beneath the hangar deck when the BOMB and KAMIKAZE came through the flight deck. Burning gas and smoke was already filling the room. I had to go through it as I ran to the down hatch, down the ladders, closing the hatches behind me sealing off the danger above.

Once inside CIC a certain calmness set in as we, without hesitation, followed the commands for gun control set ups. You bet I was scared, but I followed every command precisely with constant prayer for my shipmates exposed to the

furor above. We were kept well informed as to what was going on, especially when the ship began to list to aid washing the burning gasoline over the side.

I had faith that God was directing our Captain Dixie Kiefer and his crew to get us through. I give thanks for training we received to make us battle ready. It literally saved my Life.

Elloyd A. Rivers AM1c

We were at General Quarters when we were hit. I was on the hangar deck, at the stern of the ship near the metalsmith shop where I worked. The Kamikaze hit the ship near the forward elevator. I remember seeing smoke from the hit and became concerned about fire. I ran with other men toward the forward part of the ship. There were several planes on the hangar and flight decks which were fueled and armed. Someone ordered us to shove the planes over the side to keep them from exploding from the fire. After shoving the planes over, we ran forward to see if there was anything we could do to help put out the fire and help the guys who were injured.

After the fire was out we headed for Pearl Harbor, and then to Bremerton for repairs. I sadly remember our shipmates who were buried at sea, and those who were injured.

John A. Russell SK1c

As a storekeeper, my battle station was with a damage control party located in the after crews mess on the third deck. We were ready to go to chow (noon meal) when the first hit came. We reported to our battle stations. Most of the spaces in our area filled with smoke from fires on the hangar deck and fires in officers country, second deck forward on the port side. Some of our party carried out a search mission to the forward crews mess which was filled with thick black smoke. We carried out several crew members overcome by smoke. We then assisted in fire fighting.

Dominick J. Sacchinelli AMM3c

I was one of six plane captains that had a plane in the air on the 21st of January. A copy of the yellow sheet that the pilot signed before take-off and after landing (the latter, he never did for me, of course) follows:

When the alarm sounded I was by the forward 5 inch mount lying on the flight deck with a wheel chock as a pillow. I ran to the island. When he hit I went out to the flight deck, as the island was filling with smoke. On the flight deck I could see injured and dead. I saw Father O'Brien giving last rites. I was on a fire hose for hours.

When the second plane hit the island forward, I believe it struck a range finder. I watched him come in at the ship's starboard side. By the time I wanted to move I couldn't so I stayed flat on the deck. At this time I saw a cameraman also lying there taking pictures of the attack. I got up and got a fire hose and stayed with it until they shut the water off on us, stating they needed the pressure elsewhere on the ship. I was behind the men on the flight deck who were put-

ting water on the planes on the #1 elevator. I remained on deck until six or seven PM that evening, then went to my bunk and slept until late the next morning.

The ship sent six planes up when the strike left and mine was one of the six. It was a CAP (Combat Air Patrol) and was to intercept aircraft following our planes back to the fleet. The *Essex* CV-9 must have sent six planes for ASP (Anti-Sub Patrol).

When I stepped off #3 elevator my buddy, Richard Schillis AMM3c, greeted me and said, "I thought you were dead, but look, I was thinking of you," showing me a box under his arm which contained a rubber tube. I asked what I would do with that and he said when we jumped in the water we would have a tube. I asked how I would inflate the tube in the water and he threw the box to the deck stating, "I never thought of that." True story.

James G. Samar ARM3c

I was a gunner in a SB2C Helldiver so I kept sort of a "diary" on our strikes. It just so happens I wrote about that fateful day that same evening while in our ready room. Here it is:

This afternoon it happened! A Jap plane got through. General Quarters sounded, and in about a minute a big explosion occurred while we were in our ready room waiting for the order to "Man Your Planes"! A Jap Kamikaze dove right into and through our flight deck. All the aircrewmen got out of Ready 3 o.k. Bill Saovi had a tough time but he made it. We encountered an awful lot of smoke which came in through the air conditioner ducts. The Jap plane went right through the flight deck into the hangar deck.

Our pilots were not as fortunate. Lt. Perkins, Lt.(j.g.) Pearson, and Lt.(j.g.) Mullavey were all wounded. Many of the pilots nearly suffocated and used gas masks to get out.

We all reached the flight deck and headed aft. I was amazed at the damage to the "*Big T*" and how many shipmates were killed and wounded. The ship was burning, smoking, and listing to port.

Another Kamikaze started his suicide dive, but we got him and saw him crash in flames into the sea. Meanwhile, we were throwing bombs and ammo was going off up forward. Many wounded were taken aft on the flight deck. I met my pilot, Lt. Jim Newquist, and the Skipper, who was also injured. The third Kamikaze got through and crashed right into the island! More officers were killed and wounded. Among them were Comd. Miller, air officer, and Ens. Wehr. Ironically, Ens. Wehr didn't want to fly anymore and he ended up getting killed another way. I saw him on the flight deck and he was still alive at that time.

Our Capt. Dixie Kiefer was also wounded along with Comd. Burch, Exec. Officer. Another big explosion occurred, and at this time we thought we would have to abandon ship and made ready to do so. The fire was eventually extinguished and the list taken out. We helped move many wounded and dead. Many bodies were scorched beyond recognition. Bodies seemed to be everywhere - looked horrible! We were told there were about 140 dead and same or more wounded.

The *Ticonderoga*, once proud and powerful, was now a mess and steaming last. All planes on the hangar deck were pushed over the side. We all cleaned up the ship as best we could and cared for the wounded.

Later I saw Jap pilot remains on the hangar deck where he finally ended up. I saw the engine, one of his feet, helmet and shoe and one hand.

I took one of his 7.7 bullets and a small piece of engine which I have to this day. The following day we were still sailing southeast. More gear and planes were thrown into the sea. We buried the dead at sea with formal military service.

William C. Schneider AMM1c

I was a plane captain on a TBF at the time. The morning flight had just returned from a strike and after the plane was spotted on the flight deck, the pilot had reported a malfunctioning thermocouple which needed replacement. Chow down had been announced and I was hungry when my buddy came and suggested we get in line to eat. I told him no because I wanted to finish the job. He volunteered to have me stand on his shoulders to take the spark plug out, replace the sensor, and place the aircraft back in service, saving the time it would take to get a regular workstand in place.

Sounded like a good idea to me!

I had removed the engine cowling, taken the plug out and was preparing to install a new unit when suddenly the Marine gunner on the starboard side of the flight deck quickly turned his 50 caliber gun around and began firing over my head, tracking rapidly toward the bow.

A scant moment later a loud explosion took place amidship and, of course, GQ was sounded. The "Divine Wind" had struck. My memories of the remainder of the day are a mixture of images and thoughts.

I never did get the plug replaced before the aircraft was pushed over the side.

Don P. Selby Lieutenant (j.g.), Air Department

I was in my battle station, which was the CIC located just aft of Admiral's Plot in the island structure. We were one deck below the bridge and the air officer's battle post was immediately outside on the port side of the island.

My commanding unit officer was Lt. Cdr. Carl Ballinger, USN, now deceased. He was the fighter director officer and I was an intercept officer. We, and other shipmates, controlled and interpreted the radar and directed interceptions by the Combat Air Patrol of the Squadron.

When the Kamikaze hit the island and fires broke out, Cdr. Ballinger issued an order for all in the CIC (perhaps 25-30) to exit on the starboard side of the island and go overboard, which was a drop of 75-100 feet. I had one leg over the rail when Lieut. Gregg Ransburg yelled to get down because he thought there was an opening in the fire so we could get to the outer walkway around the flagplot, which was just forward. This we did and wound up just below the bridge where there was great confusion because of wounds, including Dixie's.

Just aft of us at the air officer's post, they were putting the dead bodies of air office Commander Claire Miller and one of our CIC sound power talkers, radarman Daugherty in litters.

I don't recall exactly how I finally worked my way down to the hangar deck as the ladder passageway up through the island was smoke filled.

I do recall a horrifying experience on the hangar deck, where the remains of the other Kamikaze lay with the brains of its pilot nearby. A severely burned man said, "Sir, can you please help me." It was only through his speech that I recognized him as a Black sailor.

And of course I recall, as I'm sure everyone else does, when Father O'Brien, the Protestant chaplain, and a volunteer Jewish line officer teamed to perform a service for our departed shipmates. Cannon saluted and the canvas bags were dropped into the sea. A terrible recollection.

Then I recall Dixie's departure in a litter and Halsey's inspection of the damage, his spindly legs in shorts.

Frederick Selley AMM2

A fellow shipmate, last name Sample, and I were working on an F6F. He was in the cockpit and I was sitting on the wing facing aft. At this particular time we had aircraft on the deck from the island aft. I don't know how many but it seems to me they were solid back to the fantail. I looked up to the cockpit to say something to Sample and immediately saw this plane drop out of the sun and head right for us. I glanced at the radar antennas and they were still. We apparently didn't know there was anything around. I think maybe Sample and I were the first to see it.

The Kamikaze was apparently aiming for the group of planes on the deck; if he had done so Sample and I would have been killed immediately, but at the last second the horn sounded for the forward elevator and it started down. Evidently, the pilot saw that hole opening up in the flight deck and he nosed up just a little and passed over us to crash into the elevator opening and create total havoc on the hangar deck. There were a lot of people on the hangar deck and a lot of them never knew what happened to them.

I never saw any panic. Everyone I saw was doing his job to the best of his ability and the Exec, Commander Burch, went from group to group of firefighters to help steady them and let them know they were doing a good job. I was on the flight deck and

saw the second plane come in from the starboard side at about deck height. I watched the five inchers firing, then the 40's and finally the 20's. At that point I retreated to the fantail as it was certain he wasn't going to be stopped. That was the plane that caused Captain Dixie and those on the bridge to be injured.

We had people either blown overboard or jumped and a lot of us were throwing life jackets over the side. We later recovered some of them that destroyers had picked up, but quite a few were lost. Finally came the saddest part - trying to identify bodies and then putting them in a canvas bag with a five inch shell, and committing them to the sea. I was relieved to find two of my close friends, George Singleton and Andy Sterling, alive and well. We were told to return to the States for repairs and it was a totally different ship than the one that began the cruise. We were veterans now, more subdued and a little more careful to wear our helmets and other gear.

John Shade AMMH2c

I had no assigned battle station and was on the fantail when the first Kamikaze hit.

A friend and I just went around helping out where we could. It was like a dream, the worst part of which was the inability to get a life jacket to a shipmate who had fallen overboard. There were a lot of brave men that day. The saddest part was bagging the bodies in preparation for burial at sea.

Harry W. Shaw AOM1c

We had just finished reloading the next strike when word was passed that there were bogies on the screen. I was on the starboard side watching the Japs do acrobatics before starting their run. The port batteries opened up and I ran over to see what they were shooting at. About half-

Photo of a Naval Helicopter, taken from the 07 level, as high as you could get on the ship. (Courtesy of E.W. Tenpenny)

way across the deck I saw splinters of the flight deck being kicked up in front of me. The "Zonie" was shooting as he made his dive on us. I dove under a fighter plane for protection and found myself inches away from a 500 lb. bomb.

The "Zonie" hit the flight deck about midship and went through to the hangar deck. I grabbed a hose from the port side and headed toward the hole in the deck, hoping with each step that the hose wouldn't reach or that some damage control crew would take the hose from me. Both happened.

Then the starboard guns opened up on a Kamikaze headed for us. It seemed to me that this aircraft passed over several ships that did not fire on it. I wondered why the other ships didn't fire at the plane, and also how it could have gotten through our gunfire which seemed to fill that section of the sky. As the plane bore down on us I tried to dig a fox hole in the flight deck; it can't be done. Fortunately for me, the plane hit the island and not me as I was about midway from the island to the fantail.

After the second plane hit us I started to help disarm and jettison the bombs from our fighters.

I won't swear to it but I think I saw an officer catch a 250 lb. bomb, as it was released from the bomb rack, in his arms and carry it to the edge of the deck and throw it overboard by himself.

Later on I was helping corpsmen carry what I thought were dead shipmates to the aft part of the flight deck. After several trips, one of the bodies I was carrying moved and I told a doctor or corpsman this man was still alive and was told they all were alive. That's why they were moved to the flight deck.

Jim Simpson RdM3c

If it hadn't been for the fact that I had early chow and had gone on watch as the air search radar operator on the third deck of the island, I might have been standing in the chow line on the hangar deck. . .not a good place to be at the time.

When the first Kamikaze hit I had barely gotten seated in front of the radar set. Ed Daugherty, who was in the watch we were relieving, said something about going topside to see the fun. After the second Kamikaze hit the island no one ever saw him again. With that hit the radars were knocked out and the compartments filled with smoke. Finally the order was given to abandon the area and everybody headed for the nearest exit.

I made it out into the fresh air through a hatch on the starboard side of the island with Lt. Cmdr. Carl Ballinger, CIC commander, but we were trapped by fire forward of us caused by burning fuel from the Jap plane almost over our heads. We discussed jumping, as opposed to burning, but the water looked awfully far down. Just then the flames died down a little and I saw Lee Lemke, another radar man, just ahead. He yelled for us to run and we tore through the fire without damage. Going around the front of the island below the bridge we came upon a badly burned sailor who could only scream. Ballinger had morphine syrettes, so he injected the man with one and tagged him. While we were there

a detail was bringing down the body of Cmdr. Miller, the air officer.

The rest of that afternoon is pretty much a blur, except that we all tried to help wherever we could. The bodies of the dead were laid out on the after end of the hangar deck and we had to file between the rows of them to get our K-Rations that evening. I have never figured out why that was done, unless it was to impress the survivors with the seriousness of the situation, or else it was just plain cruelty.

I stayed with the ship through the end of the war and was sent home in February, 1946, on points. I often wondered about that sailor we tried to help. I can't imagine he survived.

Fred E. Slick EM1c

Jan. 21, 1945, I was sitting on my bunk in my compartment when GQ sounded. I left the compartment and was going up the ladder when we received the first hit. I was knocked back. I got up the ladder again and reported to my GQ station, which was searchlights on topside. I put on my battle gear and was between the stacks and Number 1 director handling room.

I watched as the kamikaze that made the second hit was coming for us. We were hitting it but it kept on coming for its target. When we saw it wasn't going down but was coming on we hit the deck. When I regained consciousness the first thing I did was brush my hands down over my face. I had my face protected, but thank God I did this because my full beard had caught fire and was singed.

I made my way out of the area that was blazing with my clothes on fire. The following day I went up to where I had been and found one of my shoes still laced up. I had been blown out of them! They wanted me to stay in Sick Bay for my burns, but I wouldn't stay because I thought too many others needed the care. I kept working.

After we put our severely wounded aboard the hospital ship I turned in for care. My burned leg had become infected and I was in Sick Bay for 17 days. The doctor said another day or so without care might have meant losing it.

While I was in Sick Bay one of the doctors gave orders to shave my beard off. Another doctor changed the order and I was able to leave it on and wear it home when I went on first leave. Certainly had lots of good times and fun, because servicemen with beards were rare. Every girl wanted to date the bearded sailor! It was a beautiful red beard. Before I reported back from leave I had it shaved off. It was too dangerous when we were in action.

An interesting note: when I left home for the service my Mother took a Bible and cut out Psalms 91 Verse 7 that stated: "A thousand shall fall at thy side and ten thousand at thy right hand but it shall not come nigh thee." She put the verse between plastic to protect it. I made sure I was never without it in my pocket. I had it when I left for my GQ station that day. I give it credit for me being here today.

Richard Smith FC1c

I was off duty in the Fire Control Plotting Room passing some of the day and about to

leave, when the air attack alert sounded. Since this was my battle station, I manned the fire control switchboard and made the necessary switching of 5-inch 38 gun mounts to the respective fire control directors and established communications with these stations. When the forward director, which was above the bridge, was unraveled by a bomb which also killed the Gunnery Officer and his telephone talkers and wounded the Captain and many others, we had to disconnect the telephone circuits to the forward director so that we could maintain communications with the after director.

When the attack was over some of us reported to Sick Bay to see if we could help. We were directed to search the hangar deck for any disabled personnel. I remember the darkness and devastation. As I was feeling around a 5-inch 38 gun mount blister, my hand went into a bucket of water. I jerked it out with my thoughts in confusion. As I returned inboard, my waiting shipmates were startled by my appearance. It was a scary night!

As a senior Petty Officer, I then went to see how the crew manning the after director were faring and stayed there for awhile, dozing on and off.

As every surviver can recall, it was a long time between showers and a humbling experience as so many of our shipmates were committed to a burial at sea.

It was only my location in the Plotting Room, which I was about to leave at the time of the attack, that saved me from being on the hangar deck when the Kamikaze hit the forward elevator with considerable devastation to personnel and aircraft. Thank the Good Lord and may He be generous with His Graces to those He called to their rest.

Marvin D. Snider TMV3c

The sound of the guns firing, the clang of the GQ alarm, an explosion on and people tumbling down the ladder from the hangar deck, and a dying Marine. My introduction to January 21, 1945 had taken place.

Until that day I had never been present at the moment when a person died; I had dealt with the wounded or the dead, never the moment when life gurgled away.

Some of my more profound memories of that day are:

The viewing of a certain body part just lying on the flight deck.

The sailor that appeared welded to the underside of the wing of a plane near the place of the hangar deck impact.

The removal of a body from the cockpit of a plane on the forward elevator. The elevator was either going up or down as it was stopped above the hangar deck. As we removed the body I observed no cause of death, no wounds, no blood, no burns, only the pale color of death.

While evacuating wounded on the flight deck, I bent over to pick up a stretcher when the wounded sailor said, "Snider, I made it." Because of his badly burned condition I did not recognize him; all these years I have wondered who he was.

Later in the afternoon while clearing away hangar deck wreckage, I was amazed and impressed when I saw Cmdr. Burch being carried on a stretcher so he could direct damage control.

And as with all things there is humor. While clearing the ship of wreckage, which included pushing damaged planes overboard, I picked up a burned, warped, bent, and broken swab rack and started over the side with it when I was stopped and told to store the swab rack as we might need it. I do not recall where I stored the rack.

Robert W. Snyder AMM3c

It was also the day before my 22nd birthday and began, as most other days aboard the *Ticonderoga*, with early rising, breakfast, and, as plane captain on a F6F Fighter, preparing the aircraft for launching on a strike.

After launch of aircraft it was time to get lunch chow. With that over I rode the forward elevator back to the flight deck. I went over to the starboard catwalk forward of the 5-inch turret, where I kept the tie down ropes and other items needed to maintain the aircraft, and also my flak helmet, which I had hanging on a cleat there.

In just a few minutes I began to hear anti-aircraft fire from some of the escort ships off to starboard. I reached for my helmet and put it on but did not see any aircraft and wondered what all the shooting was about.

Suddenly there was a loud explosion about 40 feet behind me in the center of the flight deck, just aft of the forward elevator. I thought an aircraft had dropped a bomb but could not see any aircraft, not realizing it was a Kamikaze with a bomb aboard and he went right through the flight deck down into the hangar deck.

I still don't know why he did not plow into all the aircraft on the aft flight deck, but heard stories that someone had manned the fantail AA guns and had possibly diverted him.

Smoke and fire erupted immediately on the hangar deck where aircraft were parked. None had bombs loaded but unexpended ammo soon began to explode, sounding like fire crackers.

People trapped on the hangar deck began to try to escape through the side openings but had nowhere to go. Ropes were procured from somewhere and lowered to them and some hung on and were hauled up, but others slipped and fell into the sea, where all we could hope was that the escort ships would pick them up.

There was a depth charge sitting on a dolly awaiting loading just forward of the 5-inch turret. The turret had black smoke pouring out of it. Another hand and I, afraid the bomb might explode, bodily lifted it up and tossed it overboard. I don't know what it weighed, but it was as light as a feather.

By this time some of our 20mm and 40mm AAs were manned and shooting off to starboard at another aircraft coming straight toward the island at about 50 feet altitude. I could see his wing guns flashing as he came in. All our AAs were going but he presented a small silhouette for the gunners. I was watching him all the way until he hit the island about half way up. He did much damage, killing and injuring many personnel. The Captain, Dixie Kiefer, sustained numerous shrapnel wounds.

About this time, I was recruited to go down into officers country where there were numerous wounded and dead, to assist, as best I could, the medical personnel there. It happened to be the dentist. The person we aided had been hit by shrapnel which had come into the quarters through the wall of the forward elevator from the first Kamikaze's bomb.

After those duties I returned to the flight deck and helped man firehoses, especially onto the forward elevator, which was about one quarter of the way up with an F6F aircraft and the operator on it. It was burning fiercely.

The automatic sprinkler system had worked as advertised on the hangar deck and was producing a sea of fire with all the burning gasoline floating on top.

To get rid of this, the port tanks were flooded to cause the ship to list heavily. With everything in an uproar we thought the ship was sinking and my life jacket station was down on the hangar deck where all the fire was. I eventually found another singed one. But I put it on and kept it with me all day and had it next to me by my bunk that night.

Some of us, including myself, stood fire guard that night and that was about as eerie and ghostly a night as I think I have ever spent, with total darkness on the hangar deck.

Edward Spinks TMV2c

Just before we were hit on January 21, 1945, I was on a visual conflagration watch about midship above the hangar deck. My watch was from 1000 to 1200 hrs. It was a standard procedure to relieve fifteen minutes before the hour. My relief arrived at about 1145, we discussed the watch and I went down to the hangar deck and walked toward the stern. I did not have to report to the torpedo room until 1300 so I proceeded to the flight deck.

When we were hit I had been on the flight deck for about 5 minutes. I witnessed the first hit and saw that I wouldn't be able to get to the torpedo room right away because of smoke and fire, so I stayed on the flight deck to help with the fire hoses.

I knew I had to report to the torpedo shop, which was back aft on the starboard side, because that was my battle station. As soon as this was possible I proceeded to go there and I was in the torpedo room when we received the second hit.

The conflagration watch area was destroyed during the first attack and my relief did not survive. I think of him often and wonder who he was and where he was from.

E. Wendell Stevens ARM2c

On January 21, 1945, at the time of the first Kamikaze hit on the USS *Ticonderoga*, I was standing on the flight deck just aft of the #44 5-inch gun turret. As the 40 mms on the after deck opened fire I looked up in time to see the Kamikaze coming down and saw him hit the forward area of the flight deck by the #1 elevator. At the sound of General Quarters I went to the Torpedo Bomber Flight Crew Ready Room which was my station in that situation.

Some time later, prior to the second Kami-

kaze hit, I left the ready room to try to assist in the care of injured shipmates. At the sound of the firing of the forward starboard 20 mm guns, I looked in the direction of their fire and saw the Japanese plane coming toward the ship just above the water. I watched the final leg of his run through the anti-aircraft fire and saw him hit the forward part of the island with his port wing and, I believe, strike the port edge of the flight deck and go into the ocean.

The rest of the afternoon I assisted in carrying wounded from the upper decks to Sick Bay for treatment and care. Late in the afternoon I was on the fo'c'sle deck and attended to a critically injured shipmate who was badly burned and had a severely broken right leg, by putting drops of water on a gauze pad on his tongue. He died as I held his hand. I did not know him.

In the days after the attack I went to Sick Bay to help feed those who were injured or burned so badly they could not feed themselves. The squadron was transferred to the USS *Hancock* and we helped support the landings on Iwo Jima.

David E. Stanfield EM2c

I was an EM2c. My battle station was the Ice Machine Room on the 5th deck. I was on the hangar deck when GQ sounded. I was near the hatch to go down and did so immediately. When I was closing the round opening hatch on the third deck (living quarters), I heard what I thought was our 5-inch guns. I later realized it was the first of the two planes that hit us. About 15 minutes into GQ, one of the men on the sound-powered phones said the carrier behind us had been hit. Then, in a shocked tone, he said, "We've been hit, too." That was the sound I heard. Our speaker system was now out and the only information we could get was over the sound-powered phones, and that wasn't their purpose. We were told we were on fire and then we were told of the second plane and no details. We had no idea of the damage, our situation, or anything. We were told that we might have to abandon the ship. That turned out to be untrue, but we didn't know. We had no information on anything. About two hours later, the ship made a roll which we learned much later was deliberate. But with the talk of the ship being on fire and abandoning ship, the listing of the ship scared us badly.

Hours later when GQ was secured, I went to the hangar deck and stood there in shock. I do not recall ever seeing a more awful sight. The ship was blackened from one end to the other, planes destroyed, body bags were lying on a deck covered with water, gas and oil. A huge hole was in the flight deck and debris was everywhere. The smell was awful. I was afraid, when in the Ice Machine Room, that we would have trouble getting out, but when I saw the hangar and flight decks I knew I was very fortunate to have my General Quarters station below decks. To me, it was a miracle that we did not lose more men than we did. It must have been a nightmare to have been caught in the middle of all the fire and explosions. But we were underway and being protected by other ships in our unit. Incidentally, I knew nothing about our beloved Captain Dixie until much later.

Andrew Sterling AMM2c

January 21, 1945, started out as every other day with much apprehension and wondering what this day held in store.

About noon I was assigned the job of repairing the radar equipment on the wing of an SB2C and, while working, looked over toward the other ships and saw two Japanese planes coming in. One took a course toward the other carriers in the fleet, the other one came in on the aft end of the carrier at low altitude, just clearing the folded wings of planes already loaded and fueled for another mission.

As the planes flew over I was able to see the pilot and I could have thrown a wrench and hit the plane if I chose to do so. It appeared his destination was the area of the forward elevator. Then, all hell broke loose.

After gathering our wits we assessed the damage and tried to look after the injured and dead.

In the meantime, I don't recall the time element between the first and second impact, another plane came in at a level of the top part of the island and as he hit, some of the gunners stayed at their posts and fired continuously until the plane hit the gun mount and the island. Some of the gunners jumped overboard after being hit and others didn't survive.

At the time of the impact I was directly across on the flight deck where I was able to view the whole sequence of events.

Later, we made every effort to save the ship and assist the injured and remove the dead. As I reflect on all that happened that day, I can't help but marvel the fact these men were able to muster the strength and courage to pick up 250 lb. bombs and throw them overboard, or the many other acts of bravery displayed. I served aboard the USS *Ticonderoga* with a great group of men.

William E. Stever Bkr2c

When General Quarters sounded I was at my watch, baking. I went to my battle station, which was 5-inch gun magazine below decks putting 5-inch shells and powder on the elevator for the gun mount.

The station started to fill with smoke from the hit we took. Damage control let us up out of there and they flooded the magazine. I went up on the hangar deck and helped out with the wounded. Then I went back to clean up the bakery from the smoke.

When I was off watch I went to Sick Bay and helped feed and read and talk to the wounded. My new GQ was at 110 mm gun mount 14.

Horace S. Strong S1c

My Stomach Saved My Life!
On January 21, 1945, I was in the mess hall having dinner when we heard a thud! The first Kamikaze hit the ship and then General Quarters was sounded. I left my dinner and started for the flight deck to retrieve my battle gear. The first plane went through the flight deck, forward of the 5 inch gun, and took my battle gear along with the walkway under the flight deck.

We tried to help those on the #1 elevator but there was no water pressure. We unloaded ammunition from the planes and pushed the planes over the side.

When the second Kamikaze hit the island, everybody received an extra boost and pitched in doing anything and everything, knowing our Skipper and officers were in grave danger.

After helping the injured and disabled and doing what we could to clean up the flight deck, we had K rations and fell into our bunks, thankful to be alive!

Vincent P. Struck MM1c

I was standing in the chow line as I was scheduled to go on watch, but before we could eat they sounded General Quarters. I went to my station which was the after engine room. Just as I got there I felt the ship kind of jump. I told the fellows we had been hit and shortly thereafter smoke started coming out of the ventilators so we had to shut them down.

After the attack I went up on the hangar deck to do what I could to help. One man asked for a corpsman. He was bandaged and said his eyes hurt but the corpsman told me he didn't have any eyes. I helped carry people to Sick Bay and I was amazed when the injured would say, take him - he's worse than I am. I'm proud to have been part of the *Ticonderoga* along with all my great shipmates. It makes me sick to see the world in this condition with all the fighting.

John Stuen Lieutenant, Air Department

My duty station was the Air Operation Office just aft of the Navigation Chart Room. On the day of the attack, about noon, Lt. Bob Fleming and I were alone in the room trying to monitor where the fighters that had been launched were operating. Meanwhile, it was getting close to lunchtime so I told Bob to go get some lunch and come back to relieve me. For some unknown reason, thank goodness, Bob negated that idea and we "discussed" various reasons why the other of us should go down first. Toward the end of that discussion the big guns were heard, the 40 mm and then the 20 mm sounded. We knew something was mighty close. The thud on the deck told us we had been hit and the following announcement verified it. As the fire on the hangar deck took off, smoke began coming through the ventilators until the blowers were shut off.

Confusion reigned but common sense and training took over. Our planes were directed to land on the *Essex*. Lunch was forgotten. As the seriousness of the situation sank in, the calming words and melody of the hymn "Rock of Ages" crossed my mind. Shortly after this came the second kamikaze.

The ship had turned to get the wind abeam and we were away from the fleet without our escort, trying to stem the fire, when the second enemy plane took a run at the starboard beam. The *Essex* took some movies of the plane's approach. It shows the plane pulling up just before impact. That kept it from coming right through our office, for which we are thankful, but it devastated the forty mm gun mount overhead. All the signal flags were destroyed along with our radio communication. Only the TBs

worked. The damage control officer in charge of fire fighting was Lt. Terry Schrunk, a former fireman, who knew his job.

Everybody fanned out to help some place. I climbed up to the gun mount above and tried to help a couple of wounded men until the medics could care for them. The medical staff from the bottom to top did a fantastic job under adverse conditions.

As Captain Dixie and the Executive Officer were injured, and Air Officer Cmdr. Miller and the Gunnery Officer were killed, others stepped in to take their places. Our Navigator did an excellent job of keeping the ship moving. Coordinating all operations was the Chief Engineer, senior officer aboard.

Anthony P. Taddeo ABM3c

It started out to be a nice day. The sun was up, the skies were clear and we were at flight quarters station. Planes were being moved from the hangar deck. The maintenance men were loading the planes with gasoline, bombs, and torpedoes. The wing guns were also being loaded.

As flight deck Fire Marshall I checked around to see if the fire equipment was in good order and all my men were at their fire stations.

It got to be chow time. I let half my men go to chow. I walked down to the No. 1 elevator. I spoke to Billy Staufner who operated it. He had just brought up a plane from the hangar deck. We agreed that when the first half of the men came from chow he and I would go. Billy started down to the hangar deck. I started to walk back to the center of the flight deck. I was about 200 feet from the No. 1 elevator. I heard this loud sound and ran to get my helmet and then went back. There was smoke and fire coming from the elevator and I saw Billy's body lying on the floor. We just kept running water on the elevator as there was also a plane with a torpedo in its belly there. We had to be careful not to break the arming wire. I had to help with other fires on the flight deck. I never did get to see Billy again. I think he was only 18 years old.

We were hit at three minutes to Noon. At about 1:20 PM we received the second hit. We were just about getting all the fires out on the flight deck and had started to secure the fire equipment, when someone called me and said, "Look Out." I looked up and saw the Jap coming in on the starboard bow. I just froze and put my hands over my face. Everything went Black and got hot. The next thing I saw was some people standing over me. I was told at Sick Bay I was out about 20 minutes to a half hour. I had a head wound. My right side was bruised down to my ankle.

The next day I was able to go to the flight deck. I found out that two of my fire fighters, Miles Maher and Eddie Warren, were killed. Myself, Joe Tremer and Logan were wounded. Eddie Warren and Miles Maher had not reached their 19th Birthday.

It may be near 50 years ago but that day cannot be forgotten. The day the ship was hit flashes through your mind every morning when you get out of bed.

While the ship was in drydock being repaired I got a 25 day leave and I went to see Billy Staufner's Mother, and then I went to see Miles

Maher's Mother. Very Sad. Both boys were 18 years old.

R.H. Trent AMM2c

My job was trouble shooter on the flight deck. I think there were 4 of us. We would meet each plane as it landed to see if it was "up" or "down." If "down" we had to find out what was wrong and get it fixed. If it took longer than 15 or 20 minutes we would send it to the hangar deck. I did not have a battle station.

On January 21, my best buddy Lawrence (Larry) Miles and I had just gone to the flight deck after noon chow. Another buddy, Bob Selbe and Burgess met us and said they were going down for a cup of joe. I said I was going to get some sun - hadn't seen the sun for over a week. They went back down and I went aft to the fantail. The 1st plane hit just before I got there - no warning - no GQ - couldn't believe it.

All my battle gear was in the little shack just aft of the island. It was where the plane captains and trouble shooters had their gear. I started for the shack and got about half way when the 2nd one hit. I found out later that Miles, Selbe and Burgess were on the ladder. They told me the blast blew Selbe's arm off. They got him top side but he didn't make it. I was looking for cover, so I dived under a bomber. I looked up in the bomb bay and there were four, 500 lb. bombs. After all, everything was ready for a one o'clock strike. About that time some of the boys from V-5 Ordnance Division came and we went about tossing bombs over the side. The V-5 men would disarm them , then drop them down to us. I can't believe that only two of us tossed them over the side but we must have because there weren't many of us doing it. They also took the 50 caliber shells out of the wings. Several mates on the hangar deck were hit by exploding shells.

While we were doing this, Miles and Burgess came along and helped. None of us had a life jacket or battle gear. We started back to the shack when we saw the 3rd one coming in. Everything and everybody was shooting at him. He was about 50 or 60 ft. above the water line. After the hit we ran aft again. We went down to the hangar deck and went aft to the work shop (Hydraulics, Metalsmith, spare engines & parts, tires etc.). We broke out some inner tubes and started inflating them. Someone had heard we were going to abandon ship and we had no life jackets. Confusion was everywhere. Finally things got calmer and we went back to flight deck. The ship was listing quite a bit, but I guess that is what saved us. It kept the gasoline from starting more fires. As I said before, we had no battle stations so just milled around helping when called on. The only time I was scared was when I ducked under the plane and stared at 4 bombs hanging over me. After we unloaded the bombs and Miles showed up everything was wait and see.

Robert H. Truatt SK2c

I recall at GQ dashing from my desk in the Supply Office 9 between the flight and hangar deck, going aft and down two or three ladders during the blasts, to my damage control station to secure compartment hatches against water and fire. It was an eerie situation, out of touch with the situation above.

I sadly recall my shipmates from the supply office heading forward and down to the hangar deck to reach the twin forties on the bow. They reached that vulnerable point where the Kamikaze came through the flight deck and exploded. All of them missing in action. I recall one, Dom Mettiga SK2c, who attended Mass every single day while aboard.

When things were under control, our damage control group was released to report topside to assist in the recovery operation under way. We finally got to the fantail after devious detours through damaged areas.

We were utterly shocked at the scene of so many casualties amid the wrecked aircraft. I was overwhelmed and immobilized by the trauma of the situation. I was jolted from my state of shock by a Medic who took me in hand to assist him in administering aid to the casualties who had need for medical first aid, and words of consolation and reassurance during their stressful, painful moments. It is an experience that will long endure.

Blessed by having survived, I cannot, will not ever forget our great Skipper, Dixie Kiefer, his staff and the greatest crew a ship could have. I was honored and privileged to be a part of the "Big T" family. It is heartening to know that *Ticonderoga*, its name so historically honored, will continue to serve our country with the new CG Class *Ticonderoga* CG-47.

Jules P. Turner ABM3c

I was in the starboard catapult flight deck crew. I had just got back to the flight deck from noon chow, when off the starboard side I saw a plane dive down and back up over the USS *Langley* CVL and saw a ball of fire shoot up. At that time GQ sounded, and looking toward the stern I saw a plane diving in. I jumped into the catwalk and it hit the flight deck just aft of #1 elevator.

Jumping up on the flight deck and running over to help the fire fighters with hoses, I picked up a fur lined leather flight helmet which had a white cloth band with Japanese writing sewn on it. Because it was bloody and gory I didn't put it in my pocket. Instead, I stuffed it under one of the landing lights. After helping with hoses four of us went down to the hangar deck to help there. There was much fire and smoke. We helped move some of the wounded and helped fight fire. There were dead bodies and lots of badly burned people.

I was back on the flight deck and saw a 2nd plane come in and hit the upper part of the island. I helped by doing anything I could. That night after the ship had left the group I went for the flight helmet but it was gone - never did find out who got it. I stayed aboard ship until 1946 when the ship was a part of "Magic Carpet."

Bernard Tyson WT1c

So many of our shipmates that worked in the firerooms have passed on, not too many that I knew are left. I went aboard the USS *Ranger*, the old carrier, in 1942 and worked in the firerooms on her and the "*Big T*" until I got dis-charged. The day of the Kamikaze attack will live with us forever. My GQ Station was down in #3 fireroom. We had a great bunch of men, every one did his job. That's what made things work. So many gave their lives that we may live. Everyone did his duty and more.

Richard Valentine ARM2c

On the morning of January 21, 1945, Torpedo Squadron 80 launched 12 torpedo bombers loaded with either four 500 lb. bombs or one 2000 lb. bomb to strike against ships in Takio Harbor, Formosa. Three of our planes were hit by intense AA fire. One, piloted by Lt. Carmody, caught fire and was forced to make a water landing near a rescue sub. Lt. Smith's radioman, Frankie Piet ARM2c, was severely wounded by AA fire while photographing the damage to three ships that had been hit by our bombs. Piet's turret gunner, Bob Knapp AOM2c, attempted to render assistance to Piet on the way back to the carrier. Upon landing, Piet was immediately taken down to the medical department below the hangar deck. Frankie was my best buddy and we had planned on going to his home town in St. Augustine, Florida when we returned to the States on our 30 day leave. Since I could not see him at that time as he was being attended to by the doctors, I went up to our aircrew ready room, which was located just under the flight deck on the port side behind the side elevator, to prepare for an afternoon strike by my pilot, Lt. Young, and gunner, Joe Colenda AOM2c.

I had been keeping a detailed daily log of my combat flight time as well as what targets were hit and the results of any damage. The following is a direct copy of what I wrote that day.

On January 21, 1945, at 12:07 PM, one Japanese plane made a dive on our ship but pulled out and dropped a bomb on the USS *Langley*, a CVL in our task group. As we fired on the first plane, a second one dove out of the sun from the stern and crashed into the flight deck, 60 feet in back of the No. 1 elevator that was on its way down with a plane. About 12:15 PM the ship shot down one plane diving for the deck. About 12:30 PM one plane started in low on the water on the starboard side. It kept right on coming although the ship was firing every starboard gun point blank. It hit the forward 5-inch gun radar director control.

I remember I was suited up in my flight gear getting ready to go up on deck to our plane when I heard our guns firing. As I recall, General Quarters had not yet been sounded and the ship was hit before GQ finally came. Aircrew did not have a specific station to man so I put on my battle helmet and went up to the flight deck to observe what was happening. The aft flight deck was loaded with planes ready for the afternoon scheduled strike so I went over to the rear dual 5-inch island guns and stood behind the 20 mm guns manned by the Marines, just aft of the 5-inch turrets.

It was at that time that the Jap plane started toward our starboard side, low on the water. As every gun was firing I remember standing there cheering on the 20 mm gunners and watching as the 5-inch turret guns went off right next to me. It seemed as if everything was in slow motion as the plane kept coming through all the flak and was not being hit. As it got closer, I realized I was standing unprotected around all the planes loaded with bombs and fuel and I better get out of there. I ducked and slid under several planes headed for the port catwalk. As I got there and I jumped down, several deck plane handlers were crouched down just below deck level. Since I had on my steel battle helmet, I instinctively bent over to cover someone who did not have on any protection.

That's when the plane hit the forward island and I watched it tumble over the deck and into the water on the port side. By that time it was mass chaos and I only remember the ship listing hard to port trying to flush the flaming gas and water off the hangar deck and probably also maneuvering to avoid further attacks. I also thought several times that the ship was going to go over and thought to myself, well there are plenty of ships around to pick us up. It never occurred to me that I wouldn't make it.

After the fires were out and we were on our way back to Ulithi, I went down to the hangar deck and attempted to comfort some of the injured that were on temporary bunks and beds all over the deck. Although none of the Airgroup 80 aircrew, to my knowledge, were injured in the attack, Frankie Piet died while being transferred to the USS *Samaritan* back in Ulithi.

John J. Vender MMS3c

I write my story of that ill fated day with deep emotion and shaking hand at eighty-two.

I was a crew member in the forward mess hall chow line as the first bomb exploded overhead. I was among the wounded.

Andrew A. Vernicek AMM3c

Wake up time for V1 division and all air department was 3-3:30. Breakfast was served. I returned to the flight deck to help launch our first strike and then we proceeded to get ready for our next launch.

When the planes returned we refueled and rearmed all aircraft for the second strike. We were about ready to launch the second strike while additional planes were being brought up from the hangar deck on elevator #1 when General Quarters sounded. We all went to our GQ stations when the first Kamikaze hit the bridge where the captain was.

The second Kamikaze hit just aft of #1 elevator. Smoke and fire covered the entire area. Naturally, at the age of 17, I was frightened. I was fortunate not to be injured. I helped fight the fire, assist the injured and helped push damaged planes overboard. As the hours went by we had the fire under control and everyone seemed to settle down to do our duties.

The next day we had funeral services and headed back to Bremerton, Washington for repairs.

John Vogt AMM2c

I was an Aviation Machinist Mate 2c assigned to the V2 Division to maintain the Gruman Hellcat Fighter Planes. On the morning of January 21, 1945, I was assigned as a plane captain to a Hellcat that was to take part in a strike that

day. I was checking out my plane assigned early that morning when I heard the General Alarm and, almost at the same time, I saw the Japanese Kamikaze dive into the forward part of the flight deck. There was a tremendous explosion and a lot of black smoke. I scrambled off the flight deck to a ramp below on the port side. The smoke was thick and I don't quite recall how I got a gas mask, but put it on so I could breathe and see better. I had no fire station assignment. I then managed to get down to the hangar deck level on the starboard side away from the smoke near the fantail.

I am not sure how long it was after the 1st hit when I saw the second Kamikaze come in low and hit the island structure on the starboard side. Sometime after the second hit the ship started to list heavily to one side (approximately 30 degrees?). I felt we might have to abandon ship but the order didn't come, Thank God. After the fire was under control and extinguished we all helped to clean up the hangar deck. I will never forget the awful smell of burnt flesh while cleaning up and pushing the damaged planes into the sea.

That evening was scary, not knowing if we would be attacked again. It also was a sad time thinking about the shipmates that were killed or wounded, especially those shipmates I worked with and knew personally.

Boyd R. Watkins AOM2c

I had just got out of Sick Bay after falling off a fighter plane and injuring my leg. I was on the hangar deck, looking in a torpedo bomber that had just returned from an air strike. One of the crew members had been fatally injured.

Then all at once, the 40 mm guns opened up on the fantail. I hobbled up to the flight deck just before the first Kamikaze exploded on the front of the hangar deck.

After the explosion, the smoke from the bomb was so dense I couldn't breathe. I put on my gas mask and still couldn't breathe. I forgot to pull the tape off the canister. In all the confusion, I just jerked the gas mask off and threw it away. After that it seemed it was just pure survival.

I didn't witness the first one but saw the second one coming. I watched as long as they were shooting the 5 inch and 40 mm, but when they opened up with the 20 mm I found me a place to hide. I jumped off the flight deck and flattened out on the catwalk. Directly after I got settled, another crewman named Goforth landed right on top of me. He had the same idea.

After it was all over we prayed for dark. When night came, there was a full moon and we could see forever. We were under General Quarters all night and several Jap planes were shot down that night.

When day dawned next morning, we had left the fleet and the "*Big T*" was alone with two destroyers. What a relief after a night of no sleep.

William P. Weaver SKC

I had no one battle station but was to stand by the pay office and, if called, help any place I could.

The first plane hit the bridge, then shortly the second one came in on the flight deck. Word

came over the loud speaker to help on both decks with the wounded. My boys (pay clerks) were all assigned to a 40 mm, including the pay master.

I came on the hangar deck and what a mess - fire going, water sprinklers going, and men lying around, dead and wounded. I helped as best I could with the wounded and even helped get the Exec., Cdr. William O. Burch, to the Sick Bay (which at that time included all of the chiefs quarters).

James M. Webb FC(O)

I had the 8 to 12 watch in the main battery director located on sky one. My crew consisted of Director Officer Lt. Stephens, Assistant Director Officer Lt. J.G. Ferguson, Pointer Benham, Trainer Kenyon, Range Finder Beck, and I was Radar Operator.

Our planes were returning from a strike on Formosa when General Quarters sounded. It seemed in a matter of minutes that all our guns were firing. Apparently the Kamikazes followed our planes back in. Due to the noise and vibration of the guns firing, I didn't realize that we had been hit until I got a look at the flight deck. The crew that was to relieve us on sky one was delayed in getting there due to so much fire and smoke.

When we did get relieved, we attempted to make our way to sky two main battery director which was our battle station. It was located about 50 feet aft of sky one. It was filled with smoke from the first hit and we were unable to put it into operation. We proceeded to act as spotters with binoculars. I saw the second plane coming in at target angle zero. All the guns on the starboard side were firing at him. I watched burst after burst that looked as if they were right on his prop spinner, but he was still boring straight in. It looked as if he was zeroed in on sky two. We scattered! A shipmate by the name of Thomas and I went forward toward sky one. About halfway there I looked back and saw the rest of my crew going down a ladder to a lower level. I turned and ran in their direction. I made it back to the base of sky two and hit the deck and flattened out. I felt the heat from the explosion go over me. It hit sky one instead of sky two and completely wiped out everyone there except the ones in the top of the director. The shipmate that was with me when we started toward sky one proceeded on around the stack. He disappeared along with several others. I'll never know why I looked back and changed my direction.

Nathan E. Whitfield AOM2c

My normal duty station was on the flight deck where I operated the bomb elevators bringing up munitions from the magazines, maintained ordnance equipment on the aircraft and loaded bombs, rockets and ammunition on aircraft.

On January 21, 1945, we had been loading aircraft for strikes all morning and it was time for noon chow. Some of us had to stay on the flight deck to continue operations. Myself and another ordnanceman were told to man #2 bomb elevator and continue to bring up munitions from the magazines to reload the incoming aircraft for a turn around strike.

We had opened up the elevator and received the first load of munitions. I sent the elevator back down to the magazine; about this time General Quarters was sounded. Just seconds after GQ there was a tremendous explosion behind us in the middle of the flight deck. We were knocked several feet by the concussion from the blast. We were not physically wounded, just stunned. When I turned and looked in the direction of the explosion I saw flame and smoke all over the forward part of the flight deck. There were two men lying on the deck about ten feet from me. Apparently they had been killed instantly.

We secured the bomb elevator and grabbed a fire hose from the rack and pulled it out to the fire on the flight deck and in #1 aircraft elevator well. We lost water pressure almost immediately, but we continued to fight the fire with the pressure we had until it was apparent we were not doing any good. The water didn't have enough pressure to reach the fire.

I don't remember if some one told me or I did it on my own initiative, but I saw a need for some one to look after the wounded men on the forward end of the flight deck. There wasn't very much I could do except try to make them as comfortable as possible. I brought blankets up to the flight deck from the berthing spaces in that area and covered the wounded with them. Many of these men were suffering from flash burns and needed to be covered.

The ship's guns started firing again and I looked to see what they were firing at. I saw some Jap planes off our starboard side. As I watched I saw one Jap plane start his run in toward us; at that time I was on the starboard side. I ran to the port side of the flight deck and jumped off into the catwalk and watched as the plane somehow got through our anti-aircraft fire and crashed into the island at the #1 gun director.

After the crash, I went back across the flight deck toward the island to help wherever I was needed. As I approached the #2 gun turret, the turret Captain told me he needed me in his gun crew. One of his men had been wounded. I climbed into the gun turret and he handed me a pair of asbestos gloves that came up to my arm pits and said, "You are my hot shell man." He gave me a 30 second check-out on how to catch the 5-inch shells and toss them through the slot around the edge of the turret deck. I remained in the gun turret until 2000 that night. When General Quarters was relaxed the turret Captain released me to return to my regular duties.

I had been inside that gun turret for seven hours and had been out of touch with what had happened from fire, bomb, and water damage throughout the ship. I was unprepared for all the damage that I saw on the flight deck and hangar deck.

The first place I went was to my berthing space on the second deck and when I walked, or waded in all my friends asked me where I had been. They thought I had been killed because no one had seen me since noon. I didn't expect to find our berthing space flooded but it was about knee deep in water. I walked over to my bunk and folded my arms, and leaned onto my bunk with my head on my arms and said to myself, "What do I do now?"

I had not been there very long when some one came through the compartment asking for volunteers to help out in Sick Bay. I volunteered to go and work wherever I was needed. The doctors were performing surgery on the wounded as fast as they could get them in and out of the operating room. I helped move the wounded in and out of surgery. The area was filled with wounded shipmates. Men were lying in every available space, on the deck and in passageways, wherever we could find room to put them. The doctors could not get to the wounded fast enough to keep some of them from dying.

We were given instructions by hospital corpsmen about what to do and what not to do for the wounded. I will never forget one man who was burned from the top of his head to the bottom of his feet. He was charred black all over and he was still alive. He was suffering terribly, he begged us for some water and we were not allowed to give him any. I can see these things as clearly as if it were yesterday.

We were released from Sick Bay at about 0100 January 22. I returned to my berthing compartment and tried to get some rest before we had to get up and start another day.

I have one last thing to say. Sitting down and remembering these events was very painful to me. I had never really gone through what happened that day in detail like I had to do in order to record this on paper. After all this time, it seems like only yesterday that I lived through January 21, 1945.

Elton L. Whitney ACMMH

I was in V-2 Division, an Aviation Machinist Mate 1c. I had no regular station for GQ as I was in charge of the aircraft shops above the stern at the end of the hangar deck.

I went down for chow at no particular time as I did not like to wait in line. On this particular day, January 21, I was in the mess hall when GQ sounded, followed immediately by the explosion of the first Kamikaze. I had finished my dinner and was enjoying a piece of pie when the explosion came. I said to myself, "To heck with it, I'm going to eat this pie." Remember, I had no GQ station. After consuming the pie, I decided it was best to get on my life jacket, helmet and flash gear. I started up the nearest ladder. There was a Marine at the foot of the ladder with blood gushing from his throat and at least twenty men standing there, staring at him. I was always identified as first class by my uniform markings and I said, "GQ has sounded. Don't you have GQ stations?" All left immediately and I made sure nothing could be done for the Marine. I went up to my locker and got my helmet and flash gear, and also my life jacket. Some of the boys were trying to move planes back aft, so I got in a TBM to ride the brakes.

We cleared an area and I looked around for something else to do. I saw a great hole in the hose where all the water was escaping. I asked one of the boys to get me some tape. Fortunately, an electrician and he came back with a supply. I cut a piece of the fire curtain large enough to cover the hole and wind around the hose. The repaired hose worked and the boys did get foam on the hangar deck fire. Subsequently there was an enquiry about the fire curtain, but nobody knew about it.

Looking around for some other way to help, I saw Executive Officer William Burch on the hangar deck aft of the fire curtains and as I approached he said, "I want to go forward to see what the fire is doing and I need some back-up." There were four men with oxygen equipment there and all volunteered. I joined the party and we started forward. Smoke was so bad we couldn't see anything. We got up as far as the trash incinerator and Cmdr. Burch said, "I have seen enough." I looked around and we were alone. All the others had vanished.

When we started back, Cmdr. Burch got confused and wanted to go to the bridge but was suffering from too much smoke. I knew of a compartment in back of the stack and led him there. His shirt was so wet and he was so cold. I saw a dungaree jacket hanging on the bulkhead and urged him to put it on. It turned out to be Max Slivka's, who was told Burch was wearing it when he got to the bridge. Max's name was on the back.

We started out for the ladder but the smoke was too thick, so I took Burch up the starboard bulkhead to a railing I knew led to the hatch opening out to the catwalk. As we arrived on the flight deck, Cmdr. Burch said, "I have to get to the bridge." He took off.

I looked around and saw some men holding a fire hose in an open hatch. I said, "There is no fire down there." But they didn't believe me and went right on squirting water into an empty compartment.

As I started forward I saw the Kamikaze coming in from starboard. At the same time, some sailors carrying a wounded man in a stretcher dropped him and took off. I picked up one end of the stretcher and dragged him across the deck. The Kamikaze was still out on the starboard, coming in. I tried to lift the stretcher over the side into the catwalk but with his struggles couldn't, so I just held him and the Kamikaze hit the forward fire control and his bomb exploded in the air over the flight deck. The next day I examined the area where we were and all around were splinters of wood from the deck. We were neither one hit, but I have had a hearing problem ever since.

After the explosion, some men started to set up a first aid station on the forward flight deck. A couple came over to help me carry the wounded man over and I saw there was no first aid equipment on hand. I remembered in the compartment just aft the bow there was a large first aid chest, so sent two of our shipmates to get it. I also told some men to get all the blankets they could find in the compartment. A few days later, the man I had held in the stretcher sent word he wanted to see me. He had had a piece of propeller blade buried in his side and he had been brought up from the hangar deck.

One of those in the first aid station on January 21 was Robert Lee Selbe AMM3c. His left arm was all but severed and there was only a small bit of flesh still attaching it to his body. One of the Pharmacists who had come up to help tried to get Selbe to remain quiet, but he would not. He finally died from shock.

My Section 3 of V-2 Division had the watch for any stray fires that were constantly starting up from smouldering material stored along the bulkheads and overhead. I was Section leader and kept the men alert, as the hangar deck curtains were all destroyed and the danger was a submarine could see any light that showed. Captain Dixie stayed on the bridge until midnight and when he came down on his way to sick bay he had a corpsman helping him. They had a small flashlight and all of my section let out a yell, "Put out that D— light ." Captain Dixie explained he had been afraid of falling into the no. 3 elevator. So he was given an escort to the after ladder leading down to Sick Bay.

Vincent L. Wichert CPhoM

On the day we were hit we were off the Coast of Formosa. We had gotten into and out of the South China Sea safely after a series of highly successful strikes at Formosa, Northern Phillipines, Saigon and the Indo-China Coast. I can remember one of the other photographers saying, "I hope we run out of biscuits and bullets so we can go back to Ulithi for a couple of cold beers."

Well, we had enough stuff left for another strike or two so on Jan. 21, we took another strike at Formosa. Bogies were spotted now and then and a few splashed. There were large cloud formations overhead and the bogies were hiding in and out of those clouds.

Half of the photographers were on duty in the photo lab, the other half were top side and things were quiet at the time. We were all fairly well relaxed, drinking some joe, doing whatever work we had to do and just shooting the breeze. Suddenly the quiet was broken by the shrill sound of the bugler sounding "Torpedo Defense." I remember thinking later on, "Why didn't he sound General Quarters first?" As soon as the sounds of the bugle faded away the anti-aircraft guns started firing. There was a huge explosion, the ship shuddered and the photo lab began to fill with smoke. In the lab, we weren't sure exactly what happened. Some of the photographers stood by, getting ready to process whatever film might come in and the rest of us grabbed cameras and went top side to see what was happening.

The photo lab was situated on the hangar deck immediately below the island superstructure. I looked out at the hangar deck. I could see some flames and smoke and debris littered the deck. I grabbed a camera, took the inside ladders and passageways to topside, and when I got there I heard someone say "Kamikazes" in unprintable terms. Only then did I realize what had happened. The air was full of smoke puffs from the anti-aircraft guns, and the damage control crews had quickly organized themselves and were furiously at work putting out fires and clearing debris. Some people were trying to help the wounded.

I spotted a young, blond headed kid by the name of Jones; he was a striker in the photo lab. He was standing still, bareheaded, holding his hands over his ears. Jones was the youngest man in the lab, a likable kid, who had tried his hand at boxing in one of the intra-ship bouts we had at our smokers. He got KO'D in his first fight so he gave up boxing as a career and we used to kid him about it.

There were helmets and life jackets laying around the deck, so I hollered to him, "Jonesy, get your battle gear on." He did so, but he didn't have any more luck on the flight deck than he did in boxing. He was killed when the second Kamikaze hit.

There was a short lull in the anti-aircraft fire, then it started up again. My eyes followed the smoke puffs and I saw a small plane low on the horizon. It quickly grew into a larger plane and I could see the tracer bullets trying to track it down. I realized it was another Kamikaze headed for the control tower of the island superstructure.

I saw it hit and there was an explosion followed by fire and smoke. I was standing halfway between the island and the aft end of the flight deck. The explosion knocked me down but luckily I was untouched by the flying debris and for a while I wasn't certain what had happened. I can remember thinking, I wonder where Jonesy is? I found out later that he had been killed, his final KO.

I can't remember too much about the rest of the day, and the following day or so is not too clear in my mind. I remember eating something and trying to stay awake. I gradually got my bearings and headed for the photo lab, but the ladders and passageways were clogged by some of the crews passing the litters down to Sick Bay and helping the walking wounded. There was still a lot of smoke and I saw the Chief Photo Mate,"Hank" Bounoff, helping pass along the litters, so I laid my camera down and helped wherever I could.

The following day the ship was very quiet and all conversations were muted and soft. I never was able to find the camera.

I can remember that Dixie Kiefer and Commander Burch were wounded. The Air Officer, Commander Miller, was killed and the 1st Lt. was either killed or wounded. One of the junior officers took command. I can't remember who he was but he did a 4.0 job. Order was gradually restored and we headed out of the combat area, back to wherever we could be repaired with a couple of ships (tin cans?) as protective escort. The following day I saw the body of a Jap pilot laying on the aft end of the flight deck, guarded by a small group of Marines. I cannot recall if he was one of the Kamikazes that hit us or if he was fished out of the sea after being killed.

The more seriously wounded, Dixie Kiefer and Commander Burch among them, were transferred off and Admiral "Bull" Halsey and some of his staff came aboard to inspect the damage. The "Bull," never one for formality, wore a tired looking beat up hat, shorts and was wearing what looked like slippers or sandals. The remark went around that every Ensign and Lt.(j.g.) aboard cleaned out ships stores of shorts and sandals. They all wanted to be a "Bull" Halsey. Such jokes relieved the tensions and were an indication of the high morale of the crew. I felt proud to be one of them.

The day we buried our dead was a clear, calm day with gentle, rolling seas. The gentle swells were matched by the kindness and concern we had for each other. We had been molded by Dixie Kiefer into strong shipmates and our tragedy had welded us together even more strongly.

The repair yards at Guam and Pearl Harbor were loaded so we were sent to Bremerton for repairs. The port and starboard watches were given separate 30 day leaves and I can remember that the ship felt like a ghost ship for a while. A small crew, and the sound of repairs had a hollow ring. After three months (about) we headed back into the fleet. There was more action during which the pilots and crew of the "*Big T*" did distinguished and stellar duty. Then there were the two atomic bombs and it was all over.

Many of us had enough points for immediate discharge and were given the option of Nearest Available Transportation home for discharge, or we could stay with the ship and be part of the ceremonial fleet that was to sail into Tokyo Bay for the signing (surrender) ceremonies. I opted for home; there was a wife and a 5 year old daughter waiting for me.

M.D. Williams BM1c

I had gone to early chow about 11:30. Since it was so warm in the mess hall I had returned to my 6th Division compartment with a slice of apple pie in hand. Just as I sat down on a bench I felt concussion pressure on my ears although no GQ alarm had sounded. I quickly yelled to the 6-8 shipmates present that something was happening and we should immediately go to our battle stations. By the time I got to my Quad-40 mm gun mount on the starboard fantail deck GQ sounded. Being gun captain, I started all motors and removed muzzle covers. By this time my gun crew started arriving from their watch station on the Quad 40 mm mount of the island. Smoke was now passing by us and I commented that someone had been hit. One of my crew advised that we had been hit by a Kamikaze on the main bridge section of the island.

We were by this time connected to Fire Control and our guns commenced firing at another Kamikaze diving on us from directly astern. Our shells scored several hits on the diving plane but he kept coming and hit us in the middle of the flight deck amid-ships. As he crashed through the deck, his bombs (2-500 pounders, I believe) exploded in the area of the Admirals and Captains Quarters. It was this explosion which killed so many of our crew as they were running from the mess hall lines across the hangar deck to their battle stations.

This explosion started several fires, including some aircraft. I can remember the ship was trimmed to port in order to minimize the risk of burning fuel and to drain the water from fire hoses. Several hours later the fires were extinguished and we started to pick up the dead on the hangar deck. We found several men dead in their tracks where they happened to be when the explosion occurred. Some were going up ladders, some in the act of closing doors and one was opening a 40 mm shell canister. We had to collect all personal effects - I.D. tags, wallets and jewelry to turn over to the Chaplain's office for future disposition.

For the evening meal we distributed C-Rations to all hands. What a gruesome feeling it was that night as all the dead and wounded were laid in rows on the aft starboard hangar deck, near the entrance to sickbay.

The next morning we started transferring the wounded to our destroyer escorts to carry to the hospital ship. We also began to prepare for funeral at sea services. I believe we had three or four services over the next few days. My 6th

Division was responsible for this task, with some assistance from other deck divisions. We placed each body in a canvas bag with two 5-inch shells and sewed up the end of the bag. Several of my men got blisters from this chore.

This was the saddest time of my life and one I can never forget.

N. Frank Williams AMM3c

I had been up for more than twenty-four hours getting our TBMs in shape. Fighting had been heavy and a lot of damage had been done. Our Chief, Bill Shaffer, told me to go to his bunk in the Chiefs quarters to get some rest and sleep. It probably saved my life. Otherwise I would have shared the fate of so many others.

The gong had rung and I was rushing to get dressed and hurry to my station. Smoke was pouring in from the galley, along with three cooks trying to find a way out as the hatches were all battened down. The boys were frantic. They had climbed the ladder to the flight deck and were clawing at the closed hatch. The fire was progressing toward us via the burning paint.

I remembered our Captain Dixie had admonished us to locate escape hatches at various parts of the ship. I had taken him at his word and had scouted the ship for them. It finally dawned on me that there was one in the area. So we escaped to the fantail and the awful carnage there and started unloading bombs and pushing planes overboard. Volunteers donned asbestos suits and with Waters I went below to keep our ammunition cool.

Dr. F.E. Willing Lieutenant, Medical Department

This account of my recollections of the Kamikaze attack against the USS *Ticonderoga*, CV14 is reluctantly submitted. The intervening years have largely been spent trying to forget many of the horrible effects of war which I was forced to witness that day. I sincerely believe that had it not been for the fierce loyalty that Captain Dixie Kiefer had bred by friendly , almost fatherly leadership, and his instantaneous command to flood the empty port gasoline tanks, the *"Big T"* would have been lost.

His order to flood the tanks made the ship list to port. This forced the burning gasoline on the hangar deck to cascade over the side into the sea. Then his plea over the intercom to get the burning bomb and rocket laden planes off the hangar deck was enough to spur so many men to brave the flames and smoke that not a single bomb or rocket of our own, and there were many there, exploded on the ship. The cant of the steel deck plus the water still flowing from the heat-activated above head sprinklers allowed bombs, rockets and aircraft to be slid overboard.

However, some wing gas tanks did explode, and many rounds of the wing machine guns. At least three crewmen were killed and several others wounded by this combination. The shower/washroom/latrine area (Navy Lingo: Head) just forward of the hangar was profusely ventilated, both by these bullets and shrapnel from the primary Kamikaze. After "General Quarters Condition Able" was replaced by "GQC Baker," several occupants of staterooms far forward of the

Head were surprised to find spent bullets inside their boudoir drawers, as well as holes in the bulkheads.

My personal remembrances start with the arrival in Sick Bay, at about 1015, of a wounded photographer's mate. A Japanese anti-aircraft shell had exploded almost in his face as he manned his camera in the low-aft photo position of the converted torpedo bomber. Since the resulting trauma involved the face, I was part of the operating team.

First portent of gloom. He died on the table because a fragment of shrapnel had penetrated all the way into the center of the brain.

Some time after 1200 (the Ship's Time had nothing to do with Sun Time in the combat area. I think it was more like 2:00 pm. and we had been up since before dawn) I entered the Wardroom with my lunch tray. I remember crushed pineapple and a chicken, vegetable mixture. I had only eaten a few fork fulls when the GQ alarm sounded and, almost simultaneously, there was a severe jar and a distant sounding "Whump." At the sound of the alarm,I automatically stood, turned to run to my battle station, but reached back for just one spoonful of that crushed pineapple. Then came the "Whump" and I went to my knees wondering what all the tinkling metallic sounds that followed meant. When I took hold of the steel post supporting the hangar deck above I was amazed to find it bent almost "S"-shaped. Then I noticed a big dip in the ceiling and hanging electrical cables. Later it occurred to me that the tinkling sounds were caused by falling brackets.

Since my battle station was the after port 5-inch gun platform and battle dressing station, I rushed toward the nearest port side exit, but I was stopped en route by the sight of a cascade of fire coming down the ladder. Looking aft through another door I saw more flames. Just then I also noticed that the deck was tipping to port. Acting completely on instinct I turned to run "uphill" to starboard. Again all was flames and smoke aft so forward looked best. Smoke, but no flames. As I ran past the wall next to the forward elevator I saw it start to smoke and turn black. As I topped the ladder to the hangar deck level, but forward, I heard Dixie's call telling of the need to remove the bombs and rockets. Going aft, past my own stateroom by only a few feet, the door to the hangar deck was closed and hot but not peeling. I grabbed a large C02 tank extinguisher from its bulkhead bracket, opened the door and jumped backward as a blast of hot air and smoke blew past. Then, using the fog of C02 and foam as a shield, I stepped through only scattered flames into a vision of Hell! The overhead sprinkler system was spewing water on the hot steel deck causing steam to rise. The walls and underside of the flight deck were still burning and smoking. That area above the steel cross girders but below the underside of the flight deck had been a storage area for spare wing tanks and other aviation paraphernalia. Unfortunately it was also a favorite "sack-out" area for certain enlisted personnel.The arms and legs of several charred bodies dangled from the wreckage. Burning airplanes were scattered over the deck.

Amazingly, there were live men also on that deck, scrambling feverishly to be true to Dixie, to get those bombs, rockets and burning planes

over the side. In most cases, a crowbar or two would spring the big 500 pound bombs off the brackets that attached them to the underside of the bomber, but, in one case, the bracket broke free of the plane but not from the bomb. That made it impossible either to roll or to speedily slide it overside. Lieut.(j.g.) "Bolo" Stilwell, realizing the desperate urgency of the situation because of exploding wing tanks all about him, swept his powerful arms under that bomb and staggered and stumbled just far enough to send it into the sea.

Several days later as we limped toward Ulithi, he was asked to demonstrate how he was able to manage this feat. A 500 pound bomb was hoisted to the deck. After several minutes of strained musculature he did raise one end about a foot from the deck. So much for the power of adrenalin.

Directly in front of me, and only about ten yards away, a burning fighter plane's collapsed folding wing had caught and smashed the right elbow of an air crewman. He was unconscious but alive. One of his buddies was trying to get him loose, so I joined him. It took some doing, but we finally got him down and were dragging him toward the door I had entered when the starboard wing tanks exploded. We had been working on the port wing. The other wing was much closer to the gasoline supply and still burning. The steel helmet, which I had picked up on the way past my quarters, saved me from major damage. Just then Lt. Jim Neighbours (Aerologist or Weatherman) came out of the smoke to help get the injured air crewman on the way to the fo'c'sle dressing station.

Among the corpsmen busy were Bishop, Johnson and Saunders. An odd scene sticks in my memory: Johnny Bishop responding to the plea of a partially paralyzed seaman who had to "go" but was unable to get it out. The resigned, sympathetically fastidious expression on Bishop's face as he delicately two fingered the conduct of the penis toward the "jug" is unforgettable.

At about that time word came that medics were needed on the flight deck, so I headed for the port side ladder to the catwalk leading to the flight deck. As I ran aft toward the short ladder connecting the two, the flight deck edge was only a few feet above my head. Coming from the other direction and several feet closer to the ladder was a stalwart Marine. He hesitated briefly, but when I signaled UP with a wave of the hand, he scrambled up the ladder. As soon as his heels were out of my face, I followed. Just as my eyes moved above the deck I saw a brilliant flash from the bridge area and heard the sound of an explosion much, much louder than the original "whump." I then found myself on my back on the catwalk and heard again the many little tinkling or spattering sounds.

When I managed to regain my feet and climb the ladder I stumbled over the body of the Marine. He was riddled with shrapnel and quite dead. But that was only the beginning. There were more dead bodies than live ones on that long expanse of wood and steel.

However, I had barely started treatment of an air crewman with a badly mangled leg when I was joined by corpsmen from the fo'c'sle deck. My knapsack of medications was soon ex-

(Courtesy of R.M. Kane)

hausted, but each of the many corpsmen who were now busy giving aid had thought to bring additional supplies. Details are fuzzy for the next few hours, but I remember seeing several corpsmen and Drs. Flaiz and Scherr treating badly injured Captain Dixie, finding Commander Miller dead, Father O'Brien administering last rites. There was time spent in searching for bodies in flooded compartments below the hangar deck, and finally, the long procession of head and neck injured who were my responsibility until falling asleep on the operating table when the line ended.

Seth Thomas Wilson, Jr. S1c

I had just returned to the flight deck after eating lunch. A group of us were standing, talking, on deck next to the island superstructure when we heard a ship firing off our starboard side. I ran forward to see what was going on. As I got near the starboard 5-inch mounts our guns started firing and General Quarters sounded. I stopped running forward just as the 1st suicide plane hit the flight deck behind me. I got up off the deck, scared and confused. I couldn't get to my GQ Station, the 20 mm mounts on starboard catwalk just behind the after 5-inch mounts, due to all the smoke and flames. I joined fire fighting crews on the flight deck. I was assisting moving the wounded to the forward end of the flight deck when the 2nd suicide plane hit above the ships bridge. I don't to this day remember what time the 2nd plane hit. All I remember is being scared to death, fighting fires and helping the wounded all day and into the evening. We then started dumping debris etc. off the deck edge elevator.

William G. Yoder SK2c

January 21, 1945, was the day two Jap Kamikaze planes hit the USS *Ticonderoga* CV-14. The first plane crashed through the flight deck and landed on the hangar deck. It then exploded and caught fire. I was on my way to my battle station on the fo'c'sle (bow) of the ship. The concussion of the plane knocked me down. I lost my glasses and ID bracelet. There was fire all around me and I either had to burn alive or jump overboard. Naturally I jumped, but I didn't remember hitting the water. I must have passed out, but I came to and saw the "*Big T*" pass by. I did not have a life jacket on and someone threw a life jacket to me which landed right beside me. In 1993 I found out Joseph A. Kaskoun (who was in V-5 Div. as AOM3c) threw some life jackets to men in the water and I'm sure he helped save my life.

It was about one hour later that the USS *Ingersoll* DD 652 picked me and several other men up.

The doctor aboard the destroyer treated me for shrapnel wounds of the nose, teeth and left leg, and I was later transferred to the "*Big*

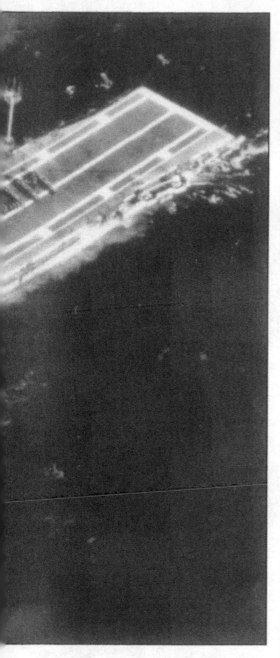

T." I received a Purple Heart later aboard the ship.

Norman J. Young S1c

I heard the P.A. system sound a General Quarters. I ran as fast as I could to my 20 mm station, on the island on the starboard side. When I ran I thought I tripped over something, but it was an explosion close to me; a small sliver of shrapnel had hit my leg.

I was the first man to arrive at the station so I proceeded to cock the guns. Then the gunner came and I took over my job as loader.

The announcement came over the P.A. system that there were many bogies in the area. There were 2 men injured on our gun station, but not seriously. After the attack, I asked permission from my gun captain to check the gun station forward of ours. When I arrived there I saw that a crewman was hit in the forehead and had died immediately. There was nothing I could do for him.

A picture of the flight deck and the two star admiral who visited the ship. (Courtesy of E.W. Tenpenny)

A bird's eye view of the Ticonderoga *under way. (Courtesy of Howard Hoxsie)*

SEA STORIES

WE WERE ATTACKED
by Anthony J. Pereira

On January 21, 1945, I had just gotten off watch at 12:00 noon and was portside at my locker after washing up, and MacDowell was amusing me with some of his B S. We heard and felt a thump and looked at each other wondering "What was That?". I said "we're hit"! The general alarm sounded and the compartment was evacuated, leaving me alone to secure my locker and finish dressing. I stepped into the aft mess hall and started moving forward when I noticed a heavy smoke screen. I paused wondering if I should go into it. Then a chief petty officer passed by and walked right into the smoke and so I followed him and could hear the water tight doors being secured behind me. Then the chief petty officer opened the hatch and went into the engine room and I proceeded to the electric shop, my battle station, repair party. It was full of smoke.

I was glad to see the repair party and that I wasn't alone. They were all wearing gas masks and putting on my gas mask, I remember thinking that from previous instructions that gas masks were ineffective to smoke. I immediately felt

water rising as the ship rolled back and forth and wondered where it was coming from as we were below the water line. I knew we were hit and was sort of afraid. At first I thought it was a torpedo or a mine. Later on, over the P A System we heard Bogie Bogie and indicating 80 something degrees so I knew that aircraft was approaching us on the starboard side, so I calculated that was where I was located. Then we heard five inch long range guns, 40mm and 20mm short range guns but it seemed like nothing was happening. I wondered why the guns weren't hitting them. Little did I know that they were kamikaze suicidal attacks. I had heard of them but never thought it would happen to us. Then I heard a thump and vibration throughout the ship and we were boxed in smoke. We had been hit a second time!

Someone requested to open the hatch and let us topside and the word came back that the hatch was open but no one was going up. The reason no one was going up was that there was too much smoke topside in the hanger and they had opened the wrong hatch. When they finally opened the right hatch we went topside. I had a three cell flashlight and the smoke was so thick, I could only see the guy in front of me. I was the third

man out. When we came to the hanger deck, I was shocked to see the condition of the ship. We moved to the starboard side and I finally breathed some fresh air.

That's when I noticed my first causality. We proceeded to pick up the wounded and take them to sick bay. I used to pal around with a kid named Jefferson whom I later found out was missing in the attack. One hundred men were killed out of approximately a thousand men on the ship. Captain Dixie was among the fallen and the senior officer took over. I often wonder why I was saved and thank God.

Scuttlebutt was that there were three kamikaze planes, I only knew of two. All this occurred between approximately 1200 hours and 1800 hours on January 21, 1945, and then at 2000 hours, I was back on my generator switchboard watch till 2400 hours midnight.

TICONDEROGA SAILOR
by Purl G. Dean, Y2c

I boarded the *Ticonderoga* on Christmas Eve, 1944. I was not "ships company." I was attached to Commander Carrier Division Six (COMCARDIV Six) and Admiral Arthur W.

MAA Force, Yokosuka, Japan, 1957. (Courtesy of Howard Hoxsie)

Radford was my commanding officer. He was not active at that time. Another admiral was running the show. I was, at that time, a yeoman second class and I was recommended for a commission by the admiral, but I was wounded in the kamikaze attack and was never promoted. I was given a medical discharge nine months later from the Jax Naval Hospital, Jacksonville, Florida, being my hometown. On August 22, 1945, a few days later, after the Atom bomb was dropped on Hiroshima. Presently I am 73 years old (January 16, 1994). VA pays me 40% disability. I should be rated for 70%, but after 40 years of claims and appeals, I gave up.

As a member of COMCARDIV six, I had no duties as the "Flag" was not active. My official designation was Intelligence Specialist, but I was rated as yeoman second class, pending promotion for a commission. The Flag Division had the "run of the ship", but stay out of their way, especially during General Quarters. We had no battle stations.

I had become friendly with a yeoman third class and palled around with him some. He was a "talker" in forward five inch gun turret. He told me to come sit with him in the next General Quarters which I had planned to do.

I was told by the older members of the "Flag" that the five inch and 40mm guns were generally long range weapons, but if I ever heard the 50 caliber machine guns start, the enemy was right on "on top" of us.

I was always a "chow hound" and was in the mess when it first opened, about 11:30 a.m. I think were at General Quarters then. I can't remember exactly, but it seems to me we had "horse cock" sandwiches. I remember going to and from chow, Bombs on Wheels ready for loading. I got back to the admiral's quarters and we had started firing the five inchers and 40mms. I sat down at a desk and started polishing a brass ash tray fashioned from a 40mm spent shell casing. It was only moments when the 50 caliber's started firing. Then I really was "concerned" and before I was to the "scared" period, All Hell Broke Loose!

The first kamikaze had crashed into the forward deck. In seconds smoke had started into the room. My first impression immediately after the blast was warm blood running down my right leg. I started to get up out of my chair to run topside and I collapsed on the floor. More and more smoke was filling the room.

Orville Woodbury, another yeoman second class from Salt Lake City, Utah picked me up bodily and carried me up one deck and when we were there the ladders were so crowded that he couldn't take me any farther.

There was small radio room next to the ladder, so he put me in there and laid me on a desk and left. That room filled quickly with 10 or 15 people. The door was "dogged."

Smoke filled the room and soon, against all orders someone opened the porthole. That helped to some degree, but it was obvious that we would all have to get out into the open.

One or two stuck their heads out of the porthole and members of the "Flag" had gone topside and dropped a line down for us to grab so they could pull us up.

The crew inside the compartment immediately said, Get the injured man out first." I didn't

argue. Some PHM/2 gave me a shot of morphine and they helped me up to the porthole. I still had my life preserver around my waist and as I went out the port the life preserver inflated and was inside the ship around my body and I was half in and half out. I could not move until a Lieutenant Rudniki from Massachusetts stabbed the inflated life preserver with his shark knife in several places deflating it. He was later awarded the Bronze Star for it. However, Yeoman Woodbury and others who "manned" the rope should be also awarded a decoration.

When I was outside the ship, they pulled me up and I watched part of the battle raging from the catwalk.

It was miserably cold. I guess the temperature was in the upper 40s or low 50s. I only had a sweater on over my shirt and dungarees. The ship must have been going about 30 knots, along with a headwind of 10 or 15 miles per hour, so it didn't take long before my teeth were "chattering" and I was shaking all over, probably from shock, as well as cold. We sat there until the battle was over and a corpsman came over with some help and moved me.

I asked the corpsman to look at my leg wound and see if it was broken. It turned out to be "compound fracture tibia and fibula right, communited, extending into the knee joint, fracture also of metatarsals and phanges." He said "No, it is not broken." I thought it was only a shrapnel wound. I tried to walk and of course the leg would not support me. The bones were literally sticking out through the flesh and skin.

I was put alongside many other wounded men and a blanket was put over me.

The battle over, members of the "Flag" came over to check on me. They were a great bunch. I wish I knew their names.

My brother in law, Bill Millward, also came over. He was a lieutenant junior grade and was with one of the air squadrons on board and was not ordered to deploy yet. After the "hits" he was unable to "take off."

He left to help jettison ammunition over board to keep the fire from exploding it and I didn't see him anymore.

A doctor came by assessing everyone's wounds and I asked him if my leg was broken and he said "No." I don't know if he was under stress or what, but a layman could diagnose a compound fracture.

The morphine was causing my mouth to be dry. I could have "spit powder." Eventually someone came by with a bucket of water and a dipper. I drank too much water. Within a few minutes I became nauseous and started heaving the chow I had eaten shortly before. It was real misery.

Somebody came up with a towel and a basin of water and cleaned me up as best they could. I did feel better, but the nausea continued.

Soon a chief pharmacist mate came by and was checking everyone lying on deck. The sun had come out by now and was blinding us. I asked the chief if my leg was broken and after feeling my toes, he also took a look at the opening in my leg. I told him to spread the wound open and get a good look. He did make some effort, but did say again the leg was not broken. So much for that.

I supposed a couple of hours passed and some

of us on deck were being moved. They put me in the chief petty officer's quarters. I was still bleeding, but the corpsman said it was good to do so and that no arteries were affected.

They put a fireproof mattress cover over the mattress and laid me on top of it so the blood would not soak the mattress. They also brought me some C rations which I could not eat, but the chewing gum was good. I used it. From time to time a corpsman would come by and check on me.

I dropped off to sleep and slept for some time. I guess four or five hours had passed since the attack.

A member of the ship's band was sent to stay with me until I was taken to the operating room.

This happened after midnight. When I arrived at the operating room, my clothes were drenched with blood. I had lain and bled for about 12 hours. Lying on the fireproof mattress cover my clothes and hair had absorbed the blood.

The doctor thought at first that I should have been attended to before this, however, when they cut my clothes off they examined me and told me "off hand" my leg was broken. Diagnosis in fact was compression fracture, compound, communited tibia and fibula right, extending into the knee joint, fractures also in metacarpals and phlanges; not diagnosed immediately was compression fracture entire spine from the axis to the coccyx, later allowed by the Veteran's Administration as a compensable disability.

They examined my head extensively as my hair was also soaked with blood and they thought I had head wounds. The blood in most places was dried. They had a corpsman literally wash my hair, not with soap, but with plain water. Fortunately, no head wounds.

They found out that the fractures were so extensive and involved parts of the tibia that extends into the knee joint and merely put a cast on my leg to immobilize it until specialists could reduce the fracture.

I was put in the officer's mess until I could be transferred to a hospital ship.

I was surprised at my "nurses." commanders and lieutenant commanders were bringing ducks (urinals) and bed pans. They were immediately "dubbed" bed pan commandos, not to their faces of course. They were good and solicitous, more so than the corpsman would have been. Also, some band members did wound dressing and more demanding routines.

After about four days we had limped back to Ulithi. Everyone was glad to be back "home."

I was in hopes I would get some mail, but such was not the case.

They transferred me to the "Good Samaritan." I left the "Ty" with nothing, but a towel; no clothes or anything. All my gear and possessions were lost.

I was put in a "preop" ward. Still nothing, but the towel. Drop off to sleep and you make one move and you are in the "buff."

I vegetated for three or four days. Doctors and nurses making rounds and checking everything possible.

Then they took me to the operating room and "set" my leg and knee. I wish I knew the orthopedist that did the work. He was a genius. I owe the use of my left leg to him.

There was a lot of muscle damage and a large

Five-inch gun crew. L to R: Pat Kitt, Leo Gauthier, Richard Jayoox, Johnny Imber, Bill Joyce. (Courtesy of Pat Kitt)

cavity in the center of my leg. They packed it with gauze so that it would heal from the bottom.

I recuperated for two or three days and they shipped all of us they could get on a PBY to send us south to New Caledonia.

It was a great day to get a final destination. Still we had only a towel to cover "possible."

That expression came from one nurse that gave me my first "bed bath." I was asking her how she was going to bathe me and she said, "I'll bathe up as far as "possible" and down as far as "possible" and you can bathe "possible." Which I did.

When we were loaded on the PBY, no small feat. Trying to get the stretcher so that it would go through the hatch with seas three or four feet was like a "sea-saw." Picture trying to put a stretcher that just would fit through the opening and the stretcher's ends alternating up and down.

On the plane we taxied out into the lagoon and went the whole distance without a take-off. They had to have a PT boat ruffle the sheet glass water so we could break the suction of the water on the PBY. Then we tried again and were airborne.

The nurses on the PBY made hamburgers for us. No "Big Mac" mind you, but meat about the size of a silver dollar with mustard, onions and pickles, the works. Food for the gods.

Next stop was the island of Manus about two degrees above the equator. Just a refueling island for ships and planes. We were put in a hospital made of Quonset huts. The island was small, only a few miles long and about the same wide.

I was placed downwind from burn cases off our ship. The odor was terrible. Putrefied flesh as well as burned odor. We were there only two days waiting for an Army C-47 to fly us to Noumea, New Caledonia, a French island farther south. While at Manus, I was annoyed by a strange occurrence. We frequently felt the earth shake and several times a day the bed would take a sharp move. I thought it was artillery practice or some demolition going on, however, when I asked a corpsman about it he said it was tremors from earthquakes. He told me, and I did, to watch the drinking water on the bedside cabinet. It was never still - always agitated. I was greatly relieved when we left Manus.

On the flight to Noumea we passed over many small islands and atolls. The beauty of the water was breathtakingly beautiful. Every shade of blue, aqua, and green blended and contrasted. I shall always remember that.

We arrived at a southern airport of New Caledonia as I guess there were no airstrips on the North.

We were then taken to an Army MASH Unit where we were fed and bathed. The food was good and the bath, too.

A quick round of Army doctors found everyone in tolerable condition and the Army nurses cared for us as was needed. Apparently the medics of the Army only did menial chores. It was nice, the feminine touch. At the Navy hospitals nurses only supervised.

After an overnight stay at this MASH unit we were loaded into field ambulances, four to a truck, and spent a few hours going over rough roads and mountains.

That was a unique experience. We all swore that the ambulance had square wheels.

There was a patient from New York City that kept screaming in pain. Everyone thought he was a crybaby. Later on in the Navy MOB Hospital, it was discovered that his femur had become unpinned and he had another open reduction made and was put in traction.

I was in the hospital until June. It was a relaxed sort of atmosphere. All the patients were stabilized and recovering. The attack was on January 21, 1945, so it was time for some healing. My leg was still in a cast. The doctor's removed it to examine the open wound. I was healing nicely, but there was still a gaping hole in my skin. They repacked the open wound in the leg with vaseline gauze and put another cast on my leg.

I was glad to have the old cast off my leg. It was soaked with blood and smelled terrible.

Easter Sunday one of the nurses insisted that all patients would go to services. We did. She and the corpsman and everyone except one post-op Marine went.

The setting of the hospital was on a high bluff that overlooked Magenta Bay. Aptly named because most late afternoons near sundown with light clouds covering the sun, everything including the hospital turned a pale purplish color. It was all really beautiful.

At Noumea, the ambulatory patients could

get passes and went into the city to the "Pink House" or to get steak and eggs, a French favorite.

I was there awaiting transportation back to the States. Eventually in late May we got a ship and were able to get back "home" to California.

On the voyage back I was placed in a cabin just above the engine room. It was like a steam room. Four times a day a man brought a bucket of water with ice floating in it. In between trips one of the men in the same cabin would go get water or soda pop for us.

One Sunday they had services in the officer's wardroom and I was picked up bodily and carried into the wardroom.

The service started and in the middle of communion we had a General Quarters. I didn't have a life jacket and my greatest fear was that a submarine would sink us, however, they secured from general quarters and we started back with the religious service, only to be jolted again by another General Quarters. I was really afraid then.

After firing a few shots and several machine gun fire they again secured from General Quarters.

The skipper was PO'ed because the first General Quarters was sort of sloppy and he had another go at it.

Back to religious services. I was put up to receive the wine. The priest gave me two "slugs." I suppose I was a little ashen and maybe he thought I needed it. I really did. It did help me calm down.

We went into port at Pearl Harbor for supplies, then finally hit San Francisco.

I was assigned to a receiving hospital at San Francisco. I was there for about a week, then transferred to Camp Lejeune in North Carolina and after a few weeks there, I was transferred to the Naval Hospital at Naval Air Station at Jacksonville, Florida. I was there until a week after the atomic bomb was dropped on Hiroshima.

I was given a medical discharge on August 22, 1945.

That ended my naval career. I was on active combat duty only 28 days. The rest of the time was spent in the District Intelligence Office, 7th Naval District, Miami, Florida.

I am 73 years old. Fifty one years after I was wounded off the Coast of Formosa. I have been awarded a 30% disability rating for my bad knee and 20% for back injury. The wound on my right leg has never closed. It still seeps blood and plasma and the scar tissue is easily abraded.

You would think 20% and 30% would add to 50%, NO WAY, the Veterans Administration awarded 30% for the knee involvement. They reason that the body is 70% efficient so the 20% is rated on the basis of 70% which is 14% making the combined rating at 30% plus 14%, 44% compensated down to 40%. I have battled with the Veterans Administration for 45 years. I have given up now—GOD BLESS AMERICA!

THE AFTERMATH OF THE ATTACK OF JANUARY 21

by J. Maury Werth, Captain, United States Navy retired

At each of the reunions which I have attended, I have heard a number of men discuss why *Ticonderoga* received no official "recognitions" for service in World War II, though she did get such for service in subsequent combat and space programs, so here is what I learned in 1945, subsequent to January 21 and prior to our return to the forward area in the closing days of the war. As most may recall, *Ticonderoga* was not at General Quarters or Condition I (for damage control) at the time that the first kamikaze hit.

As many may know, the second kamikaze aimed to the forward Mk 37 director, and came aboard about a foot above the deck of forward AA control hitting the center of the supporting base of the Mk 37. The resulting explosion not only wiped out all there (with the exception of the crew inside the Mk 37!!), but it also killed and wounded many on the open bridge. The air officer was killed, and both the commanding officer and the executive officer were wounded. What also occurred is that even after the first kamikaze, neither the forward conn (the heavily armored pilot house) nor the after conn, similarly armored, the battle stations of the captain and the executive officer, were ever "buttoned up." No bomb fragments from the enemy penetrated the overhead of the pilot house, which was the commanding officer's battle station, with very thick spinter shields to protect the survival of the commanding officer. Yet neither the commanding officer nor the executive officer were inside their battle stations when the second plane hit, and both were wounded. Since Commander Fulmer, the gunnery officer was killed, I was acting gunnery officer until they could get a commander to take over back in the United States.

It was in my capacity as gunnery officer that I went over to Pac Fleet Headquarters on our way back to the United States to inquire about our repairs, and while there to find out what were the findings on our last action reports.

The action report was not yet in any final form there, but what was called Battle Reports was in draft form. Battle Reports/Action reports were always drafted as quickly as possible, to glean "lessons learned" of both enemy tactics etc., plus actions taken by our forces and units. These were drafted on a fairly fast track, to pass the information back to fleet for their immediate use, defensively and offensively. There were already rumblings of a board of investigation as to performance of *Ticonderoga* in the kamikaze attacks. The performance of the crew in fighting the fires was exemplary. Also cited was the navigator, Commander Chase, who, at General Quarters relieves as officer of the deck and who insisted, over the objections of the captain, to making several sharp turns to starboard, so that the hanger deck could be cleared of burning gasoline, and some burning planes pushed over the side.

The first and most glaring major fault cited was the failure of Kiefer, the commanding officer to keep the ship at General Quarters for AA, and in Condition I for damage control before the first plane hit us. The CINPAC staffers pointed out that it had long been the practice, even before the kamikaze campaign began, to have all ships, particularly carriers (the preferred target of Japanese air attacks, just as it was our Navy's) that ships should remain at General Quarters from the first launch to the last landing of strike aircraft. Japanese liked to follow them back to find us. Reviewers had also found fault with the wounding of the captain and the executive officer. Both of their battle stations were inside the much more heavily protected pilot house and secondary conn, because survival of command was and is a major consideration in battle. They had subordinates who were responsible for fire fighting and damage control. They cited that shouting down from the bridge added nothing to the effectiveness of fire fighting on the flight deck.

Since I was the senior survivor of the Gunnery/AA Department, they first asked me why the ship had not stayed at General Quarters with the gun batteries. I could only answer that it was the captains decision. Since I, on air defense aft on morning General Quarter, was on the common circuit with Commander Fulmer and the bridge. When Fulmer protested to the bridge at standing down from General Quarter, the captain said "the men have worked hard and I want them all to have a good noon meal."

They asked me if the damage control officer had protested, to which I answered that I did not know. I was not on that circuit. As to why the pilot house and secondary conn had not been bottled up at any time after morning General Quarter, I had no answer to that either. I was only a lieutenant, and there were commanders and several lieutenant commanders still alive, even after the first plane had hit us, which included the air officer, Fulmer and the chief engineer, Briner. So they dropped that line of questioning, after asking the navigators views and actions.

They did not ask any more questions on Commander Briner since he already had the plant on all boilers for full speed to launch and land.

When we went through Hawaii on our return to the war zone, I again dropped by CINPAC.

The position then had been very straight forward. Since battle wounding had taken Captain Keifer out as continuing to commanding officer of *Ticonderoga*, any action against him for recall was not possible. Any official notice condemnation of him at that point in time would only hurt morale on *Ticonderoga*, if word got back to the ship.

They pointed out that Bull Halsey was almost relieved for cause after the debacle in the typhoon that resulted in the loss of three destroyers, with most of their crews, along with damage to a number of ships that the Japanese had not been able to even damage. And shortly thereafter, Halsey again came very close to causing what would have been the greatest loss of ships, and the entire MacArthur landing forces in the Leyte landings. That landing and the enormous amphibious group was saved, as history now records, by the pilots from the jeep carriers, and for the essentially suicidal assault on the huge Japanese battle fleet which had come through St. Bernadino Straits when Halsey had been decoyed to the north, and he had even failed to leave Admiral Lee's powerful units to cover that strait. Here again, Halsey had become such a hero in the eyes of the public and the fleet, that morale of the fleet took precedence, and he stayed on.

Lt. Perkins and officers of UB80 gathered around cake presented him by Cmdr. Burch for making 1,000th landing aboard "Big T". (Courtesy of James H. Klein)

The Captain and Officers of the
U.S.S. Ticonderoga
request the honor of your presence
on the occasion of the commissioning of the
U.S.S. Ticonderoga
Norfolk Navy Yard, Portsmouth, Virginia
May 8th nineteen hundred and forty four
at two o'clock P.M.

R.S.V.P.
The Commanding Officer   Newport News Shipbuilding & Drydock Co.
U.S.S. Ticonderoga   over   Newport News, Virginia

A copy of the invitation for the commissioning of the USS Ticonderoga, May 8, 1944. (Courtesy of James H. Klein)

In a leadership seminar, years later, I heard a summary which perhaps fitted Dixie.

"Leadership to bring a green, largely untried crew to battle readiness and professional competence can be done by a kindhearted and even a gentle leader, but when a unit moves into a war zone and into the indescribable violence of combat, hard, nearly harsh leadership is the key to victory or even survival."

"Kindness can kill ones own."

"Morale is not happiness...an idiot can be happy."

Douglas Southall Freeman at the Naval War College, 1949.

In closing I believe it is appropriate to add the following:

I can certainly testify personally to Dixie's thoughtfulness. I had been the #1 officer-of-the-deck soon after we left for the Pacific, drawing only night watches under weigh. When he was about to carry wounded off the ship, he had to sign fitness reports. I saw my final one from him when I went through the bureau several years later. We had crossed out all of the low marks which had been given to me (probably by the executive officer) and raised them. The principal reason that they were so low is not a part of this account.

KIA List
USS *Ticonderoga* CV-14

World War II
Ship's Company

John J. Agoglia, S1/C
Frank Alesi, COX
Raymond K. Allen, S1/C
Thomas L. Armstrong, BM2/c
George J. Arnett, PHM3/c
Emmett A. Bates, S1/C
Paul M. Bayes, AMMH1/c
Jesse G. Beasley, S1/C
Alfred M. Beauregard, S2/c
LT Reynolds F. Bess
James F. Blair, S1/C
Kenneth P Bluzard, S2/c
Thomas J. Burke, S1/C
Harry G. Burns Jr., AMM3/c
Constantino G. Busso, S1/c
Domenic Campagnone, S1/C
William H. Campbell, S1/C
Benjamin L. Cannady Jr., GM3/c
James P. Cardwell, PFC (USMC)
Byron D. Conner, S2/c
Stanley R. Conniff, S1/C
ENS John N. Cowan
John B. Cox, AM3/c
Jewet J. Cranford, COX
George W. Croley, CSMP
Claude B. Culvahouse, S2/c
Louis Czako, CM2/c
Philip M. Damico, S2/c
Robert L. Darling, S1/C
Eldred E. Daugherty, S1/C
James H. Dickens, SK
J.C. Dillard, S1/C
CDR Henry R. Dozier (CARDIV6)
Donald R. Duryea, S1/C
Calvin F. Fagley Jr., S1/C
Joseph L. Fallacaro, S2/c
Alfonso Faniel, STM1/c
Nicholas W. Frassa, S1/c
Robert E. Frazier, S1/c
CDR Herbert S. Fulmer Jr.
Frank A. Gaipa, S1/c
Carl S. Gaworecki, MM3/c
John N. Geis S2/c
LTJG Edward E. Gray
ENS Edgar A. Gregory
James E. Grubbs, S2/c
William F. Gunn, S2/c
Benjamin A. Guzman, S2/c
Beaufort Hall, STM2/c
Kenneth C. Hawkins, AMM3/c
Eugene Herrick, S2/c
James H. Higgins, S1/c
John L. Hilton, S2/c
David B. Hoehler, S2/c
John R. Hoehn Jr., PFC (USMC)
Charles J. Hollenstein, S2/c
Therman N. Holloway, ST3/c
Noah Horn, Y1/c
Julius J. Horvath, S2/c
John A. Hrosovsky, S1/c
Jospeh C. Hubiak, S1/c
John V. Hughes, PHOM1/c
Frank W. Jackson, STM1/c
Over D. Jackson, STM1/c
Kenneth G. Jambor, RT2/c
James Jeppesen, F1/c
Arthur E. Johanson, S1/c
Warren Jones GM3/c
Joseph Josick, AMM3/c
William Kean, S1/c
LT John J. Kelley, 3RD
Kenneth W. Kenny, COX

LT Owen D. Kerens
Calvin C. Kessinger, AMM2/c
Norbert S. Ketza, PHM3/c
Charles B. King, S1/C
Michael A. Koenig, S1/C
Peter J. Kooistra, S2/c
John M. Kulick Jr., RT3/c
William J. Lacalamito, S1/C
George W. Lachner, S1/c
Anthony H. Landi, S1/c
LT John S. Lavin
Bernard Lifland, S1/c
Essie D. Loucks, S1/c
Thomas Lovetere, S1/c
Douglas J. MacDonald, S1/c
John P. MacDonald Sr., COX
Kenny Magee, S1/c
Miles M. Maher, S2/c
Thomas N. Mainer Jr., FC3/c
Matt A. Mallon, AMM3/c
Carl F. Masch, ARM3/c
Edward J. Mazur, MMS3/c
Gladwell E. McCain, S1/c
William E. McCravy, S1/c
Edell McDade, STM1/c
Albert McIntyre, S1/c
Lowell D. McNeely, S1/c
Edward X. Menard, S2/c
Joseph A. Mikulcik, S2/c
CDR Clair L. Miller
Dominic A. Mittiga, SK2/c
Barney C. Morgan, S2/c
Arnold W. Mundel, COX
James E. Myers Jr., S1/c
Joseph A. Narducci, S1/c
Victor D. Nocki, S1/c
Sanford O. Olson, BM2/c
Joseph F. Oppedisano, AMM2/c
Anthony M. Patterson, S2/c
Garnet G. Porter, S1/c
Kenneth F. Rafferty, S1/c
John L. Rafter, S2/c
Stuart Rambo Jr., S2/c
Joseph L. Redmond, S1/c
Aldo Riciardello, RM1/c
Richard L. Robbins, AMM2/c
Ephraim J. Rodriguez, S1/c
Robert L. Selbe, AMM3/c
Billy B. Shelley, S2/c
Glenn W. Smiley, AMM1/c
William O. Staufner, S1/c
Dote Stone, S1/c
Sammy T. Stovall Jr., S2/c
James W. Tarver, S2/c
LT George A. Taylor
Cecil P. Terhune, S2/c
Jack Thanes Jr., S2/c
Floyd W. Thomas, S2/c
Vernon H. Thomas, S2/c
Eugene S. Thompson, S1/c
Manley N. Turner, BM2/c
Keith M. Usher, AMM1/c
William P. Valentine, S2/c
Donald W. Vincent, S1/c
Clyde E. Walker, S1/c
Eddie M. Warren, S2/c
ENS Everett T. Wehr
Horace A. Williams, BM2/c
William C. Wilson Jr., AOM2/c
Earl J. Winthrop, COX
Edmund A. Wollaston Jr., S2/c
Edward J. Wood, S1/c

Air Group 80

William B. Alexander, ARM2/c
LT Edward H. Bagley Jr.
Dan G. Booth, AOM2/c
Albert Boyer Jr., ARM3/c

Arnold C. Burnett, AMM2/c
ENS John D. Cozza
LTJG Robet F. Dickiinson
LTJG George F. Eckert Jr.
ENS Choise D. Fisher
ENS David F. Greenhagen
John E. Griffith, ARM2/c
LTJG Billie P. Hall
Charles Head Jr., AMM2/c
ENS George B. Jackson
ENS Lawrence C. Jensen Jr.
Nicholes Katsaros, ARM2/c
William W. King, ARM3/c
ENS Joseph E. Kluczinski
ENS John S. Manchester
LTJG Philip J. Manella
Russell D. Mason, ARM3/c
ENS Garland M. McGehee
Joseph T. McHugh, ARM3/c
LTJG Wayne L. Minnick
ENS William M. Nettles
LTJG Robert H. O'Reilly
LTJG John G. Patterson
Francis T. Piet,Jr., ARM2/c
ENS Edwin D. Ruegg
LT Frederick G. Tyler
Andrew A. Wadosky, ARM2/c
LTJG Robert C. Wagg
Kenneth R. Wagner, ARM2/c
Benjamin J. Walla, ARM2/c
ENS Robert K.H. Weeks
Lawrence W. Youngless, AMM2/c

Air Group 87

Normand R. Brissette, ARM3/c
LT Granville W. Cowan
Kenneth W. Grout, ARM2/c
CDR Porter W. Maxwell
LT William L. Peterson Jr.
LTJG Raymond Porter
LTJG Andrew J. Sawyer Jr.
ENS Thomas G. Schaefer
ENS William Stanley
LTJG Eppa L. Vaughan
ENS Cyrus H. Walker

Vietnam War CVA-14
Ship's Company

Edward W. White, SKC
Joe L. Williams, AO1

Airwing Squadrons

LT Richard W. Hastings	VF-51
LT Thomas B. Fallen	VF-53
LTJG Stephen G. Richardson	VF-53
LCDR Michael W. Wallace	VF-63
LT Peter F. Chemey	VF-191
LT Robert L. Miller	VF-191
LT Frank H. Harrington	VF-194
LT Michael T. Newell	VF-194
PR3 Stephen C. Cooper	VA-23
ADJ2 Ronnie L. Crepeau	VA-23
LCDR Lawrence D. Gosen	VA-23
LTJG Marlow E. Madsen	VA-52
CDR. John C. Mape	VA-52
LTJG Douglas M. Webster	VA-56
LT Richard D. Benning	VA-112
LTJG John V. McCormick	VA-144
LTJG Gerald L. Pinneker	VA-144
Capt. Michael J. Estocin	VA-192
LCDR Robert C. McMahan	VA-194
LCDR Chester L. Nightengale Jr.	VAW-195
AMH3 James L. Rush	VAW-13
AN Charles O. Dixon Jr.	Patron 4

USS *TICONDEROGA* CV-CVA-CVS 14
COMMANDINNG OFFICERS

Captain Dixie Kiefer, USN	1944-45
Cdr. Harmon V. Briner, USN	1945
Captain Giles E. Short, USN	1945
Captain William Sinton, USN	1945-46
Cdr. Warren R. Thompson, USN	1946
Lt. Cdr. W. J. Pendola, USN	1946
Cdr. Warren R. Thompson, USN	1946-47
Captain Paul W. Watson, USN	1952
Cdr. Arthur T. Decker, USN	1952
Captain William A. Schoech, USN	1954-55
Captain Andrew M. Jackson, USN	1955-56
Cdr. Harold C. Miller, USN	1956
Captain William A. Stuart, USN	1956-57
Captain Irwin Chase, Jr., USN	1957-58
Captain Wilson M. Coleman, USN	1958-59
Captain Turner F. Caldwell, USN	1959-60
Captain Robert F. Farrington, USN	1960-61
Captain Eugene G. Fairfax, USN	1961-62
Captain James G. Daniels, USN	1962-63
Captain John P. Weinel, USN	1963-64
Captain Damon W. Cooper, USN	1965-66
Captain Martin G. O'Neill, USN	1966
Captain James B. Cain, USN	1966
Captain Ward Miller, USN	1966-67
Captain Norman K. McInnis, USN	1967-68
Captain Richard E. Fowler, Jr.	1968-69
Captain William H. McLaughlin, USN	1969-70
Captain Edward A. Boyd, USN	1970-72
Captain Frank T. Hemler, USN	1972
Captain Norman K. Green, USN	1972-73
Captain George W. Bruce, USN	1973

9 Jan. 1947 to 31 Jan. 1952 in reserve.
4 Apr. 1952 to 11 Sept. 1954 SCB-27C conversion.

USS Ticonderoga *(Photography by Bruce Trombecky, courtesy of U.S. Navy Pacific Missile Test Center)*

The Many Faces of Ticonderoga

**1862-1887
STEAM SLOOP**

**1917-1918
TRANSPORT**

USS TICONDEROGA

IN MARE IN CAELESTIS

GUARDIAN OF FREEDOM

**1814-1825
ARMED SCHOONER**

USS Ticonderoga Association Veterans' Biographies

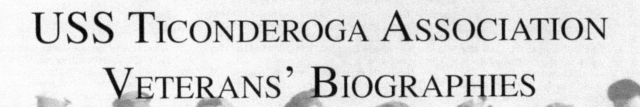

RICHARD ALFONSO, born June 8, 1923, New Bedford, MA. Enlisted in the USN in April 1942 and attended boot camp at Great Lakes Naval Training. From there he joined the USS *Card* and came to the Atlantic to hunt submarines, clearing the way for the invasion of Normandy. Transferred to the USS *Ticonderoga* in August 1944. Participated in the Battle of the Gulfs and Philippines and later served aboard the USS *Adirondack*.

On Jan. 21, 1945, he was in the attack on the Big "T". He was between watches, in his bunk below deck, reading. He heard GQ at approximately 12 noon. The Japanese planes were coming straight out of the sun at them. He ran up top deck to his GQ station, in radio central in the bridge. He sat at his station with his phones on, typing code, along with RM1/c George Olsen, Lt. Gwertz and others. There was a lot of commotion and gunfire, 5-inch, 40mm and 20mm. When he heard 20mm going off, he knew they were close. Suddenly they lost all communications topside. He took over with the JS phones. He was standing by the table with the joe pot, which was not turned off. Suddenly they heard a large explosion, which was a bomb going off in the hanger deck. Kamikaze Betty had hit the bridge. It knocked them all down to the deck. He fell forward to the deck and the joe pot fell over, spilling hot coffee all over his back. He thought the warm feeling was blood and started calling for a medic. The guys laughed about that all the way back to the States. Fortunately no one was injured in the radio shack. Except his ego.

Discharged in October 1945 with the rank of RM2/c. Married and has four children. He is currently semi-retired and continues to work for Maytag Corp.

RICHARD P. ALLEN, LT USN, born August 1928, in Chicago, IL. Commissioned January 1949; designated naval aviator September 1950 and joined *Ticonderoga* as assistant navigator in August 1957.

He served 13 months in WESTPAC as navigation division officer, OD/UW, SWO under navigators: Cdrs. Hal Vita and George Meyer. Capt. Irwin Chase, a fine man and great skipper, taught him all about navigation and watch standing. He completed two years on *Ticonderoga* in July 1959.

Retired as CDR, USN in 1970. His awards include the Air Medal w/star, European Occupation Medal, Korean Defense Medal, Expeditionary Medal, Vietnam Service Medal, Vietnam Campaign Medal w/Device, Navy Unit Commendation, National Defense Service Medal w/star.

Joined Lockheed Corp. in 1972 and retired as division manager for logistics/material at San Jose, CA in 1993. Currently playing a lot of golf. Married for 46 years to Joyce; they have five children and eight grandchildren.

GEORGE K. AMES, born in Capeville, Va. Prior to joining the Navy he worked on the construction of the USS *Ticonderoga*. Enlisted in the USN on Jan. 25,

1944, on his 18th birthday, and attended boot camp at Great Lakes, IL. He attended the Navy Electronic Schools and graduated from Primary School at Navy Pier, Chicago, on March 9, 1945, with the rank of ET2/c.

Was assigned to the *Ticonderoga* on March 29, 1945, at the Bremerton Navy Yard and was assigned to the K1 Div., with battle stations alternating between Radio Room 1 and 2. Participated in the Asiatic Pacific Area Campaign and arrived off Iwo Jima on the night that correspondent Ernie Pyle was killed and left after Japan surrendered.

Memorable experiences were of Okinawa, the Battle of Japan. His most satisfying experience was determining the cause and cure for the burps in the VHF receivers being used on the admiral's bridge. This project earned him the nickname "Megacycle Pete" and a promotion to ET1/c.

Helped decommission the *Ticonderoga* and was discharged on May 19, 1946, with the rank of ET1/c.

Married Freida and had a son, George K. and daughter, Susan A. Srite; and two grandchildren, Eric and Brian Srite.

Attended the Virginia Polytechnic Institute in 1950 as a power electrical engineer. Worked for Olin Chemical Corp. for 36 years and retired on Feb. 28, 1986. He holds one patent.

FRANK J. ANCI, born Oct. 15, 1925, Jamaica, Long Island, NY. Enlisted in the USN on Jan. 26, 1944, was sent to Sampson Boot Camp on February 2 for six weeks; and then to Newport, RI, for Big "T" detail. Arrived at the Big "T" on May 7 and was assigned to the 5th Div., Deck, forward 40mm guns. As messenger, on the bridge watches, he became first quality helmsman. Was made S1/c and was in charge of the motor whale boat #1 and operating the aft crane.

On January 21 he lunched with the mess cooks and went to the forward hangar deck to play cards with Gould and Terriel. Guns began firing and they ran to an opening to see the Japanese plane. They ran to their gun stations; GQ sounded; top of the ladder to forecastle deck; the first plane was hit on the bow. They knew the second plane was hit; the wounded were being brought up to the forecastle deck. They stood at their battle stations.

Memorable experiences were having Capt. Dixie Kiefer as their ARE man 14 command; morale of the ship's company; flying of the Victory Flag on all ships when the 3rd Fleet merged at the end of the war, they were wet behind the ears, but they grew up fast.

Later he made Coxswain and helped decommission the ship. He was discharged on April 15, 1946, three weeks shy of two years on the Big "T", with the rank of coxswain3/c.

At home he entered his father's business, a superette market until 1983. Since 1985 he has been editor of the Big "T" newsletter.

Married Carol Apicard on Nov. 27, 1965, and they have two children, Diane C. and Christopher F. He is currently a produce manager in a supermarket.

J.B. ANDERSON, born March 27, 1916, Snyder, OK. Enlisted in the USN on April 19, 1942, and attended boot training and Rangefinder School in San Diego, CA. Was assigned on the USS *Sangamon* in Norfolk VA, during the North African invasion and also the USS *Ranger*. On May 8, 1944, he was assigned to the USS *Ticonderoga*. Sailed to the West Coast via Panama Canal and on to the Philippines. Participated in the North African Invasion and the Philippines.

Memorable experience was the kamikaze attack on Jan. 21, 1945. At about 12:30 pm, GQ sounded. He manned his battle station, a five inch gun director on the bridge and was alerted to the bogies overhead. One kamikaze came through and scored a direct hit near the five inch gun director. An explosion blew the hatch open where he was standing and broke his left leg and knee, received second and third degree burns on his face, hands and legs. Seaman Woods rescued him and saved his life, receiving a Silver Star for bravery.

In Oceanside, CA, he received treatment, skin grafts and therapy. He received medical discharge on Oct. 15, 1945, with the rank of FC1/c. Awards include the ETO and Purple Heart.

Married and has three children and five grandchildren. Retired from the US Postal Service, living in Ephrata, WA.

JOHN ROBERT ARMBRUST, born Feb. 27, 1924, Continental, OH. Enlisted in the USN on May 11, 1943, and attended boot camp at the NTS Great Lakes, IL. Afterwards he was stationed at Lakehurst, NJ, and was assigned to the captain's office.

When requests for volunteers to serve on the USS *Ticonderoga* (CV-14) came, he volunteered and was assigned to K Div., where he was on board for the shakedown. He was in the executive office and later transferred to the engineering office. He was on duty in the office on Jan. 21, 1945, when GQ was sounded. He ran to his battle station in damage control when the first kamikaze hit. He served in the battles of Pacific Fleet during 1944 until the end of the war. He also served with the Blimp Sqdn. #12, Blimp Sqdn. #1 at USNB Bremerton, WA. Discharged in Bremerton, WA, on April 17, 1946, Y2/c.

Married his childhood sweetheart on July 1, 1949, and has three daughters, one granddaughter and one grandson. Retired from W-S Life after 29 years.

TRUMAN BRADLEY BAKER (BRAD) left his home in San Simeon, CA, and joined the USMC on April 27, 1960, his 19th birthday. After learning that sea-going Marines received their "blues" gratis, he signed up for sea duty.

Boarded the USS *Ticonderoga* in November 1960, and was part of the West Pac cruise from May 1961 to January 1962. For him the tour was largely uneventful, with the exception of riding out a typhoon in the Philippines (the waves did crash over the flight deck); and nearly being blown off the flight deck by jet exhaust (missed the edge by one and one half feet). Although

Vietnam was unheard of then, not noted as a stop in the yearbook, the "Ti" cruised offshore there while the pilots flew missions.

As part of his duties, he was assigned to security for Capt. Fairfax. One night, while the ship was en route from San Diego to San Francisco, he was called to the bridge. He arrived with trepidation, fearing that he might be in trouble, but the captain said, " I thought you'd like to see your house," as he pointed to a light along the cliffs of San Simeon, just north of the Piedras Blancas lighthouse. What a sight to see home as the carrier cruised past!

After he left the "Ti", he was assigned to accompany Clark's Raiders during the Cuban Missile Crisis. He ended up in the 2nd Bn., 5th Marines (H&S Co.), but was transferred to the 11th Marines one month before the 5th Marines left for Vietnam. Of his former company, approximately 15 men returned.

After his discharge in 1964, he served as a patrol officer for 15 years on the LAPD. Now retired, he has returned to the California coast, and is living in Morro Bay with his wife, Diane. He has a daughter and son from his first marriage and no grandchildren yet.

LEE R. BALDERSTON, LCDR, SC, USN, born June 5, 1926, in Omaha, NE. He enlisted in the USN Sept. 13, 1943, and was assigned to Acorn 35 and stationed on Tinian July 1944 to July 1945. Transferred to NROTC Unit, University of Idaho and discharged June 1946 as BM3.

Graduated from Idaho in May 1949 and was commissioned ensign in Supply Corps, USN. Served on USS *Dixie*; USS *Samuel N. Moore*; Astoria, OR; Adak, AK; Great Lakes, IL; and was Stores Div. Officer and assistant supply officer aboard *Ticonderoga* from August 1958-August 1960. At Naval School, Transportation Management; Naval Supply Center, Oakland, CA, and Joint Task Force 8, Oakland, CA.

He retired Sept. 30, 1966, and is proud to have served on *Ticonderoga* during a period when *Ti* went from last in the run for the Battle Efficiency Pennant to winning the "E."

Balderston is happily married and has five children and 12 grandchildren.

LEMUEL EDWARD BECK SR., born March 28, 1938, Hannibal, MO. Enlisted on June 12, 1956, served aboard the USS *Ticonderoga*, USS *Princeton*, USS *Iwo Jima* and USS *Constiation*; and was stationed at NAS Olathe, KS and NAS Grosseile, MI. Participated in battle at Formosa Straights, Quomey and Matsu Island crisis in 1958.

Memorable experiences were crossing the equator in April 1957 and when an AD blew up and caught fire aboard the ship.

Discharged on Dec. 6, 1966, from active duty with the rank of E-6. As of June 12, 1996, he had 40 years in the USN and USNR. Awards include the Expeditionary Medal, Good Conduct Medal, National Defense Medal and Naval Reserve Pistol Qualification.

Married to Mary and has a son, daughter and four grandchildren. Works as a factory worker and part-time farmer.

LESTER L. BENJAMIN, born June 24, 1914, Iola, KS. Enlisted at Des Moines, IA, on June 14, 1943, in the USNR. Was assigned as an aviation machinists mate with Div. V-2, with the rank of S2/c. Attended boot camp at Farragut, ID, on June 24, 1943, his 29th birthday, and then to Norman, OK, for 21 weeks of AMM School and training with the Marines. His next base was Lee Field, FL; advance schooling; and the start of plane captain training. His next stop was Alameda, CA, for full time training as a plane captain on SNJ trainer planes.

His orders came for them to join the Casu 6. They were being transferred to the world's best and one of the largest aircraft carriers that the Navy had at that time. Soon after they got out of dry dock at Bremerton, WA, they were allowed to volunteer for the plane they prepared to be plane captain on. His hand was one of the first to be captain of that neat "hellcat" and a perfect choice it was. However, a vacancy came up for a mechanic to take charge of the tool room that supplied all the tools on the flight deck that were needed by the plane captains. When the chiefs asked him if he would like the job since his trade as a civilian was auto mechanic, he said yes. Then they decided he could also be an emergency plane captain. The last few weeks of the action, he was put in charge as speaker of the ready room number two. At this time they brought "Railroad Riley" from the officers mess to work with him and he was in charge of the tool room while Benjamin was in the ready room or on an emergency plane captain situation. Railroad was a very special shipmate, and hopes he is still with them.

At the time of his discharge he was rated S2/c (AMM). Awards include the Victory Medal, Asiatic-Pacific w/two stars, American Area, Point system.

His wife passed away on Aug. 5, 1986. They had one daughter, two sons, two granddaughters, one grandson, three great-granddaughters and one great-grandson. He retired on Dec. 28, 1982. His last 10 years, he worked for the city of Union City, Union City, CA, as a mechanic and assistant supervisor of the maintenance department. Prior to that time he had worked as either an auto mechanic for service manager for dealerships in Iowa and California. These dealerships were Chrysler, Hudson, General Motors (Pontiac, Oldsmobile and Chevrolet Div.), Ford, Toyota, Nissan, Triumph, Volvo and Mazda. He now spends his time taking care of his home in San Leandro, CA, and belongs to VFW. He takes as many trips as possible and tries to stay in touch with his friends. He thanks all of the wonderful shipmates he met. It was a privilege to serve with such wonderful and dedicated people on the very best ship. He would be glad to hear from any of them and wishes the best of health to all of them.

ONOFRIO BIVIANO, born Aug. 24, 1925, Brooklyn, NY. Enlisted and was inducted on Jan. 24, 1944, with the USN and entered active service in New York, NY. Attended recruit training at Sampson, NY; and was assigned to MMR3/c, A Div. and stationed in the Asiatic Pacific. He participated in all WWII USS *Ticonderoga* battles.

Discharged on March 3, 1946, with the rank of MMR3/c. Awards include the Asiatic Pacific Medal w/four stars, Philippine Liberation Medal, American Theater Medal and WWII Victory Medal.

During the war when the ship was hit by two kamikazes, he was ordered up from below to help fight the fires on the flight deck which burned for a week. This was the worst disaster on the Big "T" and they limped to port still burning. They lost a significant portion of their crew that fateful day, possibly half.

Married Rose and has two sons, Salvatore and Anthony, and a daughter, Rosemarie. His wife passed away in 1994. He is now living in South Florida, owner of a local restaurant and is also in real estate rental and development.

SAL BONFIGLIO joined the USN in December 1943. He attended boot camp in Sampson, NY, and from there he was assigned to the USS *Ticonderoga* and was a member of the photo lab.

He had an early lunch on Jan. 21, 1945, as he was photographing landings from the port side of the flight deck. He heard gunfire and looked up and saw a kamikaze plane dive towards the bridge. He photographed the plane as it pulled out and veered to the right but it was followed by a second kamikaze plane which hit the deck. He then went to the starboard side to help the medics with the wounded.

After the war he was married and they had four children and five grandchildren. He was employed by the Florida and New York race tracks in their photo lab. In 1966 he moved to Florida and became president of a labor organization, which was a stage and motion picture union. He is not retired and lives in Ocala, FL, on five acres. He hopes to attend the next reunion and has donated a 16mm film from their tour of duty in January which shows the kamikaze attack.

THOMAS BANCROFT BRAINE, born Oct. 27, 1914, New York City, NY. Enlisted on May 1, 1941, and was stationed at NAS, Floyd Bennett, Brooklyn, NY; NAS, Atlantic City, NY; and CASU 23, Willow Grove, PA. Served aboard the USS *Ticonderoga*, Pacific Fleet, from the fall of 1944 until spring of 1945.

Memorable experiences include the Battle of the Atlantic; antisubmarine patrol; German submarines; China Sea; protecting the US shipping lanes in the Atlantic; servicing fleet and aircraft at CASU5; attacking the Asian coast line in the Battle of the China Sea; advancing from S2/c to AC1/c; ensign to lieutenant to operations officer CASU 23; and flight deck officer on the *Ticonderoga*.

On Jan. 21, 1945, the US fleet, including the USS *Ticonderoga*, was sailing northward in the China Sea to attack the seacoast from Hong Kong to Formosa. Having battled for days the furious 125-foot waves of a typhoon off the Chinese coast, he was taking a breather in the ward room, getting some lunch when, suddenly, all hell broke loose with the antiaircraft 40's and 5-inch guns and the GQ gong. He headed for the gangway via the hangar deck to his GQ flight deck station. Seconds before he would have emerged onto the hangar deck, he heard a sickening crash, followed by a blinding flash, which burned his eyes, and a tremendous explosion. A blast of lead-filled air rushed over his head like the death wind of the elements. "It's our turn," he thought inconsequentially as he tumbled with the sprawling mass of men blown back and down the ladder from the hangar deck to the ward room. Confusion and fire swept the ward room area as flaming gasoline poured in. Two black sailors risked their lives to close the hatch to the hangar deck.

After subduing the local fires in the ward room, he and Lt. George Martin ran to the third deck. Finding refuge in a stateroom, they called topside for help to get them out of the ghastly, smoke-filled third deck area.

Help finally arrived in a special detail from topside with permission to break water-tight integrity on the port side, which had been intentionally flooded to stop the spread of fire.

Their flight from third deck, led by an air plot chief, was immediately interrupted by another agonizing, blasting barrage of antiaircraft fire, presumably at and as the second kamikaze hurtled itself at the bridge. With a loud, jarring thud that shook the ship, the antiaircraft barrage suddenly stopped. They learned later that this kamikaze, which struck the bridge, had wounded Capt. Dixie Kieffer and AAO Ace Barton and killed AO Clair Miller. They pursued their escape aft, aiding the wounded as they advanced. Finally, with gasping, aching lungs, they emerged at the fantail and, thank God, found fresh air.

His right lung collapsed the next day. When they returned to Bremerton Navy Yard for repairs, he was transferred to Bremerton Naval Hospital for treatment and recovery. By the time he was returned to duty, Hiroshima had been leveled by a nuclear bomb. He was ordered for separation and released from duty in November 1945 with the rank of lieutenant.

Married and has two children. He is now a retired part-time teacher and tennis coach.

PETER P. BROWN, born Feb. 26, 1921, in Whitman, MA. Enlisted in the USN on Aug. 25, 1942,

assigned to the Fargo Building, Boston, MA. Instead of boot camp, he was sent to Wentworth Institute to study diesel engineering. Upon completion he was transferred to the Sqdn. AB, Quincy, MA, where he was sent to Philadelphia, PA, to Steam and Oil Burning School.

Upon completion of his schooling, he was assigned to the USS *Ticonderoga* and went to Newport News, VA to await the ship's commissioning. His duties were below in Fire Room 2. On Jan. 21, 1945, he was off duty and he heard the guns go off, he could feel the vibration from the bombing and the firing of the 20mm and 40mm, during the kamikaze attack. He was on the starboard side trying to cross over to port to his battle station, Fire Room Control. In the smoke, confusion and darkness, it was impossible. At that time the burn and smoke victims were being brought to the sick bay, and he tried to assist some of those suffering smoke inhalation. Other memorable experiences include entering the China Seas; the typhoon; occupation of Japan; and stepping out on Japanese soil.

Awards include the Asiatic Pacific w/three stars and the Philippine Liberation w/two stars. Upon discharge on Feb. 21, 1946, he married Priscilla Chamberlain. They have four sons, one daughter, six grandchildren and one great-grandchild.

He retired as a union carpenter supervisor and now spends his time managing his income properties.

WINFRED LEON BUCKINGHAM CDR USN, graduated from the USN Academy in 1949 and from

Webb Institute of Naval Architecture in 1954. He was engineer officer of USS *Ticonderoga* (CVA-14) from June 1963-June 1965 during which period *Ticonderoga* was awarded the Navy Unit Commendation and a hash mark for the second award of the Engineering "E."

He was engineering officer of USS *Kitty Hawk* (CVA-63) July 1967-February 1969 during which time *Kitty Hawk* was awarded the Presidential Unit Citation.

Retired from the USN in 1969 and worked in shipbuilding for Litton Industries, Aerojet-General and Northern Natural Gas Co. before becoming a professor of construction management at Texas A&M University in 1978. Retired from TAMU in 1989 and moved to

boyhood hometown of Tyler, TX, where he now works as a volunteer with the Literacy Council of Tyler.

Buckingham is happily married to Kathryn and they have four children: Ken, Marcia, Cheryl and Tod.

CHESTER A. BURN, born Dec. 7, 1918, Leadville, CO. Joined the USN on Jan. 2, 1942, and attended boot camp in San Diego; was then sent to two Electrical Engineering Schools; then served on the USS *Arkansas*; and transferred to the USS *Ticonderoga* in time to be a plank owner.

On Jan. 21,1945, while eating lunch, GQ sounded and he rushed to his battle station in the forward repair station. He was thrown to the deck by the first explosion. Upon arrival at the station no electrician mates were there. When the gasoline started to come down from the damaged planes, he went around putting out fires and making electrical repairs. He needed help and some of the pilots assisted him. He helped the officer in charge of flooding the ammunition and bomb storage below them or the whole ship would have blown up. He participated in all of the *Ticonderoga* battles.

Discharged in December 1946, with the rank of chief electrical mate. He was awarded the Meritorious Service Medal.

After discharge, he went on to a higher education and taught electrical electronic engineering until he started selling and servicing industrial batteries.

Married and has two sons and a daughter. One of his sons is now a naval chief warrant officer. He is presently retired.

WILLIAM JOHN BUSH, born Aug. 27, 1913, Merced, CA. Enlisted in the USN on Oct. 28, 1942, in

San Francisco, CA. Served with the 85th NCB; USS *Stack* (DD-406); Operation Crossroads; USS *Frontier* (AD-25); USS *Sierra* (AD-18); USS *Piedmont* (AD-17); USS (AFDM-8); USS *Askari* (ARL-30); FLTTRAGRO, San Diego; USS *Ticonderoga*, 1962-65, damage control assistant; and USS *Prairie* (AD-15).

Memorable experiences were the Tonkin Gulf incident and Operation Crossroads when shots were fired on board *Stack* (DD-406).

Retired on July 31, 1972, with 30 years of active duty, and obtained the rank of LCDR USN. Awards include the Navy Commendation Medal w/combat V, Navy Achievement Medal, Navy Good Conduct Medal w/one Silver Star, China Service Medal, American Defense Service Medal, American Campaign Medal, Asiatic Pacific Campaign Medal, WWII Victory Medal, Navy Occupation Service Medal, Combat Action Ribbon, Presidential Unit Citation, Navy Unit Commendation w/two stars, National Defense Service Medal, Korean Service Medal, Air Force Expeditionary Medal, Vietnam Service Medal w/stars, UN Service Medal and Republic of Vietnam Campaign Medal.

Married Catherine Borke on Nov. 20, 1937, in San Mateo, CA. They have three children and six grandchildren.

LARRY M. CHRISMAN, born June 8, 1941, Wells County, IN. Enlisted in the USN on April 3, 1961, and was on the USS *Ticonderoga* (CVA-14) from December 1962-April 1965. He participated in two Far East Cruises.

Discharged on April 2, 1965, with rank of RM3.

Awards include the Navy Unit Commendation Ribbon, Vietnam and Armed Forces Expeditionary Medal.

Married and has one adopted daughter, two stepsons and one granddaughter. He currently works as a maintenance technician.

GROVER C. CHURCHILL, enlisted at Chattanooga, TN, in June 1948 after completing Central High School. Served aboard the USS *St. Paul* (CA-73) during Korea and COMCRUDESPAC staff aboard the USS *Dixie* (AD-14) and USS *Prairie* (AD-17). Was a USN recruiter at New Orleans, LA, and Jackson, MS; attended FT Schools in Washington, DC and Great Lakes, which was split by serving on the USS *Lyman K. Swenson* (DD-729); then the USS *Comstock* (LSD-19); and Fleet Gunnery School in San Diego, CA.

Served aboard the USS *Ticonderoga* (CVA-14) as a chief petty officer from 1962-67, with two war cruises to Vietnam. Transferred to Fleet Reserve in 1970 after instructor duty at Naval Amphibious School, Coronado, CA.

Worked in various shipyards in the States, China and Brazil; civil service at Long Beach Naval Shipyard from 1986 until retirement in March 1993.

ALBERT H. CLAYBURGH, born March 7, 1909, New York City, NY. Enlisted in the USN in August 1942 as an aviation volunteer and was stationed on the USS *Ticonderoga* at Hancock.

Discharged in September 1945 with the rank of lieutenant commander.

He is a widower with three children and lives in Greenwich, CT. He is now working as a New York sales manager with the Industrial Coating Group, Inc.

ROBERT T. COBB, born Dec. 3, 1925, New York City, NY. Enlisted on Nov. 8, 1943, as an A-A Antiaircraft machine guns classification with the 7th Div.

Military locations were Portsmouth, VA; Norfolk, VA; Big "T", 1944-45; South American; Parris Island, SC; Treasure Island; Alameda, CA; Kodiak, AK, 18 months; Marine Barracks, 8th and I Sts., Washington, DC; Naval Hospital NAS; NOB Kodiak, AK; US Naval Hospital, Pugent Sound, Navy yard, Seattle, WA; US Naval Hospital, Bethesda, MD; South Pacific Asiatic Theater; Marshall Islands; Carolina Islands; Philippine Islands; Yoka Suka, Japan, 1st USMC Expeditionary Force; various other naval installations; and served aboard the Freedom Train in 1946.

Participated in the battles at Pacific Theater; Okinawa; Philippine Islands; other areas of Asiatic Theater; also served in the American Theater and during the Korean War, July 5, 1950-Dec. 30, 1950.

Discharged on Nov. 11, 1943, the first time; September 1946, the second time; and Dec. 30, 1950, the third time. His final rank achieved was sergeant USMC. Awards include the Purple Heart, Philippine Presidential Unit Citation, Philippine Liberation w/two Gold Stars, Good Conduct w/two Bronze Stars, Asiatic Pacific Theater w/one Silver Star and four Gold Stars, Combat Action w/nine Gold Stars, Koreans Service and Navy Occupation Medal.

Has five sons, one daughter and eight grandchildren. He retired as a police chief.

RALPH F. COLGAIN JR., born Sept. 21, 1923, Wilmington, DE. Enlisted on Feb. 18, 1943. Attended Fire Control School and Advanced Fire Control School from May 1943 to April 1944, in Washington, DC. Was assigned to the USS *Ticonderoga* in May 1944, at Newport News shipyard, and became a plank owner in

February 1946. After a shakedown cruise he went through the canal and out to join the fleet in the Pacific War and took part in the Pacific War serving under Capt. Dixie Kiefer.

On January 21, around noon, after chow, he went to his compartment on the third deck down to have a smoke. When GQ sounded he ran up

the starboard ladder and was behind two other men on the ladder leading to the hangar deck where his gun director battle station was on the port side when the first kamikaze exploded through the flight deck, creating a wall of fire. The first man stepped off the ladder into his eternity and the man ahead of him and Colgain were knocked down the ladder but not hurt. His battle station had been destroyed by the explosion and was surrounded by fire. They found another ladder further back that led them to the flight deck where he found another fire controlman who was caught between his watch station on the island and battle station in FC Plot. The explosion had traumatized him and he was in state of confusion. He took him back toward the fantail. At this time the second kamikaze came in from the starboard side and hit their forward gun director on top of the island. Since his battle station direction had been wiped out by the first kamikaze he made his way forward to a 40mm director on the forward starboard corner of the flight deck and remained there until dark with another fire controlman.

After returning to the States for two months for repairs, they rejoined the fleet and stayed until the end of the war.

Discharged on Feb. 19, 1946, with the rank of FC2/c. Awards include the Philippine Liberation Medal, Pacific Medal and Good Conduct.

Attended the University of Delaware and later returned to the Washington, DC area where he met and married Frances. Was married 40 years before she passed away, of cancer, one week after their 40th anniversary. Has four children and five grandchildren. In Washington he became involved in Rocket Fuel Research in the days before sputnik. As a result he had the honor of being on a team of four men who developed the rocket fuel, unsymetrical dimethylhydrazine, which was used to power the LEM from the Apollo to the moon and lifted it off the moon to return it to the Apollo and is presently used to fire control rockets in spacecraft. After several years in research and development he went into industrial sales where he stayed until he retired. He is living in Rockville, MD. Naturally he is lonely but he still has four wonderful children and his grandchildren that love him. He also belongs to the Big "T" Assn. and enjoys their annual reunions.

JAMES E. CONNOLLY, born Sept. 25, 1938, Scranton, PA. Enlisted in the USN on July 5, 1956, as a radarman 2/c, OI Div. Attended basic training in Bainbridge, MD; Class A, Radarman School, Norfolk, VA, from October 1956-March 1957.

Boarded the USS *Ticonderoga* in Portsmouth, VA, in March 1957 and left for Alameda, CA, in April 1957. Ports included the Port of Spain, Trinidad, Valparaiso, Chile, Balboa and Panama Canal Zone. Arrived in Alameda, CA, on May 30, 1957. Departed Alameda, CA, in October 1957 for Far Eastern (West Pacific) cruise. His main ports of call were Pearl Harbor, HI; Yoksuka, Japan; Iwakuni, Japan; Subic Bay, Philippine Islands; Hong Kong; Okinawa; and Manila, Philippines Islands. Returned in May 1958 to San Francisco Naval Shipyard. He spent the summer of 1958 at Basic Electronics School, Treasure Island, CA.

Departed Alameda, CA, for his second Far East Cruise in September 1958. He visited the same ports of

call as the first cruise. Returned in March 1959 to San Francisco Naval Shipyard, then on to San Diego, CA, for carrier qualification landing duty in June 1959.

Honorably discharged on Oct. 12, 1959, San Diego Naval receiving station. His awards include the 1st Good Conduct Award, Armed Forces Reserve and Armed Forces Expeditionary Forces.

Married and has three children. He is vice president of sales for a steel and metal distributor.

RUDY D'AMICO joined the USNR in March 1948, after service in the USAAC from 1945-47. Serving five years as a reservist, he requested active duty on April 26, 1955, and was assigned to USS *Ticonderoga*, R Div., as fireman with the rank of FN working in the metal shop.

In November 1955, conducting night flight operations off the coast of France, a terrible accident occurred when a jet plane tore through the nylon barrier crashing into men and planes on the launching deck. He witnessed a bloody scene of injured personnel he will never forget.

Discharged on April 25, 1957, he returned to his former craft of auto body repair. He has now established his own business which he has managed for 25 years, becoming an auto damage appraiser and virtually an expert in his field.

A native of Westport, CT, he moved to Newfane, VT, after marriage in 1985 where he is retired.

PURL G. DEAN, born Jan. 16, 1921, Melbourne, FL, grew up in Jacksonville. He attended Jacksonville College of Law. Enlisted in the USNR on Oct. 3, 1943, as Y3/c, and was assigned to the District Intelligence Office, Miami, FL. He was under Adm. Malcolm Fortson, and was subsequently assigned to the Battleship *Wisconsin*. Then out to the Pacific Theater where he was assigned to COMCARDIV VI under Adm. Author W. Radford, aboard the aircraft carrier USS Ticonderoga (CV-14), and Capt. Dixie Kieffer was the captain.

On Dec. 24, 1944, the ship was part of the 3rd Fleet. They made air strikes to cover the Luzon Invasion. He was injured in the kamikaze attacks on Jan. 21, 1945. The fleet was off the coast of Formosa (Taiwan) and he was transferred to the hospital ship *Samaritan* and various other hospitals before he was finally discharged with a medical survey.

Discharged on Aug. 22, 1945, with the rank of Y2/c. Received the Purple Heart on Guadalcanal while he was hospitalized there.

JACK DEPOULTER was inducted into the USN on Oct. 17, 1953. He learned to be a sailor at boot camp in Bainbridge, MD. On to Norfolk, VA, to Pipefitter School and Newport, RI, for Pre-commissioning School; then to Brooklyn Navy Yard and an adventure on the USS *Ticonderoga*. He was present for recommissioning The Lady, which was home for the next three years, home port was Norfolk.

The shakedown cruise was in Guantanomao Bay, Cuba. The Big "T" stopped in Philadelphia for an air show, she had the distinction of being the first to fire

aircraft from catapults while at anchor. To New York City for the sponsoring of the Ticonderoga postage stamp.

An unforgettable day was when the headlines read, "Aircraft Carrier Hits Building Coming Into Port." The pilot thought he was parking a car, not docking a ship. Their first storm was Hazel in 1954. In the three years, 21 men died, most due to flight operations accidents. After transfer to the west coast, they rounded the horn and a storm hit, buckling the armor-plated steel of the flight deck. Damage repair in San Francisco in 1957. Next port of call was Japan.

After discharge in San Francisco in September 1957, he returned home to Kennett Square, PA, and his first child. Awards include the National Defense Medal and Good Conduct Medal.

Married Joan and has two sons, one daughter, two granddaughters and one grandson. After 43 years of plumbing and 44 years in banking, he and his wife are looking forward to retirement on the Chesapeake Bay.

GEORGE WILLIAM DIEM was born Dec. 27, 1922, in East Lansdown, PA. At Philadelphia, PA, he enlisted for six years in the US Navy, reported for duty March 2, 1942, and was sent to boot camp at Newport, RI. He helped commission the USS *Pollux* in April 1942 and the USS *Santee* in August 1942. He transferred Jan. 30, 1944, to the *Ticonderoga* and commissioned her, May 8, 1944.

He was present for the attacks on the Philippines, Formosa and French-Indio China; was on board the *Ticonderoga*, Jan. 21, 1945, when she was hit by two Japanese suicide planes, causing injury to his feet; and was on board the US Army transport, *Cape Perpetua*, when she broke down and was pulled by sea-going tug to Pearl Harbor, May 17, 1945. Transferred to USS *Enterprize*, May 31, 1945, headed for the States to Bremerton, WA, to finally receive treatment for his feet (bones were out of place).

Transported 1,400 casualties from Pearl Harbor to the States, September 1945, and troops from England in October 1945. Went through a bad storm that lasted for days before arriving at Staten Island on Christmas Eve, 1945. On Jan. 18, 1946, they put USS *Guam*, *Alaska* and *Enterprise* into mothballs at Bayonne, NJ, where he stayed until Dec. 29, 1947, then sent to Brooklyn Receiving Station for discharged, Dec. 31, 1947.

After service he attended college in Ohio. Worked for the US Army Corps of Engineers until his retirement in December 1984. He was New Jersey State Commander of the American Legion from 1994-95. Diem married in May 1944 and has a daughter.

LARRY DIGAETANO joined the USN on Nov. 17, 1943, one day after he turned 17 years old. Attended boot camp in Sampson, NY; from there he went aboard the USS *Charger* in Norfolk, VA. On May 8, 1944, he was assigned to the USS *Ticonderoga*, 4th Div. Later he was promoted to coxswain and transferred to the 8th Div., which were lookouts and 20mm, to be in charge of the

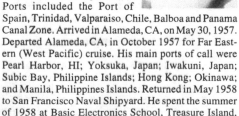

captain's gig. He later became master of arms until discharged in April 1946.

On Jan. 21, 1945, he had finished lunch and went to the starboard side of the hangar deck to check out the captain's gig. He heard 20mm and 40mm firing. He immediately ran up the ladder to the flight deck heading toward the bridge to man his 20mm gun on the starboard side of the bridge. He saw the first kamikaze plane hit the deck as he proceeded to his gun station. After manning his gun, he saw the second plane heading toward the bridge. He kept firing at the plane until it hit the bridge. He was knocked out of his gun, but was not hurt. He looked at his gun barrel and it was warped from firing so many rounds of 20mm. He and his loader changed the barrel, and stood on their battle station until after dark.

After his discharge he was married and now has two daughters and two granddaughters. He joined the West Orange Fire Dept. and retired as captain 32 years later. He is presently the sole owner of the Nu-lar Co., which deals with the sales and service of CPR equipment. On the 50th reunion of the Big "T" Assn., he was elected president of the association.

HAROLD E. DREWS enlisted in 1964 and attended basic training in San Diego, CA; and A School in Jacksonville, FL.

Boarded ship at San Diego in 1965 and served two and one half tours in the Gulf of Tonkin. Debarked ship in 1968 while docked at Subic Bay. He was flown back stateside for discharge.

JAMES DULLEA enlisted on Dec. 9, 1942, in New York City, NY. Went to boot camp at NTS Great Lakes, IL; from there to Ordnance School in Memphis, TN; graduated 3/c AOM petty officer; then on to Mercer Field, Trenton, NJ; to Quonset Point where they trained for ship operations.
Assigned to the USS *Ticonderoga* (V-5), at Norfolk, VA, he became a plank owner.

On Jan. 21, 1945, while loading planes with bombs and ammunition, he heard a loud noise overhead, looked up to see a Japanese plane overhead so low he could have hit it with a baseball. The plane crashed into the front elevator on the flight deck. They had to throw all the bombs and ammunition over the side. They had just about finished when the second plane hit the bridge. After repairs in Bremerton, WA, he made 2/c AOM and returned to the Pacific until the end of the war.

Married Marion in 1948 and has one son, Cmd. James P. Dullea, stationed in Washington, DC. He retired from Eastern Air Lines in 1986.

CHARLES A. DYER (CHARLIE), CAPT, USNR, enlisted in the USNR on Aug. 13, 1963, and reported for OCS on Sept. 23, 1963. He completed OCS and was commissioned on Feb. 7, 1964. He graduated with distinction from the Naval Justice School in Newport, RI. On April 16, 1964, he reported for duty aboard the USS *Ticonderoga* (CVA-14) which was en route to Westpac at the early stages of the Vietnam conflict.

Dyer made three Westpac deployments aboard the *Ticonderoga* in 1964, 1965-66 and 1966-67. His billets included assistant legal officer, first division officer and navigation division officer. He was a qualified officer of the deck both in port and underway. During the last 18 months of his *Ticonderoga* duty he was the GQ OOD. He received the Secretary of the Navy Commendation for Achievement for service aboard the *Ticonderoga* during the Westpac deployment of 1966-67.

Dyer was released from active duty on June 15, 1967. After his release from active duty he remained in the naval reserves and attained the rank of captain. He was awarded the Meritorious Service Medal for his service as the commanding officer of CINCPACFLT Det 920 and CINCPACFLT executive agent for naval control of shipping from Oct. 1, 1988—Sept. 30, 1990.

By special arrangement Dyer took the Law School Admissions Test aboard the *Ticonderoga* while deployed in the Gulf of Tonkin. After his active duty stint he attended the University of California Hastings College of the Law in San Francisco. He graduated in 1970. He is a member of the State Bar of California and specializes in civil litigation in the law firm of Dyer & White in Menlo Park, CA. He is a member of several professional organizations including the American Board of Trial Advocates and the National Board of Trial Advocacy.

He is married to the former Marilyn Abadie and has four daughters: Kristine, Erin, Kathleen and Kerry.

MORRIS J. EINHORN (BUZZ) joined the USN on July 4, 1942, and attended boot camp at Newport, RI. He was initially assigned to the USS *Santee* at Norfolk, VA, December 1942 and transferred to the USS *Ticonderoga* as a RM2/c in January 1944 as part of the pre-commissioning detail at the Newport News Naval Receiving Station, VA. He assisted the chief radioman in training radio operators who did not have shipboard experience, until May 8, 1944, when the ship was commissioned.

On Jan. 21, 1945, when GQ sounded, he was on duty in radio central on the O-4 deck. As soon as he was relieved, he started to his GQ station which was on the aft end of the ship on the starboard side, just under the flight deck, which was designated Radio 6. On the way to his GQ station, he had to run aft across the flight deck. The kamikaze that had dropped a bomb on the USS *Langley*, which was running aft of them, continued on to the Big "T" and dove into the forward elevator. It flew over his head as he ran aft. He heard the bullets from its machine guns hitting the deck and dove under a SB2C dive bomber which was parked on the flight deck. When it went overhead, he turned and saw it dive into the forward elevator and saw many of his shipmates flying through the air in pieces. He continued aft to his GQ station and set up emergency radio communications. Shortly thereafter the Big "T" was attacked by other kamikazes coming in from the starboard side. Some of the radio operators (there were three or four besides him assigned to Radio 6) went up to the flight deck and tried to use the machine guns in the SB2Cs to fire at the kamikazes.

After munitions personnel disarmed bombs (which had been previously loaded into planes for another strike), he helped other seamen throw them over the side. Other seamen were throwing life jackets to men who had been knocked or forced over the side by explosions and fire on the hangar deck.

After GQ was over, and they had their division muster, he learned that his best friend, RM1/c Aldo Ricciardello, had been killed, the only casualty from their division.

After his discharge from the USN, as RM1/c, in October 1945, he returned to his wife and son in Elmsford, NY. He later enlisted in the USAF and retired as a chief master sergeant in 1964. He later served as a civilian communications specialist with the US Government, retiring in 1979.

He and wife, Marilyn, later moved to Satellite Beach, FL. They celebrated their 50th wedding anniversary on April 8, 1994, at which time they had two sons, three grandchildren and three great-grandchildren.

EDWARD ELLIS, born March 23, 1934, Bronx, NY. Enlisted on Oct. 9, 1952, and served with the Patrol Sqdn. 44, NAS Norfolk, VA. Attacked Sqdn. 66 on board the USS *Ticonderoga*.

Discharged on Sept. 26, 1956, with rank of AT2.
Married Mary Lou and has three children and two grandchildren. He works as a mechanic for United Airlines.

EUGENE G. FAIRFAX was born in Vernel, UT, in 1916. He enlisted as a seaman in 1934 and retired from the Navy as a rear admiral.

He assumed command of USS *Ticonderoga* in Hong Kong in 1961 and left in July 1962. After TICO he had duty with chief of staff Carrier Division 1, WSEG, DOD, Navy Deputy JTF-2, Commander ASW Group 5, Commander Alaskan Sea Frontier, deputy inspector general, USN.

He retired Feb. 1, 1972, and lives in Albuquerque, NM.

ALBERT FASANO joined the USN on Jan. 28, 1944; attended boot camp in Sampson, NY; from there he was assigned to the USS *Ticonderoga* on May 8, 1944, and became S1/c. He worked with Chaplain Gilmore in the library and with church service.

Experienced a day he will never forget. Two kamikaze suicide planes hit the ship deck, which caused a fire on the hangar deck, killing and wounding a lot of the shipmates. Lou Izzo from his home town, which is New Haven, CT, and himself stayed up most of the night trying to help the wounded. One of his best experiences was meeting up with three of his brothers who were in the UNS, while he was out in the Pacific. He also had a twin brother in the Army. There were five of them in the service at one time.

Honorably discharged on Dec. 17, 1945 and one month later he married Donatella Ferrie, in which Chaplain Gilmore performed the wedding. He has four sons and one daughter. He is presently co-owner with his son, manufacturing precision parts on Swiss type automatic screw machines.

RICHARD B. FIELD, born Nov. 6, 1924, Brooklyn, NY. Enlisted on April 23, 1943. Served aboard the USS *Ticonderoga* (CV-14) from May 1944 until April 1945; with the NAS, Norfolk, VA; NAS Oceana, VA; NAS Atlantic City, NJ; and NATTE Memphis, TN. He participated in the battles at Philippine Liberation and Okinawa.

Memorable experiences were the typhoon in January 1945; South China Sea; and the two kamikaze hits in January 1945.

Discharged on June 16, 1946, with the rank of AOM2/c. Awards include the Navy Good Conduct, Asiatic Pacific w/three stars, Philippine Liberation w/ one star, American Theater and Victory Medal. He was recalled from the Reserves from March 13, 1951, until April 11, 1952, in NAS Jacksonville, FL.

Married and has three children and four grandchildren. He is currently retired.

FRANCIS N. FOLEY, son of Mr. and Mrs. Michael Foley of Reed St., Canaan, CT, was employed at the Pratt Whitney Aircraft Co. of East Hartford, CT, as a machinist. He graduated from Canaan High School in 1939. Enlisted in the USN in August 1942. He reported to Newport, RI, where he attended recruit training. After completing boot camp he attended Signalman's School at Newport and was assigned to the USS *Albermarle* and served in the Atlantic along the South American and African coasts. While serving aboard the USS *Albermarle* he was initiated a shellback in the Navy's traditional equator crossing ceremony.

Served for a short time on the USS *Charger*, he was assigned to this ship in August 1944. Since he had been serving aboard, he had seen action against the Japanese at Leyte, Luzon, Formosa, Indo-China, the southern coast of China, Okinawa and the final blows of the war against the home islands of Japan for which he is entitled to wear the Asiatic-Pacific Campaign Ribbon w/four Bronze Stars, Philippine Liberation Bar w/one Bronze Star, American Theater Campaign Ribbon and the European Campaign Ribbon w/two stars.

He was aboard the USS *Ticonderoga* off Japan serving aboard this mighty esset class aircraft carrier off Formosa in January when two kamikaze suicide planes got through the fighter cover overhead and the ships gunfire to crash on its decks, causing almost 400 casualties and serious fires. He served as Signalman 2/c. He escaped uninjured although his battle station was liberally riddled with shrapnel from the explosion.

Married in 1946 and had three children and seven grandchildren. Retired from the US Postal Service in 1986. They live in Canaan, CT, in the summer and Nokomis, FL, in the winter.

RICHARD FOWLER RADM, enlisted in the USN as an aviation cadet on his 18th birthday in 1942. After flight training he was assigned to VF-15 flying F6F Hellcats on board USS *Essex* in the Pacific. Credited with shooting down six and a half aircraft, he served in the Marianas, Philippines and Okinawa campaigns including the first and second battles of the Philippine Sea.

During the Korean War he flew F4U Corsairs from USS *Leyte* in the air campaigns of 1950. He commanded USS *Eldorado* and USS *Ticonderoga* in the Tonkin Gulf during the Vietnam War.

Rear Admiral Fowler has commanded two aircraft squadrons, two aircraft wings, two warships, a carrier task group, a task force, and has served in numerous other shipboard, aviation, staff and shore billets. He retired in 1974 after 32 years of service. He holds the Navy Cross, Legion of Merit, Silver Star, Distinguished Flying Cross and Air Medal.

CHARLES CLIFTON FRANCOM (CLIFF), born April 5, 1919, Payson, UT. He enlisted from college at the Oakland, CA, "E" base, soloed and was sent to Corpus Christi, TX. He became an aviation cadet on Dec. 1, 1941, and graduated as an ensign in May 1942 and immediately was assigned to VS-44 in Curacao, NWI.

In November 1944, he was assigned to VT-80 and was a plank owner on the USS *Ticonderoga* (CV-14). In August 1945 he was transferred to serve as the staff pilot to the commander Naval Air Bases in the Philippine Islands. WWII ended the day he graduated from the Advanced Instrument Flight Instructors School in Atlanta, GA.

Entered the Organized Naval Reserve Air program at Los Alamitos, CA, and served as commanding officer of two squadrons. He volunteered for Korean service and was recalled in November 1952 where he was assigned to the Naval Intelligence School (air), Anacostia. Following graduation he was assigned as assistant district intelligence officer (air), Jacksonville Naval Air Station, FL.

Was released from active duty in 1953. He re-entered the Naval Reserve program at Los Alamitos Naval Air Station being promoted to lieutenant commander and commander. He retired with 24 years service in 1966.

As a civilian again, he worked for the Rand Corp. in Santa Monica for six years, eventually going back into the school business where he retired as the assistant superintendent of schools in Orange County, CA.

Presently lives near and plays regular golf at the old Los Alamitos Naval Air Station golf course. The only claim to "fame" he will make is that he has two scenes in the picture "Fighting Lady," and that he still regularly corresponds and sees his life long friends from the *Ticonderoga*. He leaves his love and gratitude to his shipmates, many who gave much more than asked.

EDWIN J. FRIESEN was born Sept. 29, 1919, in Lake Charles. Enlisted Holloway Aviation Midshipman Program in August 1947. He began flight training in May 1948 and designated naval aviator (midshipman) December 1949. Served in VP-46, NABTC, Pensacola (flight instructor); NAS Memphis (student AE(O) School); NAS Port Lyautey, Morocco; VP-5; NAS Glynco, GA; and USNPGS, Monterey (student), before joining *Ticonderoga* as lieutenant commander (CommO) in August 1963. Was promoted to commander, October 1964, during second Westpac cruise.

After *Ticonderoga* he served at DEFCOMAGENCY, Washington, DC; Naval War College (student); COMSIXTHFLT (FLTCOMO) Gaeta, Italy; CO NAVCOMSTA Italy, Naples; COMNAVCOM, Washington, DC (ASSTDEPCOM) and DEFCOMAGENCY (ASSTDEPDIR-Programs); His memorable experiences included being in WestPac at the beginning of both the Korean and Vietnam wars; also memorable was Gulf of Tonkin incident.

He retired as captain on June 30, 1975. His decorations include the Meritorious Service Medal (2), Air Medal (4), Joint Service Commendation Medal, Navy Commendation Medal, Vietnam Service, Korean Service (3), China Service, Japanese Occupation, Korean Presidential Unit Citation and National Service.

Received BS in accounting from USF and was designated CPA in August 1983. He is now mostly retired. He and Luckey have been married since 1953 and have two children, Karl and Kandy.

WILLIAM R. FRYE was on the fantail of the USS *Ticonderoga* on Jan. 21, 1945, talking to Carl S. Gaworecki and other crewmen.

It was a beautiful day and at noontime all hell broke loose! GQ sounded and everyone ran. This was the last time he saw Carl. He ran up a ladder to see what was going on. Halfway up the ladder a marine pulled him back and went around him. When he was at the top there was an explosion. The marine fell down the ladder dead. "Why did I start up the ladder? I don't know."

His GQ station was on the emergency evaporators in the boiler room with Mike Boduch. He arrived in the boiler room but to this day he does not remember how. He put the evaporators on stand-by and reported to the main evaporator room. While waiting for more orders they could hear explosions and things falling down the stack. After the all clear, he went topside to look for Carl. He could not find him and no one had seen him. Carl was gone!

They had started out their naval service at Sampson, NY, and then to school at Wentworth Institute in Boston, MA. In January 1944 they were assigned to the Big "T". They had asked for submarine duty but were refused.

On the day of the burial at sea he was pulled to help bring the bodies from a compartment below decks to the hangar deck. The smell and feel of them when they loaded them on the stretchers was horrible. He kept looking for Carl, but did not find him. Oh God! He looked and looked but no Carl. When the bodies would slide down the ramp to the sea, all he could think about, "Is that one him?" Every parade or military function that he attends to this day he thinks of Carl and he still misses him.

On the way back to the States for repairs after the attack, a lot of the crew got sick from drinking water. What happened was that he and Mike Boduch put too much boiled compound in the water. They were told not to do that again (they didn't).

After the attack, he was on the flight deck and saw Adm. "Bull" Halsey viewing the damage. The next time he saw Adm. Halsey was in a parade in Philadelphia after the war. The parade was in his honor and he was selected to help represent the 3rd Fleet.

After repairs were made to the Big "T" at Seattle, WA, they returned to the Pacific War off the coast of the Philippines. At that time he was selected to go back to the States for schooling. He was put ashore on Leyte and assigned to the USS *General Brule* (APA-66). He arrived in the States and was then assigned to the USS *Philadelphia* (CL-41) for magic carpet duty between England, Germany, France and various ports in the United States. He visited the Big "T" after the war when she was in Philadelphia. When the *Ticonderoga* was decommissioned in 1973 in San Diego he was there as a guest of honor along with many other former crew members and men who helped build her. When the colors came down for the last time and they knew she was going for scrap, some had tears in their eyes. He cried and saluted Carl S. Gaworecki, MM3/c.

He came back to Williamsburg and settled there. He married Margaret V. Moyer over 37 years ago. They have a daughter, Jo Ann, who lives in Chambersburg, PA, and she has two children, William J. and Shawn. Also has two great-grandchildren, William P. and Joseph V. Frye. He retired from the Pennsylvania Dept. of Transportation in 1987 after 25 years of faithful service. His wife retired from Butterick, Inc. in 1990 and has taken on the job as a steward on the American Legion, Post 456.

FORREST REX GAMBREL, born Sept. 1, 1922, Continental, OH. Enlisted in the USN on May 11, 1943, Toledo, OH; spent 12 weeks in boot camp training at Great Lakes, IL; sent to Lakehurst, NJ, Blimp Sqdn. 12 and Blimp Hedron one. He was then shipped aboard the USS *Franklin* shakedown cruise. Returned to Norfolk, NJ, to board the USS *Ticonderoga* (CV-14) and was a plank owner.

Active duty included the American Theater Asiatic Pacific w/four stars, Philippine Liberation w/one star and the WWII Victory Medal.

Was astride a 500 lb. bomb when two kamikazes hit the Big "T" on Jan. 21, 1945. Being on the third deck, uninjured, he helped Capt. Dixie Kiefer's crew save the ship.

After stateside leave, he returned on the *Ticonderoga* to the Pacific Theater. He witnessed Japan's surrender to Gen. MacArthur in Tokyo Bay on Sept. 2, 1945.

Honorably discharged on May 13, 1946, with the rank of AOM2/c.

Has been married for over 42 years; has three children and 10 grandchildren. Retired BF Goodrich Co. to a farm in Hicksville, OH, on March 1, 1985.

GEORGE A. GARCIA enlisted in the USN on Oct. 13, 1942. He attended the commissioning ceremonies on May 8, 1944, and was assigned to the V-2 Div. and 20mm gun, hangar deck, starboard. In the November 1944 action a kamikaze crashed close alongside.

On Jan. 21, 1945, he was on a fire hose, hangar deck, extinguishing burning planes. Ammunition was exploding and a bomb was rolling on deck. Somehow two of them managed to roll it over the side. The sprinklers came on as they heard a second kamikaze hit the bridge. Several burnt bodies were laying on deck. He was discharged on Nov. 16, 1945.

Married while on leave and has two sons, three grandsons and one granddaughter. He was a cabinet maker-contractor and retired in 1990 after leasing his building. On Nov. 16, 1973, he was at the decommissioning of the USS *Ticonderoga* in San Diego, 28 years later.

RICHMOND D. GARRETT, born Jan. 12, 1922, Whittier, CA. Enlisted in the USN on Oct. 29, 1940; commissioned in June 1956; and retired in May 1968.

Served on the USS *Ticonderoga* (CV-14), November 1956-December 1958 as a weather officer (OA Div.). Other sea/overseas and short tours included other carriers, cruisers, sea plane tenders, COMSOPAC (Solomon Islands) and COMBATCRUPAC staffs, Navy weather facilities, fleet weather centrals, Naval Air stations, missile ranges and numerical weather facility, USNPGS, Monterey, CA.

Memorable experiences include being aboard the *Ticonderoga* dodging typhoons in WESTPAC which resulted in the ship becoming known at Typhoon-Deroga in those days.

Awards include the Good Conduct Medal, WWII American Asiatic-Pacific Campaign and Victory Medals, China Service and Japanese Occupation Medals, Armed Forces Expeditionary and Korea Service Medals.

Married Lorraine Bear in 1947, and they have three children (one is an active duty Navy captain), and two grandchildren. He is retired and living in San Diego, CA.

JAMES JOSEPH GAVIN JR., born Feb. 7, 1926, Plains, PA. Enlisted on Jan. 28, 1944, and was stationed at the USNTS Sampson, NY; USNTS Newport, RI; and the USS *Ticonderoga.* Also served aboard the USS *Missouri* and the USS *Roanoke* in the Korean War.

Discharged on May 2, 1946, and re-enlisted on Feb. 25, 1948. His final discharge was on Jan. 8, 1953.

Awards include the Pacific Theater Ribbon, American Theater Ribbon, WWII Victory Medal and the Purple Heart.

Married and had three children and five grandchildren. He passed away on Oct. 6, 1974.

WILLIAM GOWDER graduated from Central High School in Scranton, PA, in 1942. He enlisted in the USN and was sworn in on Dec. 29, 1942. His first month of boot camp was spent in the hospital at Sampson, NY, with a kidney infection. Attended Aviation Ordnance School at Memphis, TN, followed by Naval Air Gunners School at Jacksonville, FL. Worked two months on F-6-Fs at Atlantic City followed by training at Oceana, VA, for combined operations of S-B-2Cs and T-B-Fs.

Went aboard the USS *Ticonderoga* on May 8, 1944, for commissioning, but returned to Oceana as their living quarters were not finished. On May 28, they were completed and he served on the Big "T" until the end of the war.

Discharged at Lido Beach, NY, on Feb. 14, 1946, with the rank of AOM1/c.

Married and has six children and three grandchildren. Graduated from Lehigh University and worked for 38 years in the specialty steel business as a salesman and is currently enjoying retirement with wife Patricia.

ROBERT L. GRAPPI (BOB) graduated from high school in Revere, MA and enlisted in the USN the following day on June 11, 1948. After "boot camp" and completion of two vocational schools he was assigned to duty in meteorology at the Naval Air Activity at Port Lyautey, French Morroco, Africa. After a year of service there he was accepted for flight training as a naval aviation cadet at Pensacola, FL. He earned his Navy Wings and commission as an ensign in 1951.

Following specialized training in the Navy's jet transitional training unit in Texas, he received orders to Ftr. Sqdn. 91 based at the NAS, Alameda, CA, and on the aircraft carrier USS *Philippine Sea* from which he flew 101 combat missions in the Korean War. Subsequently, various tours of duty included: jet flight instructor at Kingsville, TX; aircraft maintenance officer on board the carrier *Ticonderoga*; legal officer at the NAS Moffett Field, Sunnyvale, CA; ops officer and designated as a nuclear weapons delivery pilot in Jet Attack Sqdn. 192 on the carrier USS *Bon Homme Richard*; student at the USN Postgraduate School, Monterey, CA; combat flight instructor, flight safety officer and nuclear weapons training officer at the NAS Lemoore, CA; ops officer of CAW 15 on the carrier USS *Constellation* in the Vietnam War where he flew an additional 35 combat missions in jet aircraft; and XO of Jet Replacement Air Wing Attack Sqdn. 125 at the NAS, Lemoore, CA. His selection for assignment to command of an aircraft squadron on a carrier at sea was interrupted upon the determination that his wife, Deborah, had been diagnosed as having leukemia. At that time he elected to retire from the Navy having achieved most of his career goals. Deborah passed

away just before his retirement from active duty in 1969 at the NAS, Lemoore, CA.

Earlier, Deborah had been married to Gerald Peterson and sons Gerald Howard Jr. and Terry Ford were born. That marriage ended in divorce. Bob and Deborah were married in Corpus Christi, TX. Sons: Robert Louis Jr., James Anthony, Jon Jefferson and Mark Andrew were born of that marriage.

Soon after Deborah's death and Bob's retirement from active duty in the USN, he settled with his three youngest sons in Grass Valley, CA where he started a new career and became licensed as a real estate broker. He also served as an elected public official for 10 years in the capacity of a member and president of the board of directors of the Nevada County Resource Conservation District. Additionally, he served as the executive secretary of the statewide California Assoc. of Resource Conservation Districts.

While involved in state resource activities, he met and married Barbara Lou Smith-Mack of Sacramento. She has three children from a previous marriage: Cheryl Ann, Ross Thompson and Richard Hugh Mack. They currently make their home in Nevada City, CA with several of their children, grandchildren and great-grandchildren living nearby.

E.A. GREGORY, born Feb. 19, 1910, in Laurel, MS; was the youngest son of Mr. and Mrs. John A. Gregory, who were teachers in Illinois Central Railway Employees. He was assigned to the USS *Ticonderoga* in November 1944; and was killed instantly on Jan. 21, 1945, aboard the *Ticonderoga.*

Upon his death, he left his wife of four years, Mrs. Zoie M. Gregory, and two small sons, E.A. Gregory Jr. and Kenneth L. Gregory, who at the time resided Grass Valley, CA.

WILLIAM NAVAREZ GRIJALVA, born June 25, 1924, Plymouth, CA. Enlisted in the USN on April 19, 1944, and went to Camp Peary, Wim, VA, for training.

Discharged at Bremerton, WA, on May 5, 1946. Awards include the Asiatic Pacific Area Campaign Medal (4), Philippine Liberation Medal (2), American Area Campaign Medal and WWII Victory Medal.

Memorable experience was standing at the #1 elevator when they were hit by the first kamikaze. He ran toward his battle station, not making it. He put his helmet on as shrapnel was flying. Shrapnel did dent his helmet and also got stuck in his collar bone. Two were killed behind him and another fellow from his division, plus, two others close by were wounded.

Married Jessie and had five children: Gloria (married Wally), Eddie, Rosalie (married David), Johnny (married Bertha) and Rita (married Fernando). Jessie passed away. Then married Raquel, who had two children from a previous marriage, Diana (married Augustin) and Alfred. He is enjoying retirement with his family and especially their 13 grandchildren.

R.G. GUILBAULT, RADM, a native of West Warwick, RI, served as the first commanding officer, USS *Ticonderoga* (CG-47) from commissioning Jan. 22, 1983— January 1985. This included deployment off Lebanon and demanding missile trials in 1993. Previous sea assignments included USS *Hazelwood* (DD-531), USS *Bainbridge* (CGN-25) on two separate tours. Was

executive officer of USS *Dale* (CG-19) and commanding officer of USS *Tattnall* (DDG-19).

Following his selection to flag rank, Rear Admiral Guilbault served as director, Surface Combat Systems Division (OP-35); director, Command and Control Systems Division (OP-942); Commander Cruiser-Destroyer Group 12 which included serving as Commander Battle Force Sixth Fleet, CTF-60 in the Mediterranean; Deputy Director, Space Command and Control (OP-094B) and Deputy CINC and COS CINCIBERLANT until his retirement in April 1994.

Rear Admiral Guilbault holds a MS degree in computer systems management from George Washington University. He is married to the former Huguette Coulais of Casablanca, Morocco and they reside in Alexandria, VA. He is currently the vice-president for Programs and Business Development, Federal Government Region, Digital Equipment Corp.

JOHN JOSEPH HAFFEY, born June 14, 1926, Carbondale, PA. Joined the USN on Jan. 24, 1944, and reported aboard the USS *Ticonderoga* on May 8, 1944, as part of the commissioning crew. This made him a plank owner, being one of the original crew. He was assigned to the S-1 Div., which was supply. He survived the kamikaze attack on Jan. 21, 1945, and went out on the ship's second trip to the Far East, which lasted until the end of the war.

Discharged on May 7, 1964, with the rank of SSML3/c. For his service on the *Ticonderoga*, he rates the American Theater of War Medal, the Asiatic Pacific Theater of War Medal w/five Battle Stars, the Navy Occupation Medal w/Asia Bar, WWII Victory Medal and the Philippine Liberation Medal w/one Battle Star.

Married and had one son. He worked for Bethlehem Steel in Bethlehem, PA, and later moved to Pittsburgh, PA, where he worked for rehabilitation center. He was dedicated to this work, was very kind and helped many people. He was involved in sports, especially baseball, but most of all he enjoyed traveling, camping and fishing in the United States and Canada. He passed away on Feb. 5, 1988, and is missed very much. God bless him.

NILES HAMBLIN enlisted in the USN on Sept. 6, 1957, and attended boot camp in Great Lakes, IL. After requesting to serve with his brother and many plane trips that started in Chicago, IL, and stops that included Treasure Island, CA, Hawaiian Islands, Guam, Wake Islands, Philippine Islands, and a bus trip from Manila to Subic Bay where he boarded the USS *Ticonderoga* (CVA-14). He was in B Div. for a while then transferred to F Div.

Served on the *Ticonderoga* until 1961 when he was transferred to the USS *Princeton* (LPH-5). Duties on the *Ticonderoga* included #1 fire room, mess cook, compartment cleaning, forward MK 37 director, forward starboard MK 56 system and gun plot. During his naval career he was stationed at or on: USN and MCRTC, Akron, OH; B School, Great Lakes, IL; USS *Richard L. Page* (DEG-5); FTG Guantanamo Bay Cuba; FTC Norfolk, VA.

Retired in Norfolk, VA, as a chief petty officer and moved to Kentucky where he is presently employed at the US Naval Ordnance Station, Louisville, KY.

MIKE D. HANNAS graduated from Purdue University with a bachelor of science degree and was commissioned an ensign in the USN. He was on *Ticonderoga* from 1965-67 and served in Legal, First Division and Navigation. After leaving *Ticonderoga* he entered law school and received a JD degree from the University of Missouri and designated a judge advocate. As a judge advocate he served at the Law Center, Great Lakes and as staff judge advocate NAS North Island and assistant staff judge advocate, COMNAVAIRPAC.

After a tour at BUMED, he served in the office of the judge advocate general, first as assistant division

director, Investigations Division, then as assistant division director, Claims and Tort Litigation Division until he retired in 1988. After retirement he served as the deputy general counsel to the on-site inspection agency until 1989 when he returned to the Claims and Tort Litigation Division as deputy director. He is currently the acting director.

Married Joan and has two children (one a fourth generation Purdue boilermaker graduate). His hobbies are hiking the Blue Ridge, Chesapeake and Ohio Canal; bluegrass music, reading, golfing and tennis.

WILLIAM N. HETHCOAT (BILL) E-6, was born Dec. 25, 1934, in Chicago, IL. He enlisted May 1952 as an airman apprentice.

Retired in July 1986 as (E-9) MACM, CMC (SW). His awards include the Navy Commendation Medal, Navy Achievement Medals (2), National Defense Service Medals (2), Battle "E" Ribbons (2), Enlisted Surface Warfare Insignia, Sea Service Warfare Insignia, Sea Service Deployment Ribbon, Korean Service Medal, UN Service Medal, eight Good Conduct Awards ending March 23, 1983, Vietnam Service Medals (4), Vietnam Campaign Medal, Vietnam Meritorious Unit Citation (Gallantry Cross), Meritorious Unit Commendation (2), Vietnam Foreign Service Commendation, Rifle and Pistol Marksman Medal.

His tour of duty on the *Ticonderoga* was from 1970 until decommissioning October 1973. While on the *Ticonderoga* he was in the S-6 Division as first class. In August of 1973, he was selected and converted to the master-at-arms rating. He was the first master-at-arms by rating to serve on the *Ticonderoga* since the master-at-arms rating was disestablished by the USN.

While on the *Ticonderoga* he was on two Apollo pick ups, 16 and 17, and Sky Lab. They were, as far as he knows, the only ship to have a steam room on board.

Married to the late Teauko Matsumoto; they raised five children. He would never have made the Navy a career without the support of his wife who earned every penny of her E-10 pay.

C. VERN HIGMAN, born June 25, 1922, Foster, WA. Enlisted on Sept. 26, 1942, as a Naval Aviation Cadet. He received his wings and commission as ensign on Nov. 27, 1943. After operational flight training, he was one of the first pilots assigned to Torpedo Sqdn. 80 for duty aboard the USS *Ticonderoga* with Carrier Air Group 80.

Received shrapnel wounds in his right leg during a torpedo run on Nov. 11, 1944, at Ormac Bay in the Philippines when his plane, *Round Trip Ticket*, was hit with a four-inch shell fired by a Japanese destroyer. He was one of the VT-80 pilots who were trapped in the ready room when the first kamikaze plane hit the flight deck.

Flew in air strikes in the Philippines, China Sea, Formosa, Iwo Jima and Tokyo during his tour while aboard the *Ticonderoga* and the USS *Hancock*. He served for three active duty periods over a span of 27 years retiring as a lieutenant commander on July 1, 1969. Awards include two Distinguished Flying Crosses, Air Medal and Purple Heart.

Married with five children, three step-children, 17 grandchildren and two great-grandchildren. Retired as a general manager of a hotel.

RALPH C. HINSON, born Sept. 2, 1915, Bidwell, OH. Enlisted on Aug. 17, 1943. Participated in several battles, but not on the CV-14.

Memorable experiences were in WWII when he was on the USS *Hornet* (CV-12) and the CV-14 in peacetime.

Discharged on Nov. 27, 1963, with rank of HT1. He is presently retired.

WALTER H. HOBBY, born June 23, 1926, Leicester, MA. Enlisted on Jan. 28, 1944, and was stationed at Sampson, NY; Newport, RI; USS *Wyoming*; USS *Ticonderoga* 3rd Div. on Jan. 21, 1945; and transferred to the 8th Div.

Memorable experiences were the commissioning of the Big "T"; Going through the Panama Canal; the big typhoon; Jan. 21, 1945, kamikaze hits; burial at sea; the joining of fleets and squadrons and B-29s for the surrender of Japan; and Pearl Harbor and Bremerton Navy Yard.

Discharged on April 28, 1946, with the rank of S1/c.

Married Mary Catherine Turner on April 21, 1946, and has the following children: Dale, Wayne, Bonnie Lea Vance and Drew; eight grandchildren; and one great-granddaughter. He worked as a machinist, tool maker and electrician. He now lives on the shore of James River Arm of Table Rock Lake, McCord Bend, MO. The Big "T" was a great ship.

HOWARD C. HOXSIE, born Dec. 29, 1930, Waverly, NY. Enlisted in the USN in August 1955. From 1956-57, after the conversion from a WWII carrier to a modern one, hurricane bow, angle deck, they changed home ports from Norfolk to San Francisco. The trip around the horn was devastating for several days. No one was allowed on any weather decks. Several million dollars damage to the ship caused more dry dock time in San Francisco. Crossing the equator was a blast.

Discharged in August 1959 with the rank of AB2/c. He is a widower and retired.

GEORGE S. HUBER, SSML3/c, USN, born July 2, 1914, in Gowanda, NY. Enlisted as apprentice seaman Jan. 20, 1944. Graduated boot camp in Sampson, NY; assigned to the USS *Ticonderoga* and served on board when it was commissioned into service.

In January 1945 it was hit by Japanese suicide planes while coming out of the China Sea, killing 144 and wounding 193. During this battle, one of the planes struck the ship near the 40mm antiaircraft gun that he was manning; six of the eight-man gun crew were killed and he received permanent hearing loss.

He was honorably discharged on July 2, 1945, his 31st birthday. As a result of his injuries, he was inducted into the DAV on July 19, 1982. Married 62 years to Vivian, and they have two children, four grandchildren and three great-grandchildren. Huber retired after 37 years with the state of New York as a foreman, plumber and steamfitter. He still resides in Gowanda, NY.

GENE M. HUCKLE, born in Waverly, NY, enlisted in the USN in November 1943, at the age of 17. Was stationed at Sampson Naval Training Station in Newport, RI; Philadelphia Boiler School; and aboard the USS *Ticonderoga*. He participated in all battles with the *Ticonderoga*.

Memorable experiences were of Jan. 21, 1945, when he heard guns start to fire and he went to his battle station in the number two fire room. He lost a buddy from his hometown area on this date, Eugene Herrick.

Discharged in May 1946 with rate of 2/c.

Married and has four children and a grandson, (born on his wife's birthday). Retired in 1984 from IBM. They are enjoying retirement with their family. He has been a member of the Big "T" Assn. since 1972.

JEROME HARRY JADCZAK, born Sept. 27, 1921, Detroit, MI. Enlisted in the USN on Nov. 2, 1942, and served in the Asiatic Pacific Theater. He also served at NTS Great Lakes, IL; RS NYD, Washington, DC; RS Newport News, VA; and the USS *Ticonderoga.* He served as an electricians mate on the *Ticonderoga.* He was aboard on Jan. 21, 1945, but was uninjured in the kamikaze attack.

Received honorable discharge on Jan. 19, 1946, with the rank of EM3/c. Awards include the American Theater, Asiatic Pacific w/four stars, Philippine Liberation w/one star, Good Conduct Medal and WWII Victory Medal.

After the war he became a religious brother in the Redemptorist Congregation (Catholic). He retired in 1993 with Alzheimer symptoms.

RICHARD JAYCOX, born May 20, 1925, Norwich, NY. Enlisted on Feb. 1, 1944, and attended boot camp at Sampson, NY, in Co. 151. After boot camp he was assigned to the US NT Newport, RI, on *Ticonderoga* detail. On May 8, 1944, he was stationed on the USS *Ticonderoga* (CV-14), as a seaman 2/c, 2nd Div. Once stationed on the *Ticonderoga,* he served on gun mount number four, portside.

Participated at Southern Luzon, Visayas, Central Luzon, and Northwest Luzon, Philippine Islands, December 1944; Formosa, Northwest Luzon, Sakishima Gunto, Saigon, Cam Ranh Bay, French Indo-China, South China Coast, Hong Kong, January 1945; Maloelap Atoll, Marshall Islands, Okinawa, Ryukus Islands, May 1945; Southern Kyushu, Okinawa, Minami Daito Shoto, Kita Daito Jima, Hiroshima Bay, Honshu, Shikoku, Naval Base Kure, June 1945; Kure and Tokyo, July 1945; and Northern Honshu and Tokyo, August 1945.

On Jan. 21, 1945, a little past noon, he was located at his gun station, gun number four. It was at this time that the ship was hit by a kamikaze. This kamikaze hit the ship just aft elevator one, and abreast of gun mount number two and four. At this point he heard an explosion overhead and shortly thereafter a large portion of this kamikaze's wing fell and struck gun mount number four. The gun crew, while present, threw the wing portion of this plane overboard. In doing so, cleared the gun and prepared for further action. Within the next few minutes a second plane attacked. This kamikaze struck the island or the superstructure of the ship. A large amount of damage was sustained from this attack. His first reaction, of course, was of surprise. They did not know what had hit them. It was then that the ship sounded GQ and he and the crew remained at gun mount number four throughout the remainder of this day and into the next.

Discharged on April 17, 1946, with the rank of seaman 2/c. Awards include the Asiatic Pacific Area Campaign Medal w/three stars, American Area Campaign Medal; Philippine Liberation Medal; w/one star, and the WWII Victory Medal. In late 1947 he enlisted in the US Army and was stationed throughout the US and Germany.

After serving in the US Army, he returned home, started his family and worked locally for the city of

Norwich as parks superintendent. After 22 years, he retired from the city, but continued to work full-time for the city school district as a member of the ground maintenance crew. Although he is officially retired, he finds himself working again, this time baby-sitting his grandchildren. He offers a special thank you to his granddaughter for contributing her time to this biography.

BRYCE RICHMOND JOHNSON, born Sept. 17, 1922, McCornick, UT; graduated South High School, Salt Lake City, UT, in June 1938. Joined the USN in February 1943; attended boot camp at Farragut, ID; A&E School, Norman, OK; served aboard the USS *Sable* for arresting gear training; USS *Bataan* as a plank owner; and the USS *Ticonderoga,* as a plank owner, shakedown cruise, Trinidad, plane captain F6F, SB2C, V2 Div., Liberation of the Philippines, Tokyo Bay and the Japanese surrender. Was aboard the *Ticonderoga* on Jan. 21, 1945.

Discharged in February 1946, Shoemaker, CA. Graduated Cal-Aero Technical School. Worked as a field representative for North American Aviation, F-86; research and development, Rocketdyne, Redstone, Atlas, Saturn-Apollo; chief mechanic on rocket engines and field service for Rocketdyne, NASA contracts; Litton Medical Dental Field Service; McClellan AFB in development electronic communication and command control centers and retired in August 1993.

Married Elisabeth Kondratieff and has two children, Lee Ann and Seth Richmond.

JURKERVICH survived the sinking of the USS *Arizona* at Pearl Harbor on Dec. 7, 1941. He was transferred to the Navy Communications Unit at Ford Island. During his one leave during WWII, his transport ship struck the rocks off San Francisco and sunk. He was rescued while his bride was waiting at the alter. He was married a short time later.

Was supposed to be sent to San Francisco for discharge, but there was a mix up in his orders and he was transferred to the USS *Ticonderoga.* The correct orders caught up with him in February 1946 at Seattle, WA, and he quickly received his discharge.

ROBERT M. KANE, CDR USN, Ret., born Aug. 20, 1936 in San Antonio, TX. Graduated from Texas Tech College, 1959. Attended Officer Candidate School and commissioned an ensign on Feb. 4, 1960. Reported to USS *Ticonderoga* (CVA-14) as Fox Div. Officer and later Fire Control Officer.

Duty after *Ticonderoga*: Naval Recruiting Station, Houston, TX, USS *Norfolk* (DL-1), USS *John R. Pierce* (DD-758), Republic of Vietnam, Caracas, Venezuela, USS *Midway* (CVA-41), USS *Vega* (AF-59),

Defense Intelligence School, JUSMG/MAAG, Madrid, Spain.

Medals received were: Bronze Star w/Combat "V", Defense Meritorious Medal, Joint Service Commendation Medal, Navy Commendation Medal, Vietnamese Honor Medal First Class and other U.S. and Vietnamese unit citations and campaign awards.

Retired a CDR after 24 years of service. Began second career as a realtor in San Antonio, TX. Married 36 years to Elaine Wentworth and have two daughters, Cheryl, 34 and Janet, 30 and two grandchildren, Tyler, six and Charlotte, seven.

JOE KASKOUN enlisted in the Navy V-12 Program in June 1943, and was stationed at Union College in Schenectady, NY. Was transferred to boot camp at Sampson, and on to NATTC Ordnance School, Norman, OK.

Assigned to the USS *Ticonderoga* while at Pearl Harbor into the V-5 Div. On January 21 he was on the flight deck just inboard of the island, working on a plane. He watched the first kamikaze plane dive into the deck, less than 50 feet away. Between the two hits he carried wounded and manned fire hoses. After the second hit, he unloaded bombs and ammunition from aircraft and jettisoned them over the side, along with some of the planes themselves.

Discharged in May 1946 and went to New York University as a physical education major. He earned a varsity letter on the football team and taught physical education for 35 years in the North Babylon Schools.

Married Jeanne and has four children and two grandchildren. He retired in 1986 and spends a lot of time boating and fishing in the waters off Long Island.

MARTIN S. KASMAN, born Oct. 18, 1925. Was inducted on Jan. 26, 1944, and entered active duty on Feb. 2, 1944, with F Div. Fire Control. He was on the original crew of the USS *Ticonderoga.*

When the ship was torpedoed he was lying on his bunk with his shoes off. The alarm sounded and he had difficulty putting his shoes on, this saved his life.

He passed away on Nov. 27, 1974, of a cerebral hemorrhage at the age of 49. He left three children: Joyce Robin, Bruce Charles and Andrew Todd. He never spoke of his experiences on the *Ticonderoga.*

Z. KAWASHIMA, CDR DC USN, was aboard the *Ticonderoga* in the mid-1960s during the Tonkin Gulf incident when two of their destroyer escorts were at-

tacked by the enemy. For this action they received the Navy Unit Citation Award.

Once when the *Ticonderoga* was visiting Sasebo, Japan, they held an open house. His parents had migrated from Kiyushu, Japan many years ago to the US and Sasebo was very near their old homestead. Since he was a graduate of the US Army Language School in Japanese language, he was able to greet the large crowd of visitors (men, women and children) in fluent Japanese over the ship's speaker. It was almost like a homecoming for him.

On another occasion when the *Ticonderoga* was visiting Sasebo, the ship had to leave port on very short notice because of an approaching typhoon. He was able to get back aboard okay since he happened to be at the "O" Club and got the word. Others were not so fortunate. They were still climbing up "Jacobs Ladder" while the ship was steaming out of the harbor. Others returned to the ship weeks later on Okinawa. Since they had only the clothes they were wearing when they went ashore, they looked pretty scroungy.

He discovered a case of oral malignancy on one of his young patients on the *Ticonderoga* while they were at seas. He was able to arrange for the sailor to be sent ashore to Yokosuka and then later to Bethesda Naval Hospital for very extensive treatments.

Retired December 1982 and is currently employed part-time as dental-periodontist. He and his wife, Sadako, have two daughters, Yvonne and Vita, and two grandchildren.

DANE E. KENNELL, born July 8, 1946, Gettysburg, PA.

Prior to joining the USN he had never left quiet, rural Pennsylvania. Now he had crossed the US three times, spending three months each in Jacksonville and San Diego. He had visited San Francisco, St. Augustine and Los Angeles and had spent six additional months in Le Moore, CA. When on leave he had waded in the waters of Waikiki Beach and visited his first foreign country. In 1966, at the age of 19, he found himself an ordnance man on the USS *Ticonderoga* (VA-56). The carrier, afloat in the South China Sea, was supporting the armed forces in the Vietnam War. He reminisced the whirlwind past 12 months of his life.

Enlisted on Oct. 11, 1964, and served aboard the USS *Ticonderoga* and the USS *Enterprise*. Life on the USS *Ticonderoga* was tough. Generally he worked 18 hour days, running drills to load nuclear weaponry and arming planes for sorties over Vietnam. At night he often slept on the wing of a fighter to avoid the unbearable heat below deck.

Was named sailor of the month on the *Enterprise* and was awarded the National Defense Service Medal, Vietnam Service Medal w/three stars, Republic of Vietnam Campaign Medal, Vietnam Gallantry Cross and other numerous citations for meritorious service.

Today he says, "Joining the Big "T" Assn. has been a thrill for me, because I have gotten to know the veterans of WWII. These gentlemen are some of the true heroes of our time and I salute them."

He is currently working for Indiana Aluminum Processors in Michigan City, IN.

THOMAS J. KILELINE, born Dec. 9, 1925, Detroit, MI.

Enlisted in May 1943 and was commissioned from the Naval Academy in 1949. Served as a naval aviator and in Korea.

Received his masters in aero engineering from MIT and spent three years in A-3s on the USS *Saratoga*; 6th Flt. Staff; OPS; executive officer on the USS *Ticonderoga*, 1968-69; commanding officer at Patuxent River; commander, Navbase subil; chief legislative affairs; commander, Naval Air Forces, Atlantic Fleet. Retired in 1983.

Served as president of The Retired Officers Assn., 1986-95; chair of Military Health Care Advisory Committee for secretary of defense.

Married Dornell Thompson, daughter of an aviation pilot. His oldest son is a prospective wing commander, Winson; second son was lost in a F-14; oldest daughter was a Navy doctor, lost in an auto accident; second daughter married an aviator commander. They have seven grandchildren. He and Dornell live in Mclean, VA.

PATRICK KITT, born March 31, 1917, New York City, NY.

Enlisted in November 1943; attended boot camp at Sampson, NY; served aboard the USS *Wisconsin* (BB-64); USS *Ticonderoga* (CV-14) with the 2nd Div. as part of a five inch gun crew on May 8, 1944. He participated in battles in the Philippine Islands, Luzon, Formosa, Carolines and Okinawa.

After lunch on Jan. 21, 1945, he went below deck to visit some buddies when the sound of 20 and 40mm's began. They were under attack. He made his way to the hangar deck toward the forward port side ladder leading to their battle station gun mounts. He barely got through the hatch when the forward part of the ship exploded. The first kamikaze dived into the forward deck elevator. Some of the gun crew got through but they could not do anything because the guns were knocked out. The ammunition compartment began smoking and burning, so as the shipmates were hosing him and the compartment, he went in to turn on the sprinkler system. He then teamed up with a young ensign (name unknown) to throw hot 40mm shells overboard. By then the second kamikaze hit the superstructure. They joined the men on the flight deck who were fighting the fires and hosing everything that was smoking or burning. Long work by all hands finally got the damaged ship under control.

Memorable experiences were of the new friends he made, they still keep in touch; the great times on shore leave; and who can forget Mog Mog.

Discharged in October 1945. Awards include the Letter of Commendation with Navy Commendation Medal and Ribbon.

Married Helen after his discharge in 1945. They have six children; 14 grandchildren; and two great-grandchildren.

He returned to his job at REA, and went back to the pro ring in 1946 (he started in 1938). He was in the camp of Jake (Raging Bull) LaMotta. Two other Big "T" shipmates were also pro fighters. Jimmy Hegeman of R1-Hull and George La Falgio of V1. Both have passed away recently. He wound up doing bit parts in the movies, television and commercials. It was a great experience working with some of the big names in that media. A few years later he received a Letter of Commendation with Medal and Ribbon, a wonderful surprise. Retired from Railway Express in 1975, after 36 years; pro ring in 1947, after nine years; and show business in 1977, after 20 years. He belongs to the VFW, enjoys his family, sitting around and watching the grass grow.

JAMES H. KLEIN, born July 20, 1921, Brooklyn, NY.

Enlisted in the Naval V-5 program on June 21, 1942. He received his Naval Aviator's wings at Pennsacola, FL, NAS in July 1943.

Reported aboard the USS *Ticonderoga* (CV-14) a week after her commissioning. He served aboard in Bombing Sqdn. 80. Sailed on the shakedown cruise, then through Panama Canal to San Diego then to Hawaii. Became sick and had his appendix removed at Kaneohe Naval Hospital. Two weeks later, flew out to Ulithi and rejoined VB80

Flew in the battle for the Philippines. Transferred to the USS *Randolph* (CV-15) Bombing Sqdn. 12 for Okinawa operation. Three days after reporting aboard in Ulithi, the *Randolph* was hit by a kamikaze at night. Repair ships patched them up and they went to Okinawa.

Memorable experiences include the unexpected landing. In the year 1944 he was Ensign James H. Klein, pilot of bombing squadron VB80 aboard the aircraft carrier USS *Ticonderoga* (CV-14). At Norfolk, VA, some of the aircraft of Air Group 80 were taxied to the dock and hoisted aboard the carrier *Ticonderoga*.

On Aug. 30, 1944, the remainder of the planes of Air Group 80 were to fly from Oceana Naval Air Station out to the *Ticonderoga* in the Atlantic Ocean, 100 miles off of Virginia Beach. They arrived at the carrier on schedule. When he approached the carrier, in the groove prior to landing, he received a Roger from the signal officer, Lt. Gibson. Suddenly the plane started to fall off on the port wing. He tried correcting, but, he had slipped too much altitude, and landed in the water with wheels down.

The next thing he knew, water and foam were pouring into the cockpit like a broken main. He tried unbuckling his harness, but, could not find the release (lucky he didn't, because he was still skimming across the water). The next instant he was sitting in clear green water, then up into good fresh air. The plane had been down by the nose, but the air in the empty bomb bay had caused the plane to float up to the surface. He released the harness, slowly climbed out of the cockpit onto the starboard wing. He moved to the rear cockpit and tore off the canopy and pulled out the liferaft. Seeing his travel bag with dirty laundry in it, he pulled that out also. He inflated the liferaft, then suddenly the plane started to sink by the nose. He went into the water. Looking up he saw the plane's tail, coming down on him, he paddled away from the tail noting that the liferaft was following him. The plane's tail came down across the liferaft and pulled it under. The next thing he knew he was being pulled under by his right leg. He saw the liferaft line tangled on his right foot. With the travel bag in his left hand, he used his right hand to try and get his sheath knife to cut line or leg or anything. The travel bag full of air was pulling his left arm towards the surface. Suddenly, he was traveling toward the surface, right leg first. The raft had slipped off the plane's tail and acting like a cork was pulling him to the surface. The raft was upside down. He didn't have the strength to turn it over, so he threw the travel bag on and then climbed on. He had never inflated his Mae West.

When the destroyer pulled alongside some yelled, "Throw him a line." Then, about 10 monkey fists hit him with 10 lines. There was about a six foot sea running, so, one minute he was near the deck, and the next minute, he was looking at the water line. They dropped a rope ladder and told him to come up. He mounted the first rung with the travel bag in his left hand. He couldn't climb the ladder. The chief yelled, "Leave the bag on the raft," which he did. Then he could climb the ladder. They sent a man down to bring up the liferaft and the travel bag full of sea water and dirty laundry. He spent the night on the destroyer and the next day, when the destroyer and

Ticonderoga docked, he reported aboard the Ti, less an airplane. The signal officer, Lt. Gibson, told him his port landing flap had closed. He said he never saw anyone move so fast, and Klein thought he was moving slowly, cool, calm and collected. A week later, he saw the movie taken by the Ti cameraman. He has two 8 x 10 photos showing his plane nose down in the water. He checked the Naval Archives, but, they said that the film of the crash had been destroyed.

Returned to the States and was discharged in December 1945 with the rank of full lieutenant. He was awarded the Air Medal.

As a civilian he worked in nuclear research for 37 years. He is now retired with his fine wife Doris, daughter Marilyn, son Edward, daughter-in-law Gayle, and three grandchildren: Matthew, Jennifer and Marie.

ADAM KOMISARCIK, Captain, USN, born Gary, IN, March 13, 1934. Started Flight School in NAVCAD Class 13-55. He was Assistant Navigator on TICO from June 1963 to June 1965. A memorable experience was the Tonkin Gulf incident starting the Vietnam war. In 1976 he was the navigator on the *Midway* (CVA-41) and they participated in the evacuation of the U.S. Embassy in Siagon, ending the war. Retired from the Navy in November, 1980 and started working for the Marriott Hotels at their headquarters in Washington D.C. Retired from the Marriott in 1995.

After receiving his wings in 1956, he married Geraldine (Gerry) Schultz in her hometown of Chicago. They have three children and 10 grandchildren. They all live nearby and keep them as busy as they want to be.

ANDREW J. KORDZIEL, born Nov. 12, 1925, Mineville, NY, to Peter and Mary Kordziel, both of whom were immigrants from Poland. He was the seventh of 10 children and lived in the same small iron ore mining town while growing up. The mining company allowed gardening and the pasturing of livestock in designated areas which helped families during the depression years. His parents always had a milk cow and would raise the calf plus three hogs to butcher for meat. They also had two large vegetable gardens. They all had chores to do such as canning meat, vegetables, making butter and cheese. Education and church were very important to his family. They all had part-time jobs, participated in high school sports and enjoyed hunting and fishing. He graduated from Mineville High School in June 1943 and joined the USN in January 1944.

Served aboard the USS *Ticonderoga* from May 8, 1944, until May 1946, when he was discharged. He entered college under the GI Bill, graduating from the University of Denver with a BS degree in civil engineering in June 1951. His work career was with the Federal Government, specializing in cartography and mapping.

Married Gertrude Clarke in July 1954 and they have five children and seven grandchildren, all living in the Denver, CO, area.

HAROLD (KRINOWITZ) KRANE reported for active duty and basic training USNTS Sampson, NY, on Feb. 2, 1944. On completion he was transferred to NTS, Newport, RI, for further shipboard training.

Was assigned to the USS *Ticonderoga* (CV-14) on May 6, 1944. As log room yeoman, A Div. advanced to Y3/c on Dec. 1, 1944. Reported to the captain daily with fuel and water reports and kept the engineering records.

On Jan. 21, 1944, while having lunch in the mess hall, the first kamikaze hit the ship and after GQ was sounded, he reported to his battle station number two engine room manning the phones to the bridge.

Has four children and nine grandchildren. He is now a retired design engineer of many space programs. Resides with his wife Elaine in Boca Raton, FL. He is a past president of the Big "T" Veterans Assn.

ROGER F. LANE, born Oct. 20, 1948, Catskill, NY. Enlisted with the USN on July 24, 1968, and served until May 18, 1972. Served on the Big "T" from Dec. 10, 1969, until May 18, 1972.

Worked as a legal office supervisor in the administration department on the WESTPAC Tour; on the recovery of Apollo 16; petty officer of the month in February 1971.

Married to Lou Ella Denniston and has three children: Keith W., Heather M. and Heidi L. After naval service he returned to Catskill Savings Bank and is presently vice president and senior personnel officer. He is president of the Rotary Club of Catskill from 1995-96. He successfully received a kidney transplant in May 1995.

ROBERT W. LANGE, born Jan. 29, 1926, Jersey City, NJ. Enlisted on Jan. 24, 1944; attended boot camp at Sampson, NY; and was assigned to the USS *Ticonderoga* as damage control, 3rd Deck, M Div., Forward Engine Room.

Memorable experience was meeting his brother Ed, in Pearl Harbor.

Discharged on May 19, 1946, with the rank of MM3/c.

Married Catherine in 1949 and has four sons and five grandchildren. He is currently retired.

RICHARD C. LECHTENBERG, LT, born in Calmar, IA, on Jan. 18, 1938. He enlisted in the USN on Aug. 14, 1956. Was electronics technician until advancing to officer status, March 1, 1967.

Awards include Vietnam Service Awards, Navy Commendation and Achievement Medals. He served on *Ticonderoga* from January to November of 1973 and was the ship's last electronics material officer on the decommissioning crew.

Transferred to Navy Postgraduate School where he earned BS degree. Transferred to USS *Dwight D. Einsenhower* as the CVN-69s first electronics material officer. Retired Sept. 1, 1980 as LDO LCDR.

Has been in technical recruiting ever since, owning his own company, Dick Berg & Associates.

DOUGLAS C. LEE put on his dream sheet that he wanted the steamingest ship in the fleet. He was granted his wish for the USS *Ticonderoga's* last three years were mostly at sea.

They steamed to Vietnam twice back to back. Their mission was antisubmarine and upon return from their last trip, they went north on a top secret mission to Russia. With no radar and radio, they surprised them very well indeed upon energizing their systems planes, ships and submarines, and their main objective came out to greet them.

Three spacecraft recovery missions were next: Apollo 16, 17 and the *Ticonderoga's* last mission was Skylab One. They went to places in the South Pacific that no American ship had been since WWII.

A memorable service over the USS *Houston*, a documented encounter with the famous *Flying Dutchman* around Borneo.

And the incredible last almost 40 knot, 100 mile run to San Diego. The *Ticonderoga* proved she was one hell of a ship, right up to the end.

KENNETH EUGENE LOY, born May 27, 1923, Odgen, UT. Enlisted in the USN on June 12, 1942, as a shipboard electrician. He was stationed aboard the USS *Prometheus*, USS *Hornet* and the USS *Ticonderoga*; and participated in the battles of the Pacific Theater.

He was assigned to the *Ticonderoga* detail from the *Hornet* shakedown cruise in the spring of 1944. His wife came from their home in Spokane, WA, to Newport News, VA, to attend the commissioning of the *Ticonderoga* on May 8, 1944.

Discharged on Oct. 14, 1945, with the rank of EM1/c. Awards include the Good Conduct Medal, American Area, Philippine Liberation w/one Bronze Star and the Asiatic Pacific w/four stars.

Transferred to the Naval Reserves and was called back to active service on May 20, 1951. He was then stationed aboard the USS *George Clymer* (APA-27), and participated in battle in Korea. Discharged on May 20, 1952, with the rate of EMP1. Awards include the Korean Medal, Navy Occupation, China Service and United Nations Award.

Worked in the electrical field in various places until his retirement in 1983. They live in Maple Falls, WA, during the summer and Yuma, AZ, in the winter.

FRANK LYNCH, born Nov. 25, 1926, New Bedford, MA. Enlisted on Jan. 19, 1944, and was stationed at USNTS, Sampson, NY; NTS, Newport, RI; aboard the USS *Ticonderoga*; and PSC USNB, Bremerton, WA.

Discharged on May 20, 1946, with the rank of WT3/c.

Married Barbara and had six children and 10 grandchildren. He retired after 35 1/2 years with New England Telephone Co. as a journeyman cable splicer.

DANIEL M. MADDEN went on active duty as an ensign on July 1, 1942, at Cornell University. After indoctrination he was assigned as an instructor in the new communications course for officer at Harvard University.

While an instructor, he did temporary duty on the USS *Intrepid* on her shakedown. When the USS *Ticonderoga* was launched he was assigned to the fitting-out complement in the communications department and remained with her as a communications watch officer until after the end of WWII.

On Jan. 21, 1945, he was in his room when the first kamikaze hit. He went to his battle station in the communications office in the island.

After the war he went on inactive duty. Later he served on TDY on the 6th Fleet Flagship. He retired from the Naval Reserve as a lieutenant on June 30, 1962. His wife Huan of 47 years died in 1988. He is a writer and lives in Phoenix.

MIKE MATHIAS, born Sept. 24, 1927, St. Paul, MN. Enlisted in the USNR on September 24 for the duration. He was a member of the V-1 Crash Crew, Repair 8. He was assigned to the USS *Ticonderoga*

(CV-14) from 1945-46, and participated in battle at Okinawa and others.

Discharged in 1946 with the rank of damage controlman 1/c during the four year hitch, Korean War, in the South Pacific, aboard the USS Frontier (AD-25).

Married Rose Marie and has five children: Michael, Rick, Sandy, Tim and Terry; and nine grandchildren.

He retired from USPS (postal service) after 32 1/2 years and from LIUNA (labor union) AFL-CIO. He served as general president of local 323; Mail Handlers Union of Minnesota and North Dakota; central region representative, policy and steering; committee for 18 states; and 20 years of service as union executive.

FRANK J. McADAMS III graduated from Mount Carmel High School, Chicago, IL. He went to USNR boot camp in 1959; served on active duty as HN (Corpsman) on USS Ticonderoga in the Medical Dept. from Oct. 12, 1960—Sept. 7, 1962. He made one Western Pacific cruise.

Was commissioned 2LT on Dec. 15, 1966, in USMC. He was assigned as motor transport officer, 1st Mar. Div. in Vietnam and participated in combat operations. He was awarded the Navy-Marine Corps Medal, Navy Commendation 2/V plus Vietnam Service Medals (including Armed Forces Expeditionary Medal for Laos 1961). Was promoted to CPT, USMC and released from active duty in 1970.

Graduated from Loyola University, Chicago, with a BS in history (1967) and from UCLA Graduate School of screenwriting with MFA in 1979. Won the UCLA Samual Goldwyn Screenwriting Award, first place, 1978 and 1979.

Worked as journalist, 1970-76, sports editor and general assignment reporter, *Laguna News-Post, Anaheim Bulletin*. Now teaching screenplay structure at UCLA Extension Writers Program and Adjunct Professor, USC School of Cinema/TV. Also instructor at UC Irvine Extension Writers Program and University Extended Education Cal State University, Fullerton. Commissioned in California State Military Reserve. Presently serving as lieutenant colonel deputy commander, Installation Support Group, Armed Forces Reserve Center, Los Alamitos, CA. Married Patricia Ann, December 27, 1966.

DONALD R. MCGORY, born April 24, 1937, Caledonia, NY. Enlisted in the USN on Feb. 14, 1956, and attended boot camp, Bainbridge, MD. Was assigned to the USS *Ernest G. Small* (DDR-838), October 1956-July 1957; NAS Agana Guam, August 1957-February 1959; USS *Bennington* (CVS-20), April 1959-January 1960; USS *Ticonderoga* (CVA-14), January 1960-August 1961; NTC Great Lakes, IL, October 1961-October 1963; US Naval Advisory Group, Republic of Korea, USN, April 1964-February 1966; Fleet Composite Sqdn. 10, Cuba, May 1966-May 1967; USS *Wilkerson*, (DL-5), May 1967-April 1969; USN Support Activity, Danang Vietnam, May 1969-May 1970; USN Commissary Store, Pearl Harbor, July 1970-April 1972; and the USS *Mount Baker* (AE-34), May 1972-Sept. 30, 1975.

Memorable experiences were crossing the equator aboard the USS *Small* in 1957; plank owner of the USS *Mount Baker*; two WESTPAC cruises on the USS *Ticonderoga*.

Retired on Sept. 30, 1975, as MSC. Awards include

the Vietnam Service Medal, Vietnam Campaign Medal and Good Conduct Award (four).

Currently fully retired, lifelong bachelor and living in Gorham, NY.

NORMAN K. MCINNIS, CAPT, USN, RET, born Sept. 27, 1919, in Sterlington, LA. Graduated Ouachita Parish HS, Monroe, LA; Louisiana State University, Baton Rouge, LA, 1940-42; USN flight training, Pensacola, graduated as naval aviator, September 1942.

Completed advanced training as a dive bomber pilot, November 1942 and carrier qualifications in December 1942. Reported to VS-3 in El Centro, CA, in January 1943. They deployed aboard *Yorktown* to Pearl Harbor and commenced the Central Pacific Campaign. Their first engagement was a raid on Marcus Island Aug. 31, 1943.

Other military duty stations include: 1944—training command, Cecil Field, FL; 1945—VB-75, Chincoteague, VA; 1948—General Line School, Newport, RI; 1949—Aeronautical Rocket Laboratory Lake Denmark, Dover, NJ; 1950—VA3B Air Group 4, Cecil Field, Jacksonville, FL; 1952—Albuquerque, NM for Special Weapons School.

Completed two deployments to WESPAC during the Korean War; returned to NAS to Navy War College, New Port, RI; 1954—assigned to The Joint Staff of the Air Force, Navy and Army Target Intelligence Unit in Washington, DC; 1958—VAH-9, Sanford, FL, deployed to the Mediterranean and participated in Lebanon crisis.

Returned to the States and became CO of VAH-3; squadron commander, VAH-123, Whidby Island, WA; 1961—ops officer then XO, USS *Hornet*; 1963—Imperial Defense College, London, England; 1964—CNO's staff as head of Flag Plot (OP-333) and went through the Dominican Republic crises. During this time he supervised and was responsible for the building of a river boat for Market Times Forces. Departed Flag Plot with the Navy Commendation Medal.

In 1967 received orders as CO of *Mattiponi* AO-41; 1968—*Ticonderoga* and Tonkin Gulf; 1969—Carrier Div. 3 Staff as chief of staff; 1970—Commander Fleet Air Force Norfolk with HQ at NAS Oceana, VA.

Retired July 31, 1970, then worked for McDonnell-Douglas in Long Beach, CA for 10 years. Went to Shreveport, LA, to help a boyhood friend in trouble with a commuter airline; four years later when he left, it was a thriving business. For the next eight years he continued to fix other commuter airlines.

He and wife Sal have three children: Molly, Mary and Norman Jr.

HUGH T. MCKENZIE, born March 31, 1926, Chattanooga, TN. Enlisted in the USMC on May 25, 1944, with the Marine Detachment. Attended boot camp; San Diego Recruit Depot; Sea School Training at Marine Base, San Diego; and served aboard USS *Ticonderoga* at North Island, San Diego, September 1944.

Participated in battles in five engagements against the enemy in Western Pacific from November 1944-August 1945.

Memorable experiences include being topside during the typhoon; topside on the day that all three groups of Halls's 3rd Fleet came together as one group with a fly over, the largest fleet ever assembled before or since WWII; and being topside on Jan. 21, 1945.

Discharged on Feb. 3, 1946, with the rank of private first class. Awards include campaign ribbons and Battle Stars.

Married on May 13, 1950, and raised six children. Now has five great-grandchildren. He worked as a team-

ster truck driver for 43 years. He is now retired and enjoying Walleye fishing and the good life.

FRANK J. MERRILL first went aboard the USS *Ticonderoga* for the commissioning day ceremonies on May 8, 1944. At the time he was an AMM3/c serving as a plane captain on F6F fighters with Fighting 80 of Air Group 80 stationed at Oceana, VA. Shortly thereafter they moved on to the ship. The plane captains were assigned to the V-2 Div. They went on shakedown cruise in the waters near Trinidad and Venezuela and then returned to the States for a short period before leaving for the Pacific via the Panama Canal, San Diego and Pearl Harbor and on west.

They joined the fleet in the western Pacific and first saw action in the Philippines in November 1944. After that they were involved in several actions in the Philippines, South China Sea, Okinawa and the Tokyo area. They were severely damaged and suffered heavy casualties coming out of the South China Sea when they were struck by two kamikaze planes on Jan. 21, 1945. On that day he had spotted his plane about even with the forward end of the island along with several other fighters. Pilot Andy Anderson came up to him and said that enemy planes had been reported in the area and to get the plane on the catapult, which they did. He was immediately launched along with four other F6Fs. Leonard Thorson, another F6F plane captain, and he ran down to the mess hall to get something to eat before returning to the flight deck to wait for their planes. They were still below deck when they heard and felt the impact of the first hit. They then headed for topside. The ship was burning fiercely and their bombs were rolling around on the hangar deck which was awash with burning gasoline. When they got to the flight deck they could see the large hole in the deck near where their planes had been secured. A few minutes later a second kamikaze came in from the starboard and hit the island.

After the fires were put out they headed for Ulithi where some of the wounded were transferred to a hospital ship. They then went on to Pearl Harbor and then to Bremerton for repairs. He remembers getting a 25 day leave and then back to the Pacific later in the spring.

They joined Task Force 38 and were attacking Tokyo when word came from the admiral to stop the attack, and for all planes to drop their bombs in the drink and return to the carriers. The fleet was to shoot down all bogies in a friendly sort of way. A few days later the *Ticonderoga* was honored by being chosen to accompany the USS *Langley* into Tokyo Bay. There were two or three cruisers or destroyers with them. From there they returned to Hawaii and then to Tacoma, WA, for Navy Day in October 1945. He received his discharge at Great Lakes on Dec. 10, 1945.

Presently, he is in the process of retiring from his law practice in Naperville, IL, and surrounding counties. He and his wife, Joan, have had some very enjoyable get together's with some of the V-2 Div. shipmates and their wives during the past five or six years: Leonard and Phillis Thorson, Primo and Mary Ann Rossetto, William and Pat Merges, Lawrence and Pat Miles.

CHESTER M. MIGUT, born July 22, 1925, South River, NJ. Enlisted in the USN on Nov. 20, 1943; attended boot camp in Newport, RI; Radio School, Newport, RI, and University of Wisconsin; and was temporarily stationed at Philadelphia Naval Base, PA, and Norfolk, VA. Was assigned to the USS *Ticonderoga* on Aug. 18, 1944, K-2 Signal Div. and remained there until discharged. He participated in all battles of the *Ticonderoga*.

Memorable experience was of Jan. 21, 1945, being relieved at 11:30 AM from first watch on the signal bridge. He left the hangar deck, chow line and mess hall arriving in his living compartment when GQ sounded and the kamikaze attack commenced. He was trapped below decks until about 11:30 PM. He assisted in some damage control and directed some wounded to sick bay.

Discharged on April 17, 1946, with the rank of S1/c. He received all the awards given to the *Ticonderoga* crew during WWII.

Married Sophie Marie Krukowski and now has two sons and two grandchildren. After being discharged he graduated from Seton Hall University and worked as an auditor for a number years. Later he retired as a purchasing manager.

ALLAN R. MILES, born Aug. 16, 1937, Waterbury, CT. Enlisted in the USN on Nov. 8, 1956, and attended basic training in Bainbridge, MD, electronics and FT training at Great Lakes.

Served aboard the USS *Ticonderoga*, in the FOX Div. from December 1957 until November 1960. He made three cruises with the Pacific Fleet; was part of the crew who, in 1960, won the Battle Efficiency and Operations excellence competition. The *Ticonderoga* wore the big "E" proudly. He received the Navy Good Conduct Medal and the Armed Forces Expeditionary Medal (Taiwan Straits).

Married Gloria in 1957 and has three children. The electronics training received in the USN served them well over the past 35 years that he worked in the computer industry. In February 1995 they started an early retirement, earlier than planned. They live in Andover, MN, and have four wonderful grandchildren living close enough to be with regularly. They are looking forward to their retirement.

ROBERT N. MILLER was born in San Diego, CA, and was a graduate of the US Naval Academy Class of 1940. He went to the USS *Helena* (CL-50) as the assistant engineer officer and was on board when she was attacked at Pearl Harbor on Dec. 7, 1941, and for which the ship received the Navy Unit Citation. He went to the USS *Bancroft* (DD-498) and then the USS *Lardner* (DD-487) from which he participated in the Guadalcanal and Solomon Island campaigns.

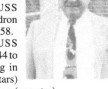

He became a naval aviator in 1943 and served as commander of various aviation units, one of which was embarked on USS *Cabot* (CVE-28). He later served as Commander Bombing Fighter 15 and as air officer and XO of the USS *Admiralty Island* (CVE-99).

During Korea he served as CO Attack Squadron 44 aboard the carrier Midway. This was followed by successive tours on the staffs of COMSIXTHFLT and COMFAIRQUONSET; student and instructor at Naval War College and Commander of Air Group 3 aboard USS *Ticonderoga*. He also served as training officer COMFAIRJAX, XO, NAS Norfolk, VA and Operations Officer on staff of COMCARDIV 1.

He took command of USS *Aludra* (AF-55) in March 1964 after a tour of duty with the JCS as actions officer in J-5, Plans, Policy and Programs. He assumed command of USS *Ticonderoga* on May 14, 1965. He subsequently became chief of staff of COMCARDIV 6 and later director of Command and Staff School at the

Naval War College. He ended his Navy Career as Commanding Officer of Naval Air Facility and deputy superintendent, Naval Post Graduate School, Montery, CA.

He retired July 1, 1971. Decorations include the Air Medal, Navy Commendation Medal and medals for service in different theaters of operations.

After 10 years of ranch life in Paso Robles, CA, he and his wife of 53 years, the former Elizabeth Broome, moved to Santa Barbara, CA, along with their four children and five grandchildren. Following a short illness, he died June 13, 1995.

EDWARD LAWRENCE MILLS, born Sept. 23, 1925, Tampa, FL. Enlisted with the USN on Oct. 2, 1942, and was assigned to the V-2 Div. Was stationed at Naval Air Station, Jacksonville, FL; NAS Vero Beach, FL; Casu 23 and 25; aboard the USS *Ticonderoga* (CV-14); Hedron FAW#8; and Casu 53 and 58.

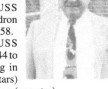

Served on the USS *Ticonderoga* from June 1944 to Dec. 5, 1945, participating in the Asiatic Pacific (four stars) and the Philippine Liberation (one star).

Discharged Feb. 7, 1946, Shoemaker, CA, with the rank of AMM2/c. Awards include the Good Conduct Medal and the WWII Victory Medal.

Retired from Eastern Airline after 33 years and he is now working as a real estate broker. He is married and has one daughter.

GEORGE L. MILLS, LT (jg) OOD, G Div. officer. He was a student at St. Patrick's Seminary, Menlo Park, CA, 1965-66. He obtained his teaching credential at Univ. of San Francisco in 1967 and started teaching at Continuation School in San Rafael in 1968.

Married Gayle Virginia Wittenmeier in 1969; Christopher Lawrence was born in 1970 and Claire Marie in 1974. He started teaching at San Rafael High School in 1976; earned his MA in education from Univ. of San Francisco in 1978 and received Award for Classroom Excellence from California Assoc. for teachers of English (CATE). Fellow of UC, Berkeley's Bay Area Writing Project - 1985.

On Christmas vacation in 1995, he visited England and Ireland with his family: Gayle, an English teacher at McAteer HS in San Francisco; Chris, UC Berkeley graduate and researcher and Clair, UCLA drama student attending U. of Birmingham for her junior year abroad. A highlight was sharing theater experiences with the family - Tom Stopards's *Arcadia* in London, Shakespeare's *Measure for Measure* in Stratford and *Singing in the Rain* in Oxford.

EDWARD MINGLE JR. enlisted on Jan. 13, 1944, on the V-6 program, at the age of 31. Was sent to Sampson, NY, for boot camp; assigned to the USS *Ticonderoga* crew, April 1; went to Newport, RI, for

training on the USS *Ranger*; then on to Radar School, Virginia Beach, VA; graduated May 7, 1944. Boarded the *Ticonderoga* on May 9 and arrived in Hawaii and given two extra weeks of radar training at Camp Cattlin; then moved from there to Ulithi. Received PO3/c, then PO2/c; was mail petty officer and police petty officer of the V-4 Div. over a year.

Upon discharge on Dec. 20, 1945, he returned home to his wife and four year old son. Went back to the florist business, which he left to go into the USN. He retired in 1965.

The Big "T" Veterans Assn. was formed in 1972 and he was elected 1st vice president in 1973; served as president, 1977-78; reunion chairman, 1975, Atlantic City, NJ; co-chairman, 1977, Norfolk, VA; and served on several other national reunion committees. Was chairman, Patriots Point, Big "T" exhibit aboard the USS Yorktown, SC, 1978-81; and secretary of the organization, 1974-77 and 1981-85.

ROBERT J. MODERSOHN, born June 6, 1924, Irvington, NJ. Enlisted in the USN in April 13, 1943 and was assigned to communications of the K-1 Div. Military locations include Newport, RI, boot camp; Chicago, IL, Pre-radio School; Takoma Park, MD, electricity and radio; Washington, DC, NRL-Radio Material School; Newport News, VA, assigned to the Big "T"; and the Pacific Theater, 1944-46 aboard the Big "T". Participated in battle at Leyte Gulf, South China Sea, Okinawa and Japan.

Discharged in Feb. 7, 1946, with the rank of ETM1/c. Awards include four medals w/six stars.

Married Olly in June 1947; has two sons and three grandsons. Worked for 3M Co. for 36 years in sales and marketing administration and retired in 1988. He is now a volunteer tour guide for the community architectural control committee.

RICHARD T. MORGAN served with the USMC from Dec. 15, 1942 until Oct. 20, 1945. Was stationed at Parris Island, January 1943 to February 1944; Portsmouth, VA, February 1944 to May 1944; Marine detachment on the Big "T", 1944-45; 20mm guns during the attack; and landed at Yokosuka, Japan on Aug. 30, 1945.

Attended Dickinson High School, graduating in 1942; received BS degree from Seton Hall, 1948; MS degree, Kean College, 1954; and PD degree at TC Columbia University, 1970.

Worked as a teacher in Bernands Township, NJ, 1950-54; Oceanside, LI, 1954-87; and Long Island University, 1969. Hobbies include art, swimming, golf, tennis and music.

GEORGE MUMPER, born May 13, 1927, Philadelphia, PA. Enlisted on May 14, 1944, and was assigned to

a five inch magazine gun. Participated in battles in the Philippine Islands; Formosa; Saigon; Marshall Island; and Okinawa.

Discharged on Oct. 30, 1947, with the rank of S2/c.

Married and has four sons and five grandchildren. He retired from the Philadelphia Police Department as lieutenant.

RONALD LEE NAEGELE, born June 15, 1942, Fennhaven, IN. Enlisted on July 4, 1960, and served aboard the USS *Ticonderoga* (CVA-14) and during the Cuban crisis.

Memorable experiences include making coxswain in 1962 and stayed until he was discharged in 1961, started as a hot caseman on a five inch gun mount until discharged. One experience he will never forget was when the other guy was firing and he was catching hot casings. He turned to throw one and heard gunfire again. He was not ready, so he ducked and it flew over his head, but he was ready to catch the next one. Also when they had been overseas for nine months and they were coming back when a plane was to fly off the ship. The engine died and the plane went off the end of the ship and the pilot died. That was a very sad time. Then a plane flew in and hit the net, which was very exciting. He and Robert Faulkenburg hitchhiked from Taswell, IN, to Long Beach, CA, and joined the USN. Their port was San Diego. They were together all four years. In the 1970s, Robert was hanging drywall in an elevator shaft and fell down the shaft and died. That was a big loss.

Discharged on June 1, 1964, with the rank of E3.

Married on Oct. 18, 1963, and has two daughters and two grandchildren. He was a tavern owner for 11 years; built log homes for two years; and then a cook at Branchville. He is now working in a prison training center and also repairs appliances, air conditioners and small engines.

FRANK R. NEUBAUER joined the USN on April 16, 1943, at the age of 17. Attended boot camp at Great Lakes, IL; was assigned to the USS *Pennsylvania*; duty in the Aleutians; assigned to the USS Hornet (CV-12), a short run; then new construction to the USS *Ticonderoga* (CV-14), plank owner, until the end of the war. His highest rank held was EM3/c.

On Jan. 21, 1945, he was eating lunch when the ship was hit. He tried to reach his battle station, which was one of the two 36 inch searchlights. The second kamikaze then hit the inland and he was unable to reach his station. He then helped out on the flight deck.

After the war he played harmonica professionally on stage, television, etc.

Married and has two sons and seven grandchildren. He is now divorced. Member of the Big "T" Assn. He loves the Big "T".

WILLIAM E. NICHOLS, born Oct. 6, 1921, Sharon, PA. Enlisted in the USN on Jan. 21, 1942. Was stationed at NTS, Newport, RI; Navy Service School, Chicago, Navy Pier; NAS, Quonset Pt., RI, CASU 22; NAS

Norfolk, VA, where he was assigned to the USS *Ticonderoga*, from May 8, 1944, through October 1945; and finally NAS, CASU 47, Saipan.

Participated in battles at Southern Luzon, Visayas, and Central Luzon, PI; Formosa; Saigon; French Indo China; South China Coast; Hong Kong; Okinawa; Marshall Islands; Southern Kyushu; Hiroshima Bay; Kure; Kure Naval Base; Tokyo; and Honshu.

Discharged on Dec. 11, 1947, with the rate of AMM1/c. Awards include the American Campaign, Asiatic Pacific w/four Bronze Stars, Philippine Liberation w/two Bronze Stars, Good Conduct, and WWII Victory Medal.

Was married for 45 years and is now a widower. Has two sons and two grandchildren, Tyler and Lacey Nichols. He retired from the state of California, office of the state architect and is now playing on a 30' boat in San Francisco Bay.

FREDERICK W. NOTTER, CPT, USNR, RET, born West Islip, NY, on May 23, 1937. Enlisted in the USNR on June 28, 1961, and was commissioned ensign USNR Nov. 15, 1961, at OCS, Newport, RI, Fox Trot Co.

Ordered to USS *Ticonderoga* (CVA-14); attended ABC School, Philadelphia, PA, November 1961-January 1962; reported to *Ticonderoga* at Bremerton, WA, Naval Shipyard, January 1962; homeported San Diego, CA, June 1962.

Second tour included Gulf of Tonkin incident in August 1964 with Maddox and Turner Joy. Served as "B" Div. and "N" Div. officer. Released from active duty Nov. 17, 1964, and entered selected Reserves. Commanded three different units and served until his retirement, June 30, 1995.

Civilian occupations were as teacher, principal, assistant superintendent and superintendent of schools in the West Islip Public Schools. Now retired and playing golf, tennis and selling real estate.

Married Frances Connelly, Nov. 20, 1965; they have four children: Kathleen, David, Alison and James. David, a commissioned supply officer, USN, serving on USS *Jarrett* FFG-33.

GEORGE E. NOWACK, born June 30, 1924, Cairnbrook, PA. Enlisted on Aug. 23, 1943, and was stationed in Newport, RI, EM School and the USS *Ticonderoga*. Participated in all the battles of the *Ticonderoga* during WWII.

Discharged on Nov. 22, 1946, with the rank of EM2/c.

Married and has three children, one of whom is deceased. He is currently retired.

J.B. NOWELL, born Jan. 1, 1926, Henderson County, TX. Enlisted on April 2, 1943, in the USN (minority cruise). Graduated from NATTC, Norman, OK, in January 1944; Catapult School at Philadelphia Navy Yard; shakedown on the USS *Franklin* (CV-13); assigned to the USS *Ticonderoga* when it was new and until the end of WWII; and was assigned to NAS Ford Island, HI, the remainder of the minority cruise.

Discharged on Dec. 31, 1946, and joined the inactive Reserve. He was called back in October 1950 during the Korean Conflict and spent 14 months at Alameda NAS and was discharged in December 1951 at Corpus Christi, TX. Awards include the WWII Victory Medal, Good Conduct Medal, Philippine Liberation w/one Battle Star, American Campaign, National Defense, Asiatic Pacific w/four Battle Stars and the Philippine Presidential Unit Citation.

Married on Dec. 2, 1949, and has three sons, all

college graduates. Worked for UOP, Inc. for 28 years as an oil refinery inspector. He retired and started his own inspection business on March 1, 1981. He trained his two oldest boys and turned the corporation over to them in 1987. His youngest son is a computer programmer in Houston. He bought a ranch in Menard, TX, with lots of deer and turkey and works a few cows. After nearly 45 years of marriage, they have a close and happy family.

DONALD J. OLEJNIK SR., born Sept. 15, 1946, Toledo, OH. Enlisted on Aug. 18, 1964, and was assigned to the USS *Ticonderoga* from September 1965 until August 1967. On Jan. 16, 1967, he was promoted to radarman 3/c.

Discharged on Aug. 15, 1967, with rank of RD3. Awards include the Navy Unit Commendation Ribbon for service during Oct. 28, 1966, to May 21, 1967, while participating in combat operations in Southeast Asia against North Vietnam military installations.; National Defense Medal, Vietnam Service Medal w/three Bronze Stars and the Republic of Vietnam Campaign Medal.

Married Adita in May 1970; has one son, FC3 Donald Olejnik, who served aboard the USS Princeton (CG-59) as a FCT3/c; one daughter, Lisa; and one grandson. He has been employed with Champion Spark Plug Co. for 27 years, presently as a senior mechanical technician in the research and development department. He has been elected to the nominating committee for the Big "T" Veterans' Assn., 1994-95.

JOHN R. OLSON (OLSZEWSKI) was born in Milwaukee, WI. Enlisted with the USN on March 9, 1943, Milwaukee, WI. Attended boot camp at Farragut, ID; Fleet Radio School, Farragut, ID; Bremerton, WA; Whidbey Island, WA, FAW6, as a radio service operator on Med. Bombers, PV-1s and PV2s; Air Gunnery School; and was transferred to the USS *Ticonderoga* on March 4, 1945, with the V-4 Div. as an ART3/c. During the invasion of Okinawa he was on the flight deck making a ARC-1 radio change on a F6F, when the GQ gong went off, followed by a voice, "Attention, Bogie Diving on Ginger," and he asked a running pilot, "Who's Ginger?," "We are, and move your —, and welcome to war." Learned how to make pink lady cocktails and acquire spare parts for radar bubbles. Also participated in battle in Japan.

Discharged on March 14, 1946, with the rank of AETM3/c. He married a wonderful girl and has four sons. His first wife passed away and he remarried a lovely lady with six children and countless grandchildren. God's been good.

Memorable experiences were his three years in the USN and all of it being memorable.

Presently retired and trying to relive those three years.

DANIEL W. OWENS born June 19, 1933, Newton, NJ. Enlisted in the USN on March 6, 1952, and was assigned to O-I Div. Discharged Jan. 30, 1956, with the rank of RD2.

Married Mary Search and has two children, Jeff and Janice. Attended Ohio State University; worked for the US Government, Picatinny Arsenal, Dover, NJ, as a member of the US Army Instrumentation Missile Team; and a logistic management specialist for 30 years with the project manager's office for mine, counter mines and demolition's.

PARKER W. PATTERSON was born in Trenton, NJ; graduated high school; attended Penn State for one year; then worked about for six months. The draft for Vietnam was nearing its peak so he enlisted in the USN 120 day delay program. As fate would have it the same day he was sworn in and the draft papers came in the mail. Reported to boot camp at Great Lakes on March 27, 1967. After attending many schools including nuclear power, he was assigned to the USS *Juneau* (LPD-10) (plank owner). In July 1970 he was transferred to the USS *Ticonderoga*, which was still a CVA and later became a CVS. The first six months he was in aft engine room. From then until his discharge he was in generator engineering and acted as division damage control officer.

Most memorable experiences were aboard the *Ticonderoga* during the Apollo and Skylab recoveries; when an oiler lost its steering and its fan tail almost hit them in the side.

Discharged on June 27, 1973, with the rank of MM2. He then worked in the boiler room at AE Staley Mfg., Morrisville, PA, for 13 years. In May 1987 he began working at Gilberton Power Co., Frachville, PA, where he is currently operations manager.

Married his lovely wife, Laura, in October 1972. They do not have any children.

ANTHONY J. PEREIRA joined the USN on Sept. 20, 1943, three months after turning 18. He attended boot camp in Newport, RI; Electrical School, Newport, RI; Boiler and Turbine School, Philadelphia, PA; and was then assigned to the USS *Ticonderoga*, Newport News, VA, (plank owner). Was assigned to E Div., generator and switchboard watch stander. Discharged May 15, 1946, with the rank of EM2/c.

After discharge he got married and has two children. Served in MSTS in Europe; stationary engineer at Polaroid; and at Bridgewater Correctional Institute. He is now retired and self-employed in real estate with gardening as a hobby.

WALTER J. PIELOCIK, born Feb. 27, 1922, Clinton, MA. Enlisted in the USN on Oct. 12, 1942, and was sent to NTS Newport, RI; NTC Jacksonville, FL; Rio Grande, NJ, CASU 23; Willow Grove, PA, CASU 24; Oceana, VA, CASU 25; and then transferred to the USS *Ticonderoga* (CV-14). Participated in every battle the *Ticonderoga* was in.

Memorable experience was of Jan. 21, 1945, he had an early chow and was just about to step out on the flight deck when the first kamikaze hit. The hatch protected him when the blast closed the hatch before he was able to step on deck. Had he been two or three seconds earlier he would have been gone.

Discharged on Jan. 16, 1946, with the rank of AMM2/c. Awards include the WWII Victory Medal, American Theater Medal, Good Conduct Medal, Asiatic-Pacific Theater Medal and the Philippine Liberation Medal.

Married on June 22, 1946, and has three children and five grandchildren. He is presently in shopping center management living in Richlands, VA.

ATLEY C. PRICE was born in Cynthiana, KY. Enlisted in the USN on Feb. 21, 1942, at the age of 25. Following the completion of basic training at Great Lakes, IL, his first duty assignment was with B Div., as a fireman in the boiler room of the Naval Armory Gunnery School located at Michigan City, IN. In February 1944 he was sent to Fire Fighting School in Philadelphia, where after he joined the crew of the USS *Ticonderoga* on May 8, 1944. Participated in all battles and campaigns in which the *Ticonderoga* was in from the date of its commissioning until his discharge.

After completing their shakedown cruise to Trinidad and through the Panama Canal, he became a permanent crew member as a WT2/c in B Div. Boiler Room where he served continuously until signing of the Armistice with Japan. Thereafter, he returned to the States aboard the USS *Wasp* and was discharged on Oct. 25, 1945, with the rank of WT2/c. Awards include the Asiatic-Pacific Medal w/four stars, Philippine Liberation Medal w/one Bronze Star and the Good Conduct Ribbon.

While stationed at the Naval Armory in Michigan City he married Evelyn and they had a son, Atley C. Price Jr. Following his discharge they moved to his hometown in north central Kentucky and spent the next 23 years farming. In 1968, they returned to Michigan City where they worked at maintaining a large apple orchard until their retirement in 1990. He passed away Aug. 5, 1994.

REAMES W. RAINEY, born March 30, 1924, Nashville, TN. Enlisted on Dec. 8, 1942, and was sent to boot camp at Farragut, ID; Diesel School; served aboard the USS *Ranier* (AE-5); the USS *Hornet* (CV-12); and the USS *Ticonderoga* (CV-14). Participated in battle in Western Carolines; Leyte; Luzon; Okinawa; and Japan.

Memorable experience was of Jan. 21, 1945, he was sitting on his bunk, second deck, port quarter with MM3/c Carl Gaworecki. When they heard the antiaircraft guns firing they ran up to the hangar deck and ran back down the hatch, they had just come up and forward on the second deck. Carl, on the hangar deck, would have been about where and when the first plane hit. He did not see Carl again, he was listed as MIA. Rainey ran to the #3 fire room and was there when the second plane hit the island. It shook the ship all the way to the bottom. He put his helmet on, the first time since it was issued.

Discharged Oct. 12, 1945, with the rank of MM3/c. Awards include the American Theater Medal, Asiatic-Pacific Medal w/five stars, WWII Victory Medal, Philippine Liberation Medal w/one star and the Navy Occupation Medal w/Asiatic Bar (clasp).

Married and has one daughter. He retired after 30 years as a fireman in Los Angeles City and 10 years as a police officer for the Dept. of Airports, Los Angeles City.

ROGER RAPP, born March 8, 1913, Albany, NY. Enlisted on Nov. 15, 1942, and was stationed aboard the

USS *Ticonderoga* and Quonset Point, Oceana, VA. Discharged on Nov. 8, 1945, with the rank of AM2/c.

Memorable experience was being a police petty officer on the shakedown to Trinidad in 1944.

Married Martha Maxson and they have a son, Roger Rapp Jr. He retired with disability from Griffith Air Base.

CHARLES F. RAU was born June 5, 1925, in Columbus, OH. He enlisted in the USNR in 1943 and completed recruit training at Great Lakes and Hospital Corps School, Bainbridge, MD. First assignment as a Corpsman was at the Navy Hospital, Charleston, SC, and from there to Lion Four during which tour he received an appointment to the Navy V-12 pre-dental program in 1944 which terminated at wars end in 1945. He returned to the Ohio State University and graduated from the College of Dentistry in 1950. The Korean Conflict provided orders back to active duty in 1951 and he augmented to USN the same year.

Duties prior to *Ticonderoga* included a brief return to Great Lakes, USS *Nereus* (AS-17), Naval Shipyard Boston, a postgraduate year at the Naval Dental School, Bethesda, FASRON 111 and NAS North Island. The two great years as dental officer in TICO from August 1960—August 1962 were followed by graduate specialty training in periodontics at Ohio State and a year of residency training at NS Treasure Island. A return once again to Great Lakes was followed by assignments to the Naval Dental Clinics in Guam and Norfolk from which he retired in 1972.

He began a career in dental education at the University of Louisville and left that after more than five years to enter private practice in Zanesville, OH. Missing the academic environment, he returned to teaching along with private practice at the University of Florida. His last academic move was occasioned by appointment as professor and chair of the Dept. of Oral Medicine/Periodontics at the University of Detroit, School of Dentistry. He was later appointed associate dean for Student Affairs and Advanced Education from which position he retired in December 1990.

Married Carolyn Grace Rau and has daughter, Kathleen; son, Michael; stepsons, Craig and Kevin; and five grandchildren. Retired to Colorado and enjoys skiing, hiking, golfing and traveling.

BRUNO ROMANOSKI served with the RSVR Unit, Wheeling, WV, and was assigned to the 5th Naval District HQ, Norfolk, VA; USS *Wyoming* (BB); USS *Sangamon* (CVE); ComFairWest HQ; USS *Ticonderoga* (CVA-14); USS *Essex* (CVA); USN Hospital, Great Lakes, IL; USN Hospital, Sampson, NY; and the USN Hospital, St. Albans.

Being a flag radioman he was assigned to the flagship *Ticonderoga*, Carrier Div. HQ and Battle Task Force Group HQ. Was assigned to radio shack duty; a battle station; and flight quarters on the starboard open side of the bridge at primary fly station overlooking the takeoffs and landings of the flight deck reporting to the ships air commander; and sometimes was assigned to the admirals bridge. Transferred to the *Essex* twice via breeches while CVA fueled the destroyer picket boat and three times to the *Ticonderoga*. Left the CVA-14 late afternoon after enemy locations were found on the island, a few hours before the ship was hit by the Japanese planes.

In 1941 he was assigned to the USS *Wyoming* radio communications for battleship squadron and Atlantic Fleet personnel being assigned to the flag office. On Dec. 7, 1941, the *Wyoming* was at Casco Bay, Portland, ME, when a message was received on the radio, "Early call to radio shack without a meal to take overall day duty. Execute Plan X. This is not a drill." He took the message to the officers lounge for the captain and another copy to the communication officer. In 1942 he transferred to the USS *Sangamon* (CVE-26) as the lone sailor aboard the ship, until weeks later when other crew members arrived aboard. While in charge of the radio shack he had to bring up to date the American and British Code Books. There were so many additions that it was one continuos job because the building of the US Naval and British Fleets. The *Sangoman* headed for the North Atlantic Patrol and escort of convoys to Britain and Russia.

Awards include the American Defense w/clasp, American Campaign w/clasp, African Campaign w/clasp and the Pacific Campaign w/nine clasps.

PHILIP ROSENBERG, born May 3, 1926, Chicago, IL. He tried to enlist but because of bad eyesight had to wait until he was drafted into the USN on June 29, 1944. After boot camp at Great Lakes and 13 weeks in Gunnery School, he was sent to Bremerton, WA, in February 1945 in a replacement draft for the USS *Ticonderoga's* Gunnery Div. kamikaze attack losses.

As the ship left the dock after repairs, he looked over the side and his only pair of glasses fell off into the water. He was assigned to the 4th Div. new twin 20mm guns, during gunnery practice on towed sleeves while en route and came close to hitting their own plane towing the target. He was quickly promoted to captain of the gun sponson and taken off the guns.

In Tokyo Bay in October 1945, he volunteered for small boat courier duty on the ship's LCVP. The big typhoon came up suddenly, the sea too rough to approach the gangway and the OOD ordered the boat to tie up at the fantail and the crew to climb up hand over hand on a knotted monkey line. He almost made it, but fell back down 30 feet into the well deck of the LCVP. The next voice he heard was his division officer, Lt. Vandermade, getting the details from the doctor in sick bay for the funeral report for burial at sea. He recovered, made all the magic carpet runs and helped mothball the ship until he was discharged as GM3/c in June 1946.

Went to college, married, has two children and three grandchildren, and is still an executive in the motivation and incentive field.

A. DARREL RUSTH was discharged at Hunters Point, CA in March 1965. He and his wife Jane have three children: Kari, Lori and Andy. They lived in San Francisco for approximately one year after discharge before returning to Klamath Falls, the town where he grew up.

He passed the CPA exam in 1970 and became a partner in a regional CPA firm in 1971. In 1986 they down-sized the practice from multi-offices to a single office in Klamath Falls.

Jane is a housewife, instrumental in raising the three kids who, hopefully, have now left the roost affording us more leisure time. Jane is very active in church and other social type activities, whereas Rusth is interested in the arts of the outdoors - hunting and fishing.. He spent 10 days in the wilderness of Idaho last year hunting elk on horseback (all to no avail).

They are looking forward to retirement at some point in the next 20 years. They have done some traveling in the past by auto to Louisiana, Florida and Washington,

DC and anticipate that probably next summer they will do the same.

JOE M. SANCHEZ, born March 17, 1941, Greeley, CO. Enlisted in the USN on March 15, 1962. Was sent to boot camp; USNTC San Diego, CA, March 1962 to June 1962, Comp. 109. He served on the USS *Ticonderoga*, with the G Div. for four years, 1962-66; made three western Pacific cruises, 1963-66; served during the Tonkin Gulf incident; and during the Vietnam War, 1965-66. He once spent 68 days at sea off Vietnam when relieving the carrier USS *Ranger*, and they blew a boiler and had to go to Japan for repairs.

Went aboard as a seaman and studied and worked his way up to GMG2 in three years. Was in charge of all 1,000 lb., 2,000 lb. bomb magazines and the bomb break out crew. His favorite overseas ports were Hong King, Subic Bay.

Discharged on June 14, 1966, with the rank of GMG2 and served two years in inactive Reserves, 1967-68. Awards include the Armed Forces Expeditionary Medal (Tonkin Gulf), Vietnam Service Ribbon, Navy Unit Commendation Ribbon, National Defense Service Medal and Good Conduct Medal.

Married Betty Jo and has three children: Joseph, Lillian and Regina; and four grandchildren. Works for Kodak Colorado Div., Windsor, CO and resides in Greeley, CO.

LARRY F. SAUM, born Nov. 21, 1942, Lima, OH. Enlisted on March 18, 1964; went to boot camp at Great Lakes NTC and Electronics Technician A School. Served aboard the USS *Ticonderoga* (CVA-14) from June 1965 until February 1968, with the OE Div. Served in the Vietnam War; Hong Kong; Susebo, Japan; Subic Bay; and the Philippines. His home port was San Diego. Discharged March 1, 1968, with the rank of ETR2.

Memorable experience was the Bob Hope Show at Christmas in 1965; the plane crash on deck at night before while show cast on island, the pilot was OK.

Married in the Philippines in 1972 and had two children. Spent 27 years at Magnavox Electronic Systems Co., Ft. Wayne, IN, as an associate electronic engineer in electronic warfare. He is a member of the American Legion Post 330, New Haven, IN.

BILL SCHNEIDER attended boot camp in November 1942 and then attended a Navy school and was promoted to AMM3/c. He was assigned to the V-2 Div. and stayed from commissioning to the end of WWII.

On Jan. 21, 1945, he was on the flight deck preparing his plane for the afternoon sortie. The 20mm gun closest to the aircraft began firing over his head, followed by the crash of the kamikaze. The afternoon

was spent frantically clearing the deck of ammunition and eventually the planes themselves. He watched the second suicide mission from the flight deck as it bore through the shells until it exploded on the bridge.

Discharged as an AMM1/c and attended MIT. He was employed by NASA as an aeronautical engineer and directed several manned programs. Retired as an associate administrator of NASA in 1980 and then served as a vice president of CSC. He again retired in 1992. He is a doctor of engineering.

ROBERT DANIEL SEILOFF, born Oct. 19, 1914, Indianapolis, IN. Enlisted in October 1941 at Bunker Hill, IN. Was assigned to ship when it was commissioned; went to the South Pacific; and spent most of his time in the print shop with the rank of Printer1/c.

Memorable experience was the suicide hit by a Japanese plane on Jan. 21, 1945; and while being re-

paired he went to Washington, DC to Litho School and was then assigned to the USS *Shenadoah* as a chief petty officer.

Celebrated 50th Anniversary with wife, Doris, in 1992. They live in Indianapolis in the summer and Sebring, FL, in the winter.

ROBERT C. SEXTON enlisted on Aug. 22, 1944, at the age of 17, from Nickerson, NE, and attended boot camp at Camp Bennion, Farragut, ID. Reported to the USS *Ticonderoga* (CV-14) at Bremerton on Feb. 22, 1945.

V-J Day was spent in Tokyo Bay; then on to the magic carpet duty until decommissioning at pier 91 in Seattle on June 20, 1946.

Awards include the Good Conduct (seven awards), American Campaign, Asiatic-Pacific (two stars), WWII Victory Medal, National Defense (second award), Navy Occupation and the Philippine Liberation Medal.

Retired as senior chief radioman on Nov. 2, 1970. In 1990 he retired from Ft. Lewis College, Durango, CO, and is enjoying time with wife, Karen, son, daughter and their families.

HARRY W. SHAW, born Sept. 9, 1922, Long Branch, NJ, moved to Ft. Randolph Canal Zone with his family at the age of 18 months. After seven years they moved to Ft. Monroe, VA; five years later they moved to Eustis, FL, which has been his home of record to date.

Enlisted in the USN on July 8, 1941; went to boot camp in Norfolk; then to AOM School; and was assigned to the USS *Ranger*. In January 1944 he joined the fighter of Air Group 80 and boarded the Big "T" in Norfolk in June 1944, with the rank of AOM1/c.

Left the ship in Bremerton in April 1945. The next 15 years were on the beach; Militon, TN; Key West; Port Lyautey; Naples; Oceana; and Sanford. In Sanford, in April 1960, he boarded the USS *Saratoga* for several med cruises; then aboard the USS *JF Kennedy*; to Jacksonville and retirement as an AVCM in December 1970.

Married Maria in Rome in 1952, while he was stationed in Port Lyautey. They have two children. When he retired he worked for General Electric, sheriff's office and then USPS where he retired in 1985.

CLEMENT J. SKORUPKA, born Aug. 1, 1923, Wallington, NJ. Enlisted on Jan. 4, 1943; attended boot camp at Great Lakes; sent to NATTE Memphis; Daytona Beach flight operation; NAS Wildwood, NJ; NAS

Oceana, VA. Served aboard the USS *Ticonderoga* (CV-14) and the USS *Bennington* (CV-20) in the Philippines, Iwo Jima and Okinawa.

Memorable experiences were dive bombing Manila Bay shipping, diving bomb the Japanese cruiser Santa Cruz at Pt. Luzon.

Discharged Oct. 11, 1945, with the rank of ARM2/c. Awards include the Distinguished Flying Cross, four Air Medals, VB80 and BV82.

Married Verne and has two children, Anne and Clement. Retired after 34 years with Bendiz Aviation (now Allied Corp.), Tetenboro, NJ.

WILLIAM VITO SPERDUTS, born Feb. 13, 1926, Somerville, NJ. Enlisted in the USN on Jan. 12, 1944; attended boot camp in Sampson, NY; and served aboard the USS *Ticonderoga* in May 1944, where he was assigned to the forward flight elevator V-1 Div.; and also served aboard the USS *Liddle*. He participated in the Philippine Liberation.

Was in the mess hall having lunch when the kamikaze plane attacked the ship. He immediately ran to his fire station. The elevator where he had been a short time ago was engulfed with smoke and flames. He remembers seeing sailors on fire jumping over the side. Only one ship stayed in the area in the hope of picking up any survivors in the water. The captain refused to abandon the ship so they headed back to port. On the way back the ship was like a ghost ship, it was virtually silent. If anyone made the slightest sound the men would jump 10 feet in the air.

Discharged May 5, 1946, at Lido Beach, Long Island, NJ, with the rank of S1/c. Awards include the American Theater Medal, Asiatic-Pacific Medal w/four stars, WWII Victory Medal and Philippine Liberation Ribbon w/one star.

Married in April 1950 and had four children and seven grandchildren. Was employed at RBH/Inter chemical Corp. for 19 years, when another company took over and they decided they did not need him and four other supervisors, so he was let go. He was then employed by Raritan Supply Co. In 1982 he fought perhaps his biggest battle against cancer and kept his enemy at bay for 10 1/2 years. He passed away on Aug. 1, 1992.

JOHN A STAMPER was in the USN from October 1945—November 1967 as follows: NTC San Diego, CA, 1945-46; *William C. Cole* (DD-641), March 1946—December 1948; *Shelton* (DD-790), December 1948—September 1952; *Leray Wilson* (DE-414), February 1953—May 1954; *Douglas A. Munro* (DE-422), June 1954—June 1956; Ship Repair Facility, Yokosuka, Japan, July 1956—August 1958; Naval Station Tongue Point, Astoria, OR, August 1958—August 1959; Columbia River Group Pacific Reserve Fleet, Astoria, OR, August 1959—October 1960; *Ticonderoga* (CVA-14), April 1961—November 1965; *John R. Craig* (DD-885), November 1965—November 1966; Naval Inactive Ship Maintenance Facility, Bremerton, WA, November 1966—November 1967.

During his career he went from seaman recruit to master chief machinist mate and SPCM and was a qualified gas generating mechanic. While in the *Ticonderoga* he was the leading chief in the Auxiliaries A Div. He made two WESTPAC cruises while attached to the ship.

After retiring from the Navy in 1967, he moved back to Utica, MO and built a house on the home place where he was born. He worked for and retired from the Missouri Dept. of Corrections after 20 years. He and his wife Viola love to camp and travel.

FRED STELIANOU joined the USN on Jan. 18, 1944. He was sent to Sampson, NY, for boot camp then to Naval Air Technical Training Center, Norman, OK, for aviation machinist mate and radioman training. He completed aerial gunnery training in Corpus Christi and Kingsville, TX, before being sent to NAS Alameda, CA, for duty with the Pacific fleet.

With assignment aboard the USS *Ticonderoga* in the V-2 Div., he was a plane captain in charge of a TBF Avenger. His combat duty in the Western Pacific included the Philippines, Okinawa and culminating in Tokyo Bay. He was discharged in May 1946 as AMM3/c.

After discharge in Bremerton, WA, he was appointed postmaster of Lyndonville, NY, a position he held for 40 years. He was active in public service serving as trustee and mayor of Lyndonville and councilman of the Town of Yates. He is married and has one daughter and one grandson.

ANDREW STERLING (SEDENSKY) age 23 and married, enlisted on Dec. 7, 1942. He attended boot camp at Great Lakes, NTC, Navy Pier, specialized training in airplane engine repair at the 87th and Anthony, Chicago, Cape May, NJ ,and Oceana, VA. He was then assigned to the USS *Ticonderoga* in May 1944 as AMM2/c in V-2 Div.

On Jan. 21, 1945, he was assigned to repair radar equipment on the wing of an SB2C so he was on the flight deck at the time of the two attacks by the kamikaze planes and witnessed them both after which he helped assess the damage and helped look after the wounded and dead.

After discharge on Oct. 14, 1945, he returned to his wife in Ohio, later moving to Arizona and returning to Ohio in 1954. He has two children and two grandchildren. He worked in construction, retiring in 1980.

RICHARD J. STOHR from Cincinnati, OH, enlisted in the USNR in 1963. Having been promoted to airman in 1964 and graduated from the University of Cincinnati in 1965, he completed pre-flight training and was commissioned ensign in October 1965. He was designated naval flight officer in August 1966. His first fleet tour was flying in P-3Bs in VP-10. In 1969 he was assigned as flag lieutenant for COMNAVAIRLANT, in 1971 he augmented the USN and graduated from the US Naval Postgraduate School with an MS in management.

Lt. Stohr then reported as ASCAC officer in Tico. He qualified as fleet OOD Underway; was JOOD for Apollo 16; OOD for Apollo 17; and bridge VIP tour guide for the first Skylab astronaut recovery. ASCAC was very active in the RIMPAC and UPTIDE exercises as well as the quick reaction deployment in Vietnam. In 1973 he was selected for the Initial Cadre for S-3A Fleet Introduction and was assigned as a TACCO instructor in VS-41.

Following discharge from active duty in 1975 he rejoined the USNR and was a TACCO and mission commander in P-3s in VP-4549 and VP-68. Following promotion to CDR he commanded VP-4549 during 1983 and 1984 with deployments in Rota, Bermuda and Lajes. His last tour was as head, Inshore Undersea Warfare Section (OP-372K) as the CNO program sponsor for IUW. Capt. Stohr retired from the USNR in 1991.

Civilian employment from 1975 to 1994 in the Washington, DC area included: presearch, tractor, analysis and technology, Cypress and currently secretary and treasurer for Quadleta, having worked on DoD and Navy programs such as S-3/P-3, F/A-18, SSN-21, IUSS, SONAR systems and transducer repair. In 1963 he married Beverly Ann Lotz and they have two sons.

EDDIE W. TENPENNY, born Sept. 10, 1947, Woodbury, TN. Enlisted on April 11, 1965, and served aboard the USS *Ticonderoga* (CV-14), 1966-68. Participated in battle on the Yankee Station North Vietnam.

Memorable experiences were many, but two he remembers quite well. The first one was the fire on the USS *Forrestal* on July 29, 1967; and the second was the capture of the USS *Pueblo* on Jan. 23, 1968. When the *Pueblo* was captured, they were on Yankee Station and deployed to Korea.

Discharged on Sept. 7, 1968, with the rank of AK3. Awards include the National Defense Service Medal, Vietnam Service Medal w/four Bronze Stars, Navy Unit Commendation w/one Bronze Star, Republic of Vietnam Campaign, Gallantry Cross Medal w/Palm and Armed Forces Expeditionary Medal for the *Pueblo* incident. Also at a later date he was issued sea service and overseas ribbons.

Married Killeen from Rochester, NY, and a graduate from the University of Miami. They have two pets, one cocker spaniel and one cat. He is currently on active duty with the TNANG.

LEONARD THORSON a farm boy from the prairies of South Dakota, enlisted in the USN on Dec. 1, 1942. He took boot training at Great Lakes, IL. From there he was sent to Navy Pier, Chicago, IL, for AMM School. He went to Radar School at Memphis, TN, and to Gunnery School at Pennsacola, FL. His next assignment was at Atlantic City, NJ, where Fighter Sqdn. 80 was being formed. His duty was as a plane captain. After several months training he went aboard the Big "T" on June 13, 1944, in the V-2 Div.

On Jan. 21, 1945, he was having chow when GQ sounded. He immediately headed for the flight deck as that was where his battle station was. Before he ever got to the hangar deck a marine practically fell at his feet and died from shrapnel. When he got to the flight deck he started fighting fire and helped push damaged planes overboard. He came out of the war without a scratch, but lost several close buddies.

After his discharge he went back to farming and ranching. He was married in 1948 and has four children and seven grandchildren. In 1984 he retired and sold his ranch to one of his sons. He and wife Phillis bought a small acreage near Philip, SD, where he keeps busy gardening. They spend their winters on the gulf coast of Texas. He was one of the 10 crew members who attended the first Big "T" reunions at New Port Richey, FL, in 1972.

JOHN J. TIERNEY, born March 19, 1925, Brooklyn, NY. Enlisted in the USN on March 18, 1943; attended boot camp at NTS Sampson, NY, from March 18, 1943 to May 1943; Electrical School at NTS Detroit, MI, June 1943 to October 1943; pre-commissioning crew at USNS Newport News, VA. Served aboard the USS *Hornet* (CV-12) from October 1943 to February 1944; and the USS *Ticonderoga* (CV-14), E Div., from

February 1944 to April 1946. All battles he participated in were during WWII aboard the *Ticonderoga*.

Discharged April 6, 1946, with the rank of EM2/c. Awards include the Good Conduct Medal, WWII Victory Medal, American Campaign Medal, Asiatic-Pacific Campaign Medal w/five stars, Navy Occupation Service Medal, Philippine Liberation Ribbon w/two stars and Philippine Presidential Unit Citation.

Graduated St. France Prep High School, Brooklyn, NY, June 1946; and Polytechnic University, New York, with BEE degree in June 1954. Worked for Murray Mfg., Brooklyn, NY, from February 1950 to October 1962, with his last position being product engineer; Grumman Aerospace Corp. (now Northrop Grum Corp.), Bethpage, NY, holding positions of engineer on the Lunar Model program and engineering positions on various aircraft programs (E-2A, A-6A, F-14C and others), and finally as program manager of the E-2C program. Retired from Grumman in November 1990.

Married Marion on June 10, 1961, and they have four children.

EDGAR S. TROTTER JR. was born Oct. 13, 1939, in Little Rock, AR. He graduated from Memphis State University in 1961 and went to OCS being commissioned an ensign, USNR in November 1961. Reported to USS *Ticonderoga* January 1962 where he was Auxiliaries Division Officer and engineering administrative assistant. He made two Western Pacific cruises (was cruise book editor on second cruise).

Left ship in June 1965 and married Carolyn Roe. He reported to Navy Supply Corps School; February 1966, reported to USS *Lindenwald* (LSD-6) as supply officer. Ship was decommissioned in December 1967. Became supply officer of Commander Naval Special Warfare Group, Atlantic until December 1969.

Was supply officer of Mobile Construction Bn. 1 from July 1970—April 1972. Made deployments to Puerto Rico and Diego Garcia. Was Material Division Officer at Naval Construction Battalion Center, Davisville, RI, May 1972—July 1974. Went to foreign duty as the supply officer at US Defense Liaison Group in Jakarta, Indonesia from October 1974—January 1977. Was supply officer of Naval Air Reserve Unit, Pt. Mugu, CA from March 1977—July 1980. Was supply officer of Naval Astronautics Group, Pt. Mugu, CA from July 1980 until retirement in February 1982. Received Armed Forces Expeditionary Medal, Navy Unit Commendation Medal and the Naval Commendation Medal. Now working as a general supply specialist for the Naval Surface Warfare Center, Port Hueneme, CA. Actively involved with the Boy Scout Program, he has three sons: John, Edgar III and Henry.

JOHN F. TROUT served with the USN from June 1941 to January 1946.

He was on board the USS *Ticonderoga* in December 1945, following the surrender on Okinawa and Japan.

THOMAS W. UHRON, born Dec. 6, 1924, Chambersville, PA. When he enlisted he was assigned to radio central. He participated in every battle of the Big "T" from commissioning to the end of the war.

Memorable experience was the kamikaze attacks

in January 1945. Discharged Dec. 6, 1945, with the rank of RM2/c.

Married and has two sons. The youngest, Mark, is a graduate to the Naval Academy and is now a full commander. Uhron is a retired insurance broker.

RICHARD VALENTINE, born Feb. 7, 1925, Chicago, IL. Enlisted on Feb. 5, 1943; attended boot camp, Great Lakes, IL; Radio and Radar School, Memphis, TN; Aviation Gunnery School, Hollywood, FL; operational training in torpedo bombers, Ft. Lauderdale, FL; aviation radioman in Torpedo Sqdn. VT-80 aboard the USS *Ticonderoga*, May 1944 to January 1945; then VT-80 transferred to USS *Hancock* in February 1945; then stateside to NAS Alameda, CA, for reassignment as aviation radioman in a PBM/PBY Sqdn. at NAS Banana River, FL, until discharge.

Served through 20 torpedo or bombing missions of the Philippine Islands, Formosa, French-Indo China and Hainan while attached to the *Ticonderoga*; six bombing missions of Japan, Iwo Jima and Okinawa from Jan. 28, 1945, to March 9, 1945, while attached to the USS *Hancock*.

Memorable experiences were of his first combat mission on a torpedo run on ships in Manila Bay. They lost their wingman on the way down. As they passed over the Japanese ship, he was strafing the deck and could see them firing back at them. He realized then that these missions were not going to be easy. The other mission that was impressive was their support of the invasion of Iwo Jima. They had a ringside view from 10,000 feet as the invasion began with their ships spread all the way to the horizon.

Discharged March 2, 1946, with the rank of ARM2/c. Awards include the Air Medal, Asiatic-Pacific Campaign Medal, American Theater Campaign Medal and WWII Victory Medal.

Married Jean and has three children; and five grandchildren. Received BSEE degree from the University of Illinois; spent 36 years with two electronic companies on every NASA space program through 1986. He is now retired.

JON R. VEARD, born Aug. 26, 1941, Elyria, OH. Enlisted on Aug. 25, 1959; was stationed out of San Diego, CA, for two and one half years; attended boot camp at Great Lakes Training Center; trained in Philadelphia, PA, in catapults and arresting gear.

Memorable experiences were going to Hong Kong, Manila, Japan and the Philippines; and cruising the South China Seas at the beginning of the Vietnam conflict.

Discharged Aug. 25, 1962, with the rank of petty officer 3/c. He was awarded the Good Conduct Medal.

Married for over 31 years to Joy and has three children and two grandchildren. He is self-employed as a property manager and developer.

A.J. WAGNER served on duty station as a telephone operator, landing pattern plane check for landing signal officer and landing signal platform (fly four).

Has five children: Betty Jean, Steve, Kevin, Barbara and Chris; and three grandchildren: Matthew, Danielle and Jake. He retired as superintendent, sulfuric acid and co-generation production at Conserve, Inc., Nichols, FL.

ROBERT O. WALKER, born Oct. 15, 1925, Bradford Township, Clearfield County, PA. Enlisted in the USNR in July 1943, with assignment to Torpedo Sqdn. 87, as an aviation radioman 3/c combat air crew.

Greatest memories of service on the USS *Ticonderoga* were being on the strike when the Japanese battleship Hyuga was sunk in July 1945. His pilot Ltjg. Paul W. (Jake) Boyd was awarded the Navy Cross for a direct hit on the Hyuga. Also, returning to the ship after being recalled from their last strike on Japan. The whole crew was in the cat walks and superstructure. What a welcome home! He has often wondered who was doing the work below deck.

Discharged in July 1946 and entered Indiana State Teachers College, Indiana, PA. After two years he enlisted as NAVCAD and went to Pensecola, FL, for flight training. Resigned in 1949 when budget cuts made a career as a naval aviator seem to be an impossible dream.

Returned to college at ISTC, graduating in 1951. During his senior year the Korean War began and an Army ROTC unit was opened at ISTC. He joined up and after graduation he was commissioned a 2nd lieutenant in the Regular Army. He missed combat during the Korean War, and trained recruits and draftees. Served in Korea (post war), Okinawa, France and in Vietnam as deputy assistant chief of staff, intelligence (G-2), XXIV US Army Corps. Upon his return from Vietnam he served as executive officer at the US Army Intelligence School. His final tour was in Germany as Chief Exploitation Branch, Product Division, office of assistant chief of staff intelligence, US Army Europe.

Retired in June 1973, with the rank of lieutenant colonel military intelligence, with 26 1/2 years of service.

Married Rovena Stepp, of Ford City, PA, in July 1950. They have two daughters, Jayne and Susan; and six grandchildren.

WILLIAM WALLER JR. (BILL) left the *Ticonderoga* and the West Coast in March 1963 and headed to Norfolk, VA for his last tour of duty with the Operational Test and Evaluation Force. Following slightly over three years of testing the latest electronic, countermeasure and navigational equipment, he retired from the Navy July 31, 1966.

The next morning he started a career with IBM. For the next 25 years, he was involved with installing computers and computer programs for IBM in the Norfolk Virginia Beach area. His job consisted of making the computer do whatever the salesman had promised the customer it would do. During this time he was fortunate to be twice assigned temporary duty to the IBM German Development Laboratory to ring out new unannounced computers and the associated software. He retired from IBM Aug. 31, 1991 but continues to work about half-time for various IBM customers doing pretty much the same thing he did for IBM for 25 years.

His wife Neola taught the highest level math offered by Frank W. Cox HS, Virginia Beach for 30 years and retired in 1993. Last fall she was invited to be a delegate to the first US—Russia Educational Conference and he was invited to come along. They were able to add Moscow and Saint Petersburg to their list of places visited. They continue to travel every chance they get.

They have a son Jeffrey Scott and daughter Mary Ann McKenney.

WILLIAM PAUL WEAVER, born July 17, 1910, Wilson, NC. Joined the USN on Aug. 6, 1928, Norfolk, VA, and was assigned to the S-1 Div. in charge of the disbursing office. Served on various ships and stations for the next 20 years. His first, as a boot to Washington, DC; then to New London, CT, for sub duty; kicked out of school for one hour late (sub) getting underway. Then went to San Juan, Puerto Rico, to open a pay office, the same at Antigua, BWI. Received his orders to the USS *Ticonderoga* in Antigua in September 1940.

Went back to the States to Newport News, VA, for duty with the Big "T" detail, helped open and set up disbursing and supply offices. He was on board when it was commissioned. He was on board the Big "T" the Saturday night before commission and spent that night (his first) in the chief quarters.

Was first chief in charge of the chief's mess and his main duty being in the disbursing office. He was in every battle of the Big "T" from the first to the last.

Memorable experiences were of when the first plane hit. He was in the pay office getting records together when he heard the word "all hands help with the wounded," etc. He was on top side in minutes. He will always remember helping Comdr. Burch to the sick bay, half his clothes gone and the rest being burned. His battle station was the five inch forward battery, but was called off to go to the disbursing office for what records they could save.

Awards include the Good Conduct w/four bars, American Defense w/fleet clasp, American Campaign Medal, Asiatic-Pacific Campaign w/four bars, WWII Victory Medal (2) and the Philippine Liberation Ribbon w/one bar.

Married a young girl whom he met in San Juan. She was there with her brother, an Army doctor. She left San Juan a month before he did and they met in Miami and married on Jan. 31, 1944. They have two children, of which their daughter is a doctor.

J.P. WEINEL, ADM, born and raised in Columbia, IL. He graduated from the USN in 1939. He served in the cruiser *Chester* and destroyer *Mavry* until 1942, then took flight training. During WWII he saw combat as a destroyer officer, a fighter pilot and an amphibious staff officer.

After the war he served on the carrier *Antietam* as assistant AW officer. He commanded Fighter-Bomber Sqdn. 98, Fighter Sqdn. 14 and was also Commander Air Group 5. During the Korean War,

he was Air Officer on Valley Forge for three hours. During this period he was operations officer of Carrier Div. 5 and served two tours in the Pentagon.

Promoted to captain in 1957, he was on the faculty of the NATO DEF COL in Paris, France. He also attended the National War College in Washington, DC. He commanded the *Great Sitkin* and in July 1963 he took command of *Ticonderoga*. Adm. Weinel considers the following year in *Ticonderoga* the best duty of his entire career. He was chief of staff of first fleet. He then returned to Washington as a member of the Chairman Joint Chiefs of Staff.

Promoted to rear admiral in 1966, he commanded Carrier Div. 3 and during the Vietnam War he commanded Task Group 77.0 in command of all naval forces in the Gulf of Tonkin. This was followed by a series of high level planning assignments in the Pentagon as assistant deputy chief of naval operations for Plans and Policy; director of Plans for the Joint Chief of Staff and assistant to the chairman, Joint Chiefs of Staff.

Promoted to four stars in 1944, he served as the US military representative to NATO in Brussels, Belgium. Adm. Weinel returned in 1977. He now resides in California with his wife, Ann.

His decorations include five Distinguished Service Medals, two Legions of Merit, Air Medal, Presidential Unit Citation, Navy Unit Citation and the Vietnam Cross of Gallantry.

J. MAURY WERTH enlisted in the USNR as a volunteer on Nov. 6, 1935, while still in high school, to compete for appointment to the Naval Academy. He would have been too old to have sought one through the fleet, after high school graduation. Entered the USNA in June 1935; graduated; and was commissioned on Feb. 7, 1941. By then he had sea duties of six months aboard the USS *Texas*; four months in four pipe destroyers USS *Yarnall* and USS *Simpson*. He was ordered to USS *Raleigh* (CL-7) based in Pearl Harbor. On December 7, although torpedoed, bombed and strafed, they were still able to be the first ship to commence firing, and knock down four planes, one of which still managed to crash into the USS *Curtis*. The CL-7 served in south, central and the North Pacific through the Aleutian campaign.

Ordered to the USS *Ticonderoga* (CV-14) upon her launching on Feb. 7, 1944. In May 1945 he was ordered to COMCARDIV 7 as assistant operations, logistics, navigator, task group 38.5, then occupation duty in Japan at the war's end. They demobilized CARDIV 7 and CARDIV 6 and he was ordered as executive officer on the USS *Purdy* for fleet and occupation duties in the Mediterranean until mid 1948.

Subsequent sea duties included captain on the destroyer USS *Bordelon* and USS *Ad Everglades*; commander of the Escort Sqdn. 14 for 10 months; Lebanon Crisis; followed by 10 months of deployment in joint training exercises in Brazil, Uruguay, Argentina and Columbia, in that order; followed immediately for two months was deployed again as chief of staff, Flotilla 2. Overseas shore duties consisted of Brazil, England, assistant chief of staff, logistics, Naval Forces in Europe and the Mediterranean. Spent 16 months ashore in Vietnam with the US Army from Hue at the 17th parallel to Mekong Delta to Cambodian border, including urgent construction of 1,000% increase in cargo piers of DaNang, QuiNhon, CamRon Bay, Vung Tao and Saigon. Final duties in the States were joint staff, operations officer for special activities involving Green barets, Vietnam, Laos and Cambodia; superintendent of the Naval Observatory with stations in Washington, DC, Flagstaff, AZ, and Argentina.

Retired in September 1970, after 35 years with the USN, which included 15 years of sea duty, 10 of which were deployed away from home; two years ashore overseas in the war zone (peace time); and one year total, TAD overseas while on shore duty in the States. Earned the Army Air Medal, but the USN would not permit such for non Airedales; two Purple Hearts, Legion of Merit and Bronze Star.

Married in November 1945. Bought and managed three western Maryland farms for nine years and a real estate broker for 17 years. Served major voluntary public service: four years opening up Appalachia for that neglected region; four years fund raising for Rotary International to eradicate polio from developing nations; 12 years with the scientific development council; and to the College of William and Mary in oceanographic and riverine research necessary to reverse the disaster of the last 80 years to the Chesapeake Bay and the watersheds that feed it.

JOHN WILLIAMS, born April 25, 1943, Philadelphia, PA. Enlisted in the USN on Aug. 1, 1962, at the age of 19. After completing boot camp at Great Lakes Naval Training Center, he was ordered to the USS Ticonderoga, where he was assigned to A Div. Station two (steam heat) in the forward diesel generator room.

Most of his tour was during the peace time except for the start of the Vietnam conflict in mid 1964. In August 1964 he lost 90 percent of his vision and was flown to Clark AFB in the Philippines for tests. From there he was flown to Philadelphia Naval Hospital where he underwent testing at Wills Eye Hospital. After six months of treatment for blocked optic nerve, he was discharged in February 1965 from the USN for medical reasons. He held the rank of fireman.

Memorable experience was his whole tour aboard the USS *Ticonderoga* and the crew he worked with.

Married Elizabeth and has four children. He is now an over the road driver for National Brands of Philadelphia. They reside in Philadelphia.

JACK C. WHITE, born Jan. 31, 1917, Monroe, MI, was the son of Lovell and Bessie (Clark) White. Graduated in 1935 from Monroe High School and worked as an agent for Metropolitan Life Insurance Co. until his retirement in 1970.

Served in the USN from July 23, 1943, to Nov. 28, 1945, as a machinist mate 2/c aboard the USS *Ticonderoga*. Received the American Defense Medal, Asiatic Pacific Defense Medal and Philippine Liberation Medal.

Attended school at Con Edison in New York and Wentworth Institute in Boston. He also attended Henry Ford Community College in Dearborn.

Married Marguerite Miller Feb. 11, 1939, in Napoleon, OH. They have two children, Dennis R. of Port Huron and Marigail Stubleski of Monroe; eight grandchildren living and one deceased; and 11 great-grandchildren. They celebrated their golden anniversary in 1989. He was a member of the Calvary United Methodist Church; served the church as chairman of the finance committee, architect for the new church building, Sunday School teacher, chairman of the trustee board, a youth group leader for eight years, choir member, communion steward, president of the Men's Brotherhood and Boy Scout leader. He was also active in basketball, baseball and volleyball at the church. Served as president of the Monroe Underwriters Assn. and taught business insurance classes at Monroe County Community College and was an electrical leader for 4-H. He passed away on June 22, 1995.

BOB WINNEBERGER and a buddy went to join the USM, but they were closed. They saw this USN chief and he said join the Navy, you will always have a bed and food. They did on July 9, 1942. Attended boot camp at Quonset Point, RI; from there went aboard the USS *Ranger* (CV-4); made ship fitter 2/c; served in the Atlantic with the *Ranger*.

In December 1943 he was assigned to the USS *Ticonderoga*, since it was not ready, he had a 30 day leave and then went to Welding School. In May 1944 he went aboard and helped put her in commission and was assigned to the plumbing shop. There he made ship fitter 1/c.

On Jan. 21, 1945, when they were hit, he was in charge of repair two. Like everyone else he fought fires and tried to stay alive.

Awards: Purple Heart, Bronze Star, five Silver Stars, Battle Stars, Good Conduct Medal, American, European and Asiatic-Pacific Campaign Medals, and WW II Victory Medal. Discharged Dec. 11, 1945.

After discharge he moved back to Baltimore, MD. Married and two children and one grandchild. He became part-owner of Mechanical Contractors Co., Inc. He retired after 37 years and moved to Florida to enjoy the sun and fishing.

JAMES H. WRIGHT, born Jan. 29, 1922, Hatboro, PA; graduated from Hatboro High School in the Spring of 1941; and enlisted in the USN on Aug. 1, 1942. He was assigned to the USS *Ticonderoga*. During his military career, he was decorated with the WWII Victory Medal, Good Conduct Medal w/six OLCs, Purple Heart, Bronze Star, Philippine Liberation Ribbon, National Defense Service Medal, American Campaign Medal, Asiatic-Pacific Campaign Medal and Naval Reserve Medal.

Served in many positions with the USN: aviation machinist mate, 1942-45; flight engineer, 1946-47; technician training instructor, 1947-49; librarian, technical publications, 1949-50; assistant fighter line chief, 1950-56; quality control supervisor, 1956-58; assistant engineering chief, 1958-61; VP, line chief, 1961-63.

Discharged on Jan. 15, 1963, and spent the next 10 years in the fleet Reserve where he retired as a chief petty officer.

Has maintained the aircraft that have fought four conflicts, including WWII, Korea, Vietnam and Desert Storm and proudly maintained 14 types of aircraft to include: F3A, F4A, F6F, TBF, SB2C, F4U, R5D, F9F, P2V, SBD, C-47, C-130, C-135 and C-141.

In March 1964 he entered the Federal Service as a C-135 aircraft maintenance technician. Shortly thereafter, he was promoted to work leader (WL-10) and became the NCOIC of the T-56 engine test cell. In 1968 he was promoted to WS-12 and became the TF33 propulsion branch foreman and was then promoted to propulsion flight foreman (WS-15) in 1983. He is an active member of the NRA, Masons, Elks and Shriners. He was also selected as the 21st AF nominee to HQ for the prestigious Elder Statesman of Aviation Award in 1992.

Above and below: USS Ticonderoga *(CG-47), Pacific Missile Test Center, Point Mugu, CA. (Photographer, Bruce Trombecky)*

Index

The biographies are not included in the following index since they appear in alphabetical order in the biographical section of the book.

OUR SHIP'S PRAYER

Invoked at the Commissioning of the
U.S.S. TICONDEROGA, (CV-14) 8 May, 1944

Most high and mighty ruler of the universe,
    By whom our nation hath been established
    In freedom and preserved in union;
We thank Thee for our heritage which is rich
    In heroic examples of self-sacrifice
    In the interest of freedom and justice.
We thank Thee, too, that Thou hast not withheld from us
    The opportunity to participate
    In the heroism of our fathers.
Mindful of our past and present we pray for this ship.
    O God bless this ship.
    May she be in Thy hands an avenger to all
Who have disturbed the peace of the world.
    May she strike terror into the hearts of those
    Who plan slavery for fellowmen.

Father in Heaven, we invoke Thy blessing upon this ship.
    Make her the Champion of all those who are crushed
    By tyrrany and despotism.
May she have the greater glory of being an instrument in
    Thy hands for creating the Kingdom of God upon earth.
    Most merciful God bless this ship.
Bless him who is her Captain and all who have authority
    Under him that working together we may please
    Him to Whom belongeth all authority.
As our home, may this ship be a place where each forgets
    Himself in the interest of the common good. May each
    One follow the example of Him who lived to serve.
May the Lord bless us and keep us; may the Lord
    Make His face to shine upon us and be grcaious
    Unto us; and bring us to a righteous and enduring peace.
                                    Amen.

CARRIER AIR GROUP

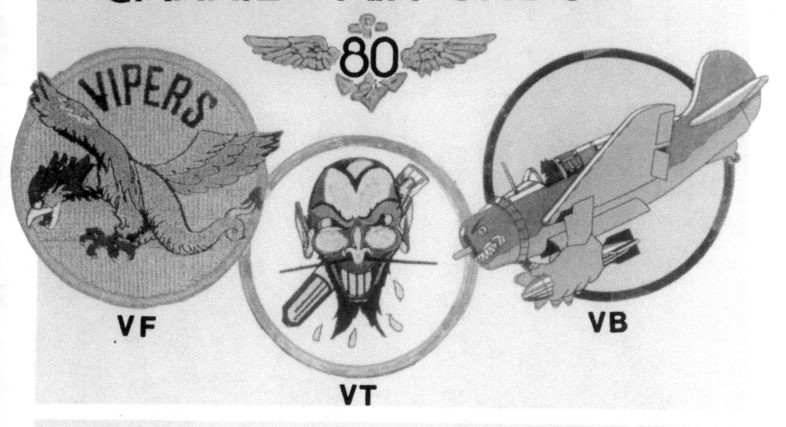

80

VF

VT

VB

VT-80 Pilots, 1944-45, USS Ticonderoga.

Printed in the USA
CPSIA information can be obtained
at www.ICGtesting.com
JSHW050357030424
60428JS00015B/550